Also by Gerald Marzorati

A Painter of Darkness

Late to the Ball

Seeing Serena

GERALD MARZORATI

SCRIBNER

New York   London   Toronto   Sydney   New Delhi

Scribner
An Imprint of Simon & Schuster, Inc.
1230 Avenue of the Americas
New York, NY 10020

First Scribner hardcover edition June 2021

SCRIBNER and design are registered trademarks of The Gale Group, Inc.,
used under license by Simon & Schuster, Inc., the publisher of this work.

For information about special discounts for bulk purchases,
please contact Simon & Schuster Special Sales at 1-866-506-1949
or business@simonandschuster.com.

The Simon & Schuster Speakers Bureau can bring authors to your live event.
For more information or to book an event, contact the Simon & Schuster Speakers Bureau
at 1-866-248-3049 or visit our website at www.simonspeakers.com.

Interior design by Erich Hobbing

Manufactured in the United States of America

10 9 8 7 6 5 4 3 2 1

Library of Congress Cataloging-in-Publication Data has been applied for.

ISBN 978-1-9821-2788-6
ISBN 978-1-9821-2790-9 (ebook)

For Roger Angell

There are years that ask questions, and years that answer.
—Zora Neale Hurston,
Their Eyes Were Watching God

Culture does not make people. People make culture.
—Chimamanda Ngozi Adichie,
We Should All Be Feminists

CONTENTS

Seeing Serena

INTRODUCTION

It was the last weekend of September 2018 when *Saturday Night Live* kicked off its forty-fourth season. Three weeks earlier, Serena Williams had played Naomi Osaka in the US Open women's final, a match that was among the most bizarre and controversial in the history of professional tennis, a match made memorable by Williams's clashing loudly and unceasingly with the chair umpire, Carlos Ramos. Three weeks is a long time ago in the digital-age news cycle, but there, on *SNL* that Saturday night in early fall, was the comedian Leslie Jones, crashing the "Weekend Update" sketch in a one-shoulder silhouette tennis dress with a tulle skirt—like the dress Williams wore at the US Open—and waving a Wilson Blade 104, the racquet Williams uses. It was meta-comedy: Jones burst into the skit, insisting, in a dead-on Serena impersonation, that she was owed an apology, hilariously mashing up Serena's already notorious tirade aimed at the chair umpire in the women's final—Williams believed *she* was owed an apology for being charged with a violation she felt implied that she was cheating—with her, Jones's, accusatory rant that a planned Serena skit had been cut from the show. One of the "Weekend Update" anchors tried to reason with Jones, as she yelled and swung phantom fore-

INTRODUCTION

hands: The Williams-Osaka match was old news. But what made the bit work was that the match *wasn't* old news, that it was still being brought up, mulled over, parsed, argued about. . . . I couldn't remember the last time a sports controversy, or any sort of pop-culture controversy, had remained a part of the general conversation for so long. What was it? Or better, what was it about Serena?

Watching Leslie Jones as Serena Williams for a minute and a half: that's where the idea for this book began. *What was it about Serena?* The "it" was complex, singularly so, which made the idea alluring. There was her indisputable greatness as a tennis player, which, as someone who wrote frequently about tennis, I was familiar with. But there was her broader presence in the culture, too: as a striving woman from a striving family, as a powerful woman, as a sometimes angry woman, as a wealthy woman, as a fashion-conscious woman, as a woman who was a social media "influencer," as a working woman with a baby, but above all—or better, perhaps, at the root of it all—as a Black woman who'd, beginning with tennis, forged a commanding presence in one essentially white realm after another. Williams struck me, and I sensed struck others, too, as someone ever present—a global celebrity—but not quite apprehended. And the more you thought about her, the more myriad-minded you grew. That was alluring to me, too.

This is not an authorized book. I got no special access to Williams or those closest to her. That would have entailed making it her book, ultimately, which was not what interested me. She has told her own story in many forms and many forums and will no doubt continue to do so. I wanted, simply and not so simply, to *see* her in all the ways I could: watch her, describe her, listen to her, follow her (in the new conditions of seeing created by Instagram, etc.), interpret her, situate her. My tools were sports writing, biography, reportage, and cultural criticism. The narrative armature of the book is Williams's return to tennis after giving birth to her daughter and her quest to win another Grand Slam or two, to tie and maybe break a long-standing record and win a major as a mom. I spent a year on the women's tour, watching live nearly every match Williams played, attending her press conferences, talking to players, coaches, journalists, and others. I also read what others had written about her, and I read more broadly dozens of books— novels, memoirs, volumes of history—and essays (on topics ranging from race to feminism to what is known as critical sports studies) that informed, challenged, and (re)shaped my thinking. I understood, too, and that understanding only deepened in working on this book, that Serena Williams, like all today who achieve the measure of fame and celebrity she has, exists in the public imagination as a sum of myriad projections (by her detractors) and longings (by her admirers). Were these pressures that molded whom she came to be? (And because she is a Black woman finding success in white realms, those projections and longings have had a way of being charged.) There was no way of knowing, or no one way of knowing, Serena Williams—of seeing her. In the end, this book is one (yes, white male) writer's way, or ways.

The form I chose for the book is prismatic, collage-like. The point was to see Serena Williams from as many angles as I could. It is Serena Williams's complexity, even beyond her greatness on court, that has made her the most consequential athlete of her time, and it is my hope that this book, in its way of telling, evokes and somehow deepens that complexity.

Part One
Melbourne

1

Serena Williams was waiting, restless to get on with it. She adjusted and readjusted her big Beats by Dre headphones. It was important to loosen up and crucial to get focused. She stretched, reaching back with her right hand to clutch her right foot, leg bent and drawn up behind her, while her left arm reached farther and farther forward. It's a common enough stretch now in tennis, good for slowly engaging the quads and groin and opening up the chest. In yoga it's not only a stretch but a balance pose, Lord of the Dance, Natarajasana. It's described as dancing while remaining still and understood to embody and perhaps convey to a practitioner the sagacious notion of *changing* while remaining *changeless*. That was one way to see Serena Williams.

She was back in a tunnel somewhere in Rod Laver Arena, the main tennis venue of the Australian Open. Held each year in Melbourne at the end of January, the Australian Open is the first of the four major or Grand Slam tournaments on the annual tennis calendar. The last two weeks of January are high summer in Melbourne, with hot afternoons that stretch past seven before surrendering in spectacular sunsets toward nine. The streets east of Melbourne's city center that I would walk late each morning on my way to Melbourne Park and "the tennis," as Melbournians say, had a Victorian feel: terrace housing, bungalows, tidy squares with their lawns and well-tended rosebushes. Melbournians themselves seemed to have deeply internalized the Victorian enthusiasm for sport. They biked and ran and played; they filled their newspapers and news sites with sports stories; they poured into Melbourne Park for the tennis, passing one of the world's largest cricket grounds, known simply as the G, on their way.

Along with its warm afternoons and congenial vibe, the Australian Open is known for its dedication to enhancing what has come to be called the fan experience. Which is why I could see Serena Williams stretching—she was poised and pixelated on each of two giant screens suspended at either end of the 14,800-seat arena. Cameras had recently been installed at various points along the hallways and passageways that lead from the players' locker room to the Laver court. Williams was back there somewhere loosening and psyching herself up. The idea, according to tournament officials, was to take ticketholders "behind the scenes," where they might, up on the jumbotrons, get a special glimpse, an unvarnished glimpse—a captivatingly candid glimpse—of a favorite player. Telecasting had transformed sports, beginning in the 1960s, turning games and matches into shows; perhaps no better evidence of the thoroughness of the transformation is that those attending a live sporting event now spend a lot of their time staring at a screen.

But where or what was behind the scenes for Serena Williams? She had more than 10 million followers on Instagram, who, every day or nearly every day, glimpsed her practicing, glimpsed her lounging with her husband, glimpsed her in a sandbox with her fifteen-month-old daughter, glimpsed the tacos she was about to have for Sunday dinner. These glimpses were not of anything candid. They were glimpses of presentations. Most everything on Instagram was, in some way or another, a presentation: an extension of the idealized, curated self, a transmission of "brand." But then so, in essence, was what was captured by the new cameras leading to courtside at Rod Laver Arena. Williams surely understood this. And she knew how to captivate. On a summery, sun-splashed afternoon, Serena Williams was doing her stretching on the enormous screens in what, for all the world, appeared to be a chic black trench coat. Those seated around me at courtside, the women especially, oohed and aahed.

Williams was herself captivated by self-presentation, and all that it could summon: mystery, unapproachability, allure, mastery, exoticism, glamour, power. It was there, if you spent the time looking that I had, in the interviews she gave, the fashion shoots she participated in, the posts she created for Instagram, how she entered a room full of reporters, how she walked onto a tennis court and went about her game. She expected to be gazed upon. What contemporary sports icon, what global celebrity, did not? The British psychotherapist and essayist Adam Phillips has written, "We seek attention without quite understanding what the attention is that we seek, and what it is in ourselves we need attending to." Maybe, for Williams, it had to do with growing up with four older sisters who fussed over her clothes and hair. Maybe it was that, even as she was being molded by her parents, from the time she turned four, to be a tennis champion, she dreamed of being an actress. Maybe it was learning to play tennis on glass-strewn public courts in South-Central Los Angeles and being puzzled over by youths who'd come to shoot hoops or buy dope. Maybe it was that she'd spent so much time as a child and teenager in the shadow (on the tennis court, in the media) of her sister Venus, fifteen months older than Serena, and more reticent. Venus had been first to deal with the attention and the racial and social dislocation that came with being a Black female tennis prodigy, and then a Black female tennis star—and dealt with it by becoming ever more quietly self-contained. Maybe worrying her personal presentation had to do with Serena's thinking she was ugly, or thinking she was attractive. She had said both, at one time or another.

Serena Williams had been answering questions about herself, after her tennis matches and not only after her tennis matches, since she was a preteen, by which time she was already drawing a great deal of attention: a personality before she could reasonably be expected to be a person. The *New York Times* sent a reporter to an obscure tournament in Canada in October of 1995 because, at the age of fourteen, she was to play her first professional match there. (She lost badly. Her opponent, Annie Miller, herself only eighteen, said afterward, "I guess I played a celebrity.") Williams over the years would say all sorts of things, to reporters and into television cameras, about who she was and how she looked. It was not always clear what she actually thought or believed—if, for that matter, she always knew what she thought or believed, or if she really wanted to let on to her questioners what she thought or believed. Did she say things that, at the moment, she thought or believed? Or did she say things—and this was the temptation of any public figure—to construct how she wanted to be perceived? All this was, in its own way, when you pondered it, captivating, too.

That she was Black in what was still a white girl's game; that she was broad and muscular in ways no player on the women's tour had ever been; that she was coming to tennis from where no one had come before, from Compton, known nationally and internationally during her childhood mostly for its turf wars between the Bloods and the Crips, for its murder rate, and for its gangsta rap; that she was coached at first solely by her father and mother, who themselves had never played tennis but taught themselves, from books and videotapes, so that they might, in turn, teach their daughters—Serena, like her sister Venus before her, was going to be puzzled over, scrutinized, interpreted. From the start, Serena seemed to have an intuitive sense of this. Playing white girls in front of white crowds in a game that savored its starchy traditions, she gave every indication of embracing her role as the outsider, the proud and enormously gifted (and thus complicating to detractors) Other, heralding a transformation. She would expend little energy trying to fit in; she and her sister mostly kept to themselves those first years they were on tour. On court, and off it with the media, Serena exuded strength and confidence, emotional exuberance: if she was going to attract attention, she should be a subject of it, not an object. She sought agency and would struggle to obtain it, not by making compromises, not by making nice, but by making room—cultural space—for exactly who she was. She would make her presence felt and her otherness electrifying. The black trench she was wearing that January afternoon in Melbourne? It wasn't the half of it. As the match was about to begin, she shed it to reveal she was set to play in a fifties-pinup-like, kelly-green romper and black fishnet tights. Another wave of oohs and aahs swelled courtside.

This first-round match was the first official match of the year for Williams. Entered in the main singles draw of the Australian Open were 128 women, as in all the Grand Slam tournaments— the four most prestigious, lucrative, and, with regard to ranking points, critical of the year's tennis events, with 2,000 points bestowed on the winner, 500 more than for winning the year-end Women's Tennis Association's final, and double the amount earned by the champion of even the biggest of non-Slam tour tournaments. A player's WTA ranking—a rolling, cumulative system updated every week throughout the season—affected sponsorship deals and media attention and young, fragile egos, but, more tangibly, affected seeding in tournament draws: what caliber of player you would play, and when you would play her, during a tournament's unfolding. At a Grand Slam, only a quarter of the women were seeded, one through thirty-two, based almost exclusively on their WTA ranking, and these seeded players were carefully spread through the draw, so they would, by design, not meet other top players on court until the third round of play, at the earliest, late in the first week of the two-week-long tournament.

In the first round, seeded players met opponents ranked No. 50 or No. 84 or No. 103: struggling newcomers, fading veterans, career-long also-rans. Williams was seeded thirteenth, which corresponded to her current WTA world ranking. Her opponent in the first round, Tatjana Maria, was a thirty-one-year-old German who had won precisely one singles title in her many years on the WTA tour; whose career-high ranking (reached two years earlier) was No. 46; and who was unseeded. The first set of their match was done in eighteen minutes. It didn't seem to take even that long. Maria didn't win a game. Williams would win the match 6–0, 6–2, doing little more than serving and returning serves, devastatingly, and be off the court and back in the locker room in less than an hour.

Maria spoke afterward of how she and Williams were actually neighbors in Florida, in a gated community in Palm Beach Gardens, where Williams had lived for much of her adult life, first in a ten-thousand-square-foot home she shared with her sister Venus, and, more recently, in her own place, one of a number of houses and apartments—in Florida, Los Angeles, Paris, and elsewhere—she shared with her husband, the tech entrepreneur Alexis Ohanian and their young daughter, Alexis Olympia Ohanian Jr., whom her parents called Olympia. Players, women and men, and from all over the world, establish residency in Florida or Monte Carlo or Dubai—for the weather and the favorable tax rates and, as was the case in the gated community where Maria and Williams lived, for the proximity to elaborate tennis facilities.

Maria said that she had never had a neighborly tennis practice with Williams. Williams had come over for a barbecue, Maria said, and their daughters had played together once or twice. Tennis play-ers were seldom home; their season stretched from January into November. Big show courts such as Rod Laver Arena, Maria went on to say, were, for Serena, "like her home." Maria meant the famil-iarity and comfort Williams had in front of large crowds, crowds that, as on this afternoon, mostly cheered for Williams. Maria meant, too, that Williams possessed a knowledge of how the Rod Laver acrylic-coated hard-court surface played—she'd played and practiced on Laver so many times, and Maria, never. (Williams had, in her long career, won the Australian Open seven times; Maria, not once, not even close.) Maria was thinking out loud, as players will do after being overwhelmed in a match, telling herself how the result might have been different on another court, another day. The attraction of sport is that it provides spectacle with so few illusions. But that doesn't stop those who play from harboring them.

2

Serena Jameka Williams was thirty-seven years old as she began the 2019 season. She had been a professional tennis player for more than twenty-three years. For 319 weeks of those many years, she had been ranked No. 1 and would likely have been ranked No. 1 for more weeks than that had she chosen to play the number of tournaments most players played, rather than choosing, instead, to take stretches of time away from the game to pursue interests beyond the sport—an interest in fashion design, for example, and, in time, an interest in not wearing down as she aged. She had won twenty-three Grand Slam singles titles, one short of the record held by the Australian Margaret Court. It was hard to find anyone arguing that Margaret Court, a great tennis player, was a greater tennis player than Serena Williams. Margaret Court had won many of her major titles at the

Australian Open when some of the best players in Europe and the United States passed up the event because it was so far away, and also because it had for years been held in December, close to the holidays. Still, tying and surpassing Court's record mattered to Williams. It was a reason she was still playing tennis at thirty-seven. (Among the top women playing singles, only her sister was older than Serena.)

Williams had earned, by the end of 2018, nearly $90 million in prize money, more than any other woman had ever won, in any sport, and more than double that collected by her sister Venus, who was second in all-time earnings among active players on the WTA tour. Serena's net worth, which would include, along with prize money, real-estate holdings, returns on investments she'd made, and especially endorsement deals secured for her by her longtime agent, Jill Smoller, was estimated by *Forbes* magazine to be $225 million. (In 1990, Zina Garrison, an American women's tennis player ranked No. 4 in the world, and Black, could not get so much as a sneaker sponsorship.) Beyond the money, Williams had dominated a sport in her time as no other woman in this century had. (Only the record-making Alpine skier Lindsey Vonn, in her prime, and the extraordinary young gymnast Simone Biles could make a conversation of it.) Williams had also, with her power but not only her power, changed the way women's tennis got played and, to no small extent, as a long-standing champion, brought to the sport girls who might well never have picked up a racquet were they (or their nudging parents) not inspired by her example. Finally, there was her recognition and fame. In the United States, only two athletes, the golfer Tiger Woods and the NFL quarterback Tom Brady, had, in her time, achieved broader public awareness, and her Q Score—a polling metric designed to gauge an individual's or product's familiarity and marketing appeal—was above average among Americans of nearly all income levels and age groups. Further, she'd achieved *worldwide* sports stardom as no woman before her (and no NFL quarterback) had. As the Australian Open got underway, ESPN was producing a list of the world's most famous athletes, using three metrics to determine global popularity: how frequently an athlete's name was searched online; how much money the athlete generated from endorsements; and the number of followers he or she had on social media. Williams wound up No. 17 on the list—soccer stars dominated the top spots—and was the only woman in the top twenty-five. She was, in sum, by most any calculation, the greatest player in the history of women's tennis—the queen her most avid fans worshipped her as—and the most renowned woman athlete of all time.

And something, or someone, more than that. Williams entered her thirties at a time when being Black and female, especially if immixed with wealth or stardom (or both), began to make for an especially galvanizing admixture. Michelle Obama; Beyoncé and Rihanna; Stacey Abrams's run for governor of Georgia and Kamala Harris's seeking the Democratic presidential nomination (followed by her being selected as Joe Biden's vice presidential running mate and, in November 2020, being elected vice president as the first woman and first woman of color to hold that office); the continued TV presence of Oprah, the women of color on *The View*, and the emergence of Shonda Rhimes as a prolific television and audio producer; the many novels being written by women of color and suddenly being published and read—Black women had a place and a voice in America as at no time before. Williams was caught up in this time, her time, as a person always is. But with her achievements and her celebrity, she was having a role in shaping her time, too. The efforts and accomplishments of Williams and these other women were contested, their struggles to gain success hard fought. Among the things dividing America in the second decade of the twenty-first century, the emergence of powerful Black women, women who were no longer going to be pushed to the side of their own lives, was a pronounced, if not always enunciated, matter of contention. Some people feared these women, hated these women, white men, mostly, or anyway most vocally—hated them, in no small part, for being formidable Black women.

A sense of being feared and disliked can reinforce a self-understanding that you see things more clearly than most—which, in turn, if expressed, can make you someone with something to say that others want to hear. Michelle Obama would poll at the end of 2018 as the most admired woman in America, and her memoir, *Becoming*, would sell more copies than any autobiography in history. People were drawn to Michelle Obama, to the story of how she struggled and triumphed. The same could be said of Serena.

Williams was of this moment in America, was a factor in shaping it; and the moment, in turn, fueled Williams's widening stature beyond the tennis court. It wasn't just her Grand Slam triumphs that mattered (though they mattered a lot), but the compelling particularity of who she was, a particularity she, with her embrace of celebrity, made millions aware of. Hers was a self she struggled with—on court, on TV, on social media—but not to struggle out of. Williams's rise as a figure in popular culture, it could be argued, helped lead to a broader interest in, and apprehension of, others who might look like her, come from places like where she came from, exhibit the dauntlessness she did, suffer the disappointments and discontinuities she did, annoy and inflame as she did, impose themselves as she did, revel or rage as she did. That she could and would navigate all this surely led others to think, *If she could do it, I can do it*—not that they *could* do it, not necessarily, but that wasn't the contract one had with one's cultural icon. And a cultural icon is whom she'd become. It wasn't that there was an intimate understanding of her, any more than there was, say, of Beyoncé. Icons, nevertheless, embody meanings, encapsulate stories, epitomize situations. Women of color, white women, too, girls of all ages, and enough men, for that matter, looked to Serena Williams for meaning, for direction, for affirmation, for reassurance, for inspiration.

This, all of it, had made her one the most absorbing figures of her time, and one of the most famous women on earth: *Serena*. Williams had always conscientiously spoken of the Black women who came before her in tennis, such as Althea Gibson and Zina Garrison, and of earlier tennis-playing feminist trailblazers, such as Billie Jean King—spoken of them as heroes. But Williams was something else, a woman in sports without antecedent. It could be said that she'd become the most consequential athlete America had produced since Muhammad Ali. She had not and would not take the bold and direct political stances Ali had. She was raised a Jehovah's Witness and, it appeared, continued to adhere to tenets of the denomination, including its ban, based on its distinctive reading of the Gospels, on voting or participating in any way, through statements or actions, to change a government or its policies. She never protested a war or lent her name to fights against laws that were seen to thwart the freedom, safety, or progress of women or minorities. But then, Muhammad Ali had slapped his first wife for what she chose to wear and had views, informed by *his* faith as a follower of Elijah Muhammad and his Nation of Islam, that women were to remain, for the most part, silent and obedient to men. It could not be more clear what Serena Williams would think about something like that. To be shown respect, to be unbeholden and powerful and free to express herself as and when she saw fit: here were the principles she embodied, always had. And that, in 2019, was a political stand, and one she was thoroughly and forcefully identified with. For Serena Williams, the personal, if only the personal, was political. That, too, suited the moment, a moment with identity politics and gender issues at the fore.

"I feel like with my platform, the things I do, the different boards

I sit on, we really talk about equality, gender equality, role equality, pay equality, how important that is," she'd said when I asked her one afternoon in Melbourne how she saw herself as a public figure. Williams held no office, but she was, in her way, a new kind of pop politician, with a loyal following most elected officials would envy.

3

Could it last? Excellence in athletics is so perishable—and with it, attention. To watch greatness in sport is to be transfixed by promise, then transcendence, then decay, and then to be transfixed no longer. This was not easy for any athlete to accept, and for Williams, who had faced so many challenges, this had to loom among the largest: she *loved* celebrity, the attention it brought, though she was always careful, as celebrities tend to be, to say otherwise. Over the years, she had at times spoken of being tired of tennis, the grind of it, but she had always found a way back to it. She was so good at it, and it is not easy to abandon what you are very, very good at. She craved competition, too, which meant—and this is difficult for all of us who aren't athletes, never mind great athletes, to comprehend—exposing herself to the possibility of losing. She hated to lose, deeply hated it. She needed to sense what losing might make her feel, might do to her sense of self-worth, and prevent it. That is what winning is for most sports stars. But now she was in her late thirties, beyond old by tennis standards. How much more winning was there for her?

And what was there for her beyond her tennis career? Were there ways to maintain the cultural status and power she'd earned? She seemed—through fashion and business, through the statements she was making in interviews and on social media—to be exploring that. What might be possible for her, beyond tennis, would not be bound by tennis—would be more than what had been available upon retiring to, say, Chris Evert. Williams's money and social-media presence, her ambition and the social and cultural paradigm shifts underway in America, would assure that. She wasn't going to coach or run a tennis academy or provide commentary on TV during Wimbledon. It would be a future, if she could pull it off, more along the lines of what had been brought about by the Barbados-born pop singer turned global taste arbiter and lifestyle entrepreneur, Rihanna.

In recent years, Williams had said, when asked, that she would like to tie or break Margaret Court's record of twenty-four Grand Slam championships. That was a reason to keep going, even as she reached an age when most women who have played singles tennis decide to retire. Williams had won her twenty-third major in 2017, in Melbourne, beating easily enough her older sister Venus in the final, 6–4, 6–4. With that win, Williams surpassed Steffi Graf as the all-time leader in Grand Slam wins earned in the Open era: the *real* record, to many inside tennis. The Open era began in 1968, when the Grand Slam tournaments finally agreed to allow professionals to compete. Professionals were, until 1968, all men and by and large the best male players, mostly under contract to one of two leagues; male amateurs, or lots of them, professed a frayed Edwardian snobbery about money while accepting payments under the table for travel and living expenses. Billie Jean King and a few others were the first women to turn pro, signing contracts when a small women's section of the male National Tennis League was formed in the spring of 1968. The depth of the women's game in the years before the Open era was nothing like what it would become, beginning in the 1970s and 1980s: money attracted talent. Steffi Graf, as a result, faced much tougher competition than Margaret Court, who, along with her many Australian Open triumphs at a time when top players often skipped the event, won most of her Grand Slam titles before the Open era began. That's why some journalists and fans considered Graf's Open-era record of twenty-two Grand Slam titles, not Court's twenty-four Slam victories, the one to beat, which Williams did in Melbourne in 2017. Graf, the dazzling German who had honed the power-baseline game that the Williams sisters would master and elevate, dominated women's tennis in the late 1980s and through the 1990s. She retired in 1999, and it was reasonable to assume that the women's game would never again see anything like her. Then Serena Williams came along.

Serena's 2017 Australian Open win over Venus, along with earning Serena her twenty-third major title, returned her to No. 1. Then thirty-five, she was the oldest woman to ever reach No. 1. The real news, though, would only be disclosed a few months later, by a photo of Williams posing sideways in a yellow one-piece bathing suit that she may or may not inadvertently have posted on Snapchat: she was pregnant. She'd been playing eight weeks pregnant in Melbourne and knew. She and Ohanian, then her boyfriend—a founder of the news-aggregation-and-discussion website Reddit, and a tech-world influencer—would be having a child come September. It seemed clear from the start that Williams was looking forward to the joys of being a new mom. It seemed clear, too, that she understood how becoming a mom heightened and deepened, complicated and could vex, the challenge of winning that next major title, or two. This life change would, as well, draw renewed attention, magnified attention, to the unfolding story of Serena Williams and—in a moment in which the struggles of the working mother had emerged as a cultural-political topos—add a dimension to her pop-icon status. Could she win another Grand Slam *as a mother*?

4

In a 2009 women's semifinal match at the US Open, Serena Williams played the terrific, no-ball-gets-by-me Belgian Kim Clijsters.

Williams lost the first set; and then, trailing 5–6 in the second, and serving, down 15–30 in the game, she was called for a foot fault on a second serve. A foot fault—when a server's foot, even the smallest part of it, is deemed to nick the baseline she's serving from behind before the serve is completed—is like any other service fault: if it is called on a second serve, the result is a loss of the point. Serena's foot fault made the score 15–40. Williams believed she did not foot fault; the Hawk-Eye camera system on the court in Arthur Ashe Stadium did not track foot faults, so she had no appeal. Furious, Williams threatened to shove a tennis ball down "the fucking throat" of the line judge who made the questionable (if only because rarely made) call. Williams was immediately penalized a point for that by the chair umpire, which meant she'd lost the game and thus, incredibly, the match as well. (Later, Williams was fined more than $80,000 for obscenely threatening the line judge, a woman named Shino Tsuru-buchi.) It would become, along with numerous rain delays and Juan Martín del Potro, age twenty, stunning Roger Federer in the men's final, what people remembered about 2009 in Flushing, Queens.

But a remarkable story was on the other side of the net that night, too. Clijsters, at age twenty-six, had only recently rejoined the women's tour after two years away. She had retired from the game to have and care for a baby. She'd played an exhibition match, then decided, with a why-not shrug, to get back to competing for real. Ranked far from the top one hundred, due to her lengthy maternity absence, she'd gained entry into the Open only by way of a wild card, a free pass of sorts that Grand Slam officials typically extend to veteran players returning from injury, or to teenage wunderkinds poised to join the tour. After her victory over Williams, Clijsters would go on to win the title at that US Open. Her cherubic daughter, Jada, toddled onto the court for the trophy presentation. It was something: Jada held by her mom, who was also managing to hold the large trophy. "We had planned Jada's nap time for later than usual so that she could be here tonight," Clijsters said during her on-court interview, and the crowd giggled and roared.

Only two other women before Clijsters in the Open era had won majors after having children. The Australian-aboriginal great, Evonne Goolagong, won two: the Australian Open in 1977, seven months after having her daughter, Kelly, and then Wimbledon, in 1980. Margaret Court had won *three* majors as a mom. That was it: three women who'd earned major titles as moms. Could Williams, returning to play in 2018, become the fourth? Could she win a Slam as a mom? It would not be easy. Court and Goolagong, like Clijsters, had been in their midtwenties when they became mothers. Williams would be an older mom, edging beyond her midthirties, and an older player returning to the game.

Any challenge, a real one, is suffused with threat and vulnerability. "When I realized that I was pregnant, I was like, 'Oh, my God. How am I going to play?'" That was Williams's first thought after learning she was pregnant. That's what she said on camera near the beginning of a five-episode HBO documentary, *Being Serena*, a self-serving enough but also a revealing enough and, in moments, deeply moving documentary conceived by Williams and produced, in partnership with HBO, by the original-content division of the talent-management company IMG, which is owned by William Morris Endeavor, where Jill Smoller, Williams's agent, is an executive. The creators of *Being Serena* began working on it not long after her pregnancy was revealed in 2017, and the series premiered in the spring of 2018 as she returned to the tour. *How am I going to play?* If you have read the many memoirs by athletes that grapple with late-career doubts about continuing to play (the most moving of these, on this facet of an athlete's life, being *The Game*, by former Montreal Canadian goalie Ken Dryden); if you have spoken to onetime tennis greats; and if you have spent time around Serena Williams, it was not a stretch to hear in her wistful uttering of those words that she could well be conveying this:

Could I ever regain my champion's form after taking off the time, at age thirty-six, to have a baby? And this: Could I find the time to train hard enough, once I'd had the baby and was ready to, to get good enough once more to win tournaments? And this: Could I handle the grind of a tennis tour, even one limited to Grand Slam tournaments and a few others, with a baby in tow? And this: Could I win another major or two? And this: If I couldn't, and if I didn't play at the highest level, at the championship level—at *my* level—how would I handle that? And, finally, this: If I couldn't train properly or handle the tour with a daughter in tow or regain my greatness or win a major or handle being something less than great, then what was next for me?

Ultimately, what Williams was conveying, most revealingly and movingly, if not always because she meant to, was this: fear. That was something Serena Williams was not about conveying.

How am I going to play? When I watched and heard Williams say that, what came to mind was this passage from Joan Didion's novel *Play It as It Lays*:

"Something real was happening: This was, as it were, her life. If she could keep that in mind, she would be able to play it through, do the right thing, whatever that meant."

By then, in May of 2018, when *Being Serena* was airing, it was not at all clear how Williams was going to play it through. What did seem clear was that many fans, and many others who had not paid much attention to tennis, were invested in her finding a way. When fear sneaks up on someone looked to as the embodiment of gladiatorial fearlessness, it compels. Celebrity motherhood seemed to, too. Celebrity idolatry, as *People* magazine figured out years ago, and as Instagram has digitally and exponentially magnified, fevers with the onset of a wedding, a breakup, or a pregnancy. A new wave of attention, devotional and febrile, swelled around Williams in the spring of 2018, as she returned to tennis and talked about becoming a mother in the HBO documentary.

5

Her pregnancy through the spring and summer of 2017 had been troubled only by heartburn. She'd done the breathing exercises and prepared for labor with a doula. All of this was public knowledge. There she was, healthy and visibly pregnant, a near nude, on the cover of the August 2017 issue of *Vanity Fair*. Soon after, it would be revealed that she had secured an entire floor at St. Mary's Medical Center in West Palm Beach, Florida, to deliver her daughter on September 1, by induced birth.

Then much of what could go wrong did go wrong. Williams had been in labor nearly fourteen hours and was beginning to have contractions when the baby's heart rate began to plunge. She had an emergency C-section. For the procedure, she went off the blood thinners she'd been on since suffering a blockage in an artery in her lungs, a pulmonary embolism, in 2011. The day following the C-section, she began feeling short of breath and feared that blood clots were once again forming in her lungs—fears she expressed to the doctors, who, she would later say, did not at first believe her. This is a documented fact of life for many women giving birth, Black women in particular. (A Black woman is three to four times more likely than a white woman to die in childbirth in America.) The doctors did agree, eventually, to perform a CT scan, which proved Williams right: blood clots had traveled to her lungs. She was put on an anticoagulant drip. The blood thinner helped her lungs but caused her to hemorrhage from the C-section incision. She would undergo three postdelivery surgeries before she was able to leave the hospital and would, once home, remain in bed for weeks recovering.

She and Alexis Ohanian married in November 2017, in New Orleans, having rented the Contemporary Arts Center there for the occasion. The decor had a theme: *Beauty and the Beast*. No explanation was proffered as to why. The guests included her friends Kim

Kardashian and Eva Longoria, Beyoncé and Jay-Z, and they sat on sofas and watched Williams come down the aisle in a white wedding dress designed by Sarah Burton for Alexander McQueen. (Burton had also designed the wedding dress worn by Kate Middleton, when she married Prince William and became the Duchess of Cambridge—which Williams may or may not have considered.) All this was celebrity news. A month later she played her first tennis match since delivering Olympia, not an official tour match but an exhibition, in Abu Dhabi. Star players such as Williams can earn hundreds of thousands of dollars, maybe as much as a million dollars, maybe more—no one knows for sure—for the hour or two it takes to play a glorified practice match known as an exhibition. Williams lost the exhibition match to Jeļena Ostapenko, a twenty-year-old Latvian, who, the previous spring, unseeded and barely known, had won the French Open. Williams knew she was not ready to play, play for real, and passed up the Australian Open the following month.

She rejoined the tour in March of 2018 at Indian Wells, in the California desert, carrying considerable postchildbirth weight, evidently slower, and struggling with her footwork, especially when forced to change direction. She served well but sprayed her ground strokes every which way. In her third-round loss to her sister Venus, she made forty-one unforced errors in two sets. It would get worse. She lost the following week in Miami to the young Japanese phenom Naomi Osaka in the first round, in straight sets. At the French Open—which began just after *Being Serena* aired, and fans learned of her difficult pregnancy and recovery—she was forced to withdraw with a pectoral injury. She would make a deep run in her next tournament, at Wimbledon, the most prestigious of the Grand Slams, where she had won seven previous times. She reached the final and had her first chance to secure a twenty-fourth major trophy, but lost in straight sets to the German Angelique Kerber, whose left-handedness and defensive relentlessness had frustrated

Williams and her game before. Although Williams hadn't had to face a top-ten player to reach the final and looked slow and winded at times, she left London having reached a Grand Slam final. If Williams was suffering in some way, it wasn't showing.

But it would soon enough. Back in the United States for the month of hard-court tournaments leading up to the summer-ending US Open, the last major of the year, she entered the small Silicon Valley Classic, in San Jose. In the first round, against England's Johanna Konta, who was in the midst of a near-disastrous season, Williams suffered the most lopsided loss of her career, winning only one game. She'd later say that just prior to the match she'd learned of the release from prison of the convicted murderer of her older half sister, Yetunde—shot in 2003 while sitting in an idling SUV with her boyfriend outside a Compton crack house, by a gang member said to be guarding the place. Williams then withdrew from the next tournament in which she was scheduled to play, in Toronto. She would subsequently explain to *Time* magazine, and on social media, that she was suffering from postpartum depression. On Instagram she stated that she "felt I was not a good mom," but that she had come to understand that it was "totally normal to feel like I'm not doing enough for my baby." If Williams was contending, physically and emotionally, with being the mother of an infant, and if that created uncertainty about whether she'd be able to win another Grand Slam, interest in her was in no way fading. Williams was forging and sharing a narrative of being a struggling working mom, on Instagram and cable TV and elsewhere, and it was proving as galvanic as anything she'd ever done.

6

Serena Williams has the most beautiful service toss in tennis—aesthetically pleasing, effortlessly smooth, the ball gently rolling off the fingertips of the left hand of a player whose game is anything but gentle. Beautiful, too, in the functional sense of being everything a service toss should be at the highest level of the game, which simply, yet not so simply, comes down to being consistent and functional.

Most humans have a dominant arm and hand. Most tennis players are taught to serve with that arm and hand and thus, when serving, toss the ball with their nondominant arm and hand. As a result, every point in tennis begins with a player depending on an arm and hand that he or she otherwise does nothing critical with. Here's what that developmentally secondary and underutilized arm and hand need to do: cradle the ball delicately, with all the fingers; firmly straighten the arm and slightly turn the forearm (without tightening the grip on the ball); and lock the elbow. Then, with the shoulder, not the arm—a completely unnatural movement—raise this oddly deployed limb calmly and continuously to the height of the eyes (while doing all sorts of other things with the dominant arm and hand, the legs, and back) and release the ball with a relaxed but controlled force such that it slowly and precisely reaches a height to meet the racquet, fully extended above. Got it?

Serena Williams, again, does this better than any other player, Roger Federer and other male players included. As a child, she practiced her serve unceasingly. She got bigger, yes, and used those muscular thighs (much of the power in any tennis shot comes from below the waist) and strapping shoulders to hit first serves that have topped 125 mph. That's nearly unheard of in women's tennis. But here is something rarer: her beautiful toss has no "tells." Even most good servers indicate to the returner, with the positioning of their toss, what kind of serve is coming: out front for a flat serve, out wide a bit toward the racquet-hand side for a slice, above the crown of the head for a topspin kick serve. When Williams is playing her best, her toss is in precisely the same place for all her serves. An opponent can't lean, can't guess. Or can, but helplessly.

That, more or less, was how Williams would reach the final of the 2018 US Open. If she was continuing to suffer from postpartum depression, there were no signs. Her serving was remarkable and carried her. No one had seen more of Williams's serves than her sister Venus—twenty-five, thirty years of them. In their third-round match, in a packed and lively Arthur Ashe Stadium, on a mild Friday night that marked the start of Labor Day weekend, Venus simply had no clue where Serena's serves were headed. Venus guessed wrong, leaned wrong, stood flat-footed, and quietly despaired—just as Serena's opponents in earlier rounds did, and those in subsequent matches leading to the US Open final would do. True, of the ten aces Serena struck, it wouldn't have mattered even if Venus had guessed right: they were simply too good, too exacting, painting the lines. But, beyond the aces, many Serena serves that Venus got a racquet on never got back over the net, and many others that she did get over the net landed short and smack in the center of the court—balls Serena could pounce on to take control of the point. Serena won nearly 90 percent of her first-service points. (Seventy-five percent is considered a terrific day on court.) She drubbed her sister, 6–1, 6–2.

Eight days later, in the US Open final, her first serve was, for stretches, nowhere to be found. Nerves? So much was riding on her winning, not just one more Grand Slam final to tie the record Margaret Court held, but a championship earned as a working mother. That was the story line being promoted by ESPN, which would broadcast the match—a late-afternoon Saturday match, not a prime-time match—to an audience that would prove to be the second largest in the network's years of telecasting the US Open. (The largest? Serena versus Venus, evening quarterfinal, 2015.) That was the story line reinforced by the Nike ads and the Chase ads featuring Williams that had been filling the commercial breaks on ESPN in the days before the final. That was what was being written about in the newspapers and on the blogs and in posts on social media. And all of it weighed squarely, had to, on Williams's shoulders.

Her opponent? Naomi Osaka had beaten Williams in Miami months earlier. Her coach, Sascha Bajin, had previously been Williams's hitting partner in practices. Osaka would, or could, know Williams's patterns: where she tends to hit her forehand early in a rally; to where in the service box she will try to direct her serve if she is behind in a game. Osaka had been playing clean and fearless tennis on her way to the US Open final, her first major final. She was twenty years old. She was the daughter of a Haitian father and a Japanese mother and had grown up worshipping Williams, had modeled her game on Williams's game, had told reporters after defeating Williams in Miami that she loved her and loved any chance to play her. So what if she was defeated by Williams in New York in a final in front of a crowd roaring for Serena? She was playing with nothing to lose. You can often tell a player is tight if the follow-through on her strokes appears stiff and shortened—clenched muscles, stiffened by nerves, curtailing and decelerating the swing. Osaka was not tight. From the start, she was swinging free and hard.

Osaka would outplay Williams from the beginning of the match to the end. She hit more aces than Williams; she had fewer double faults on her serve than Williams (who had *six*, some in pivotal moments); she took control of more points than Williams, moving her side to side and leaving her gasping for breath; she won more baseline rallies than Williams; she made fewer errors than Williams. She broke Williams's serve four times and won the match, 6–2, 6–4. But that is neither why nor how the match will be remembered.

The crowd was subdued as the second set began. Williams had been routed in set one and would have to win the second and then a third, deciding set if she was to come back and earn the championship, a big ask. Early in the second set, with Williams already having held her serve and leading 1–0, and Osaka serving and one point from holding, the chair umpire, Carlos Ramos—Portuguese, still youthful-looking in his midforties, widely respected on both the men's and women's tours—issued an official warning to Williams. He'd espied her coach, Patrick Mouratoglou, seated in Williams's courtside player's box, urging Williams, with hand gestures, to begin rushing the net during points—a tactic to cut off the longer rallies Williams was mostly losing, and to shorten points to preserve her energy. Coaching during a match was permitted on the WTA tour, but not at Grand Slam matches, which are overseen by a different governing body with its own rules, the International Tennis Federation. Code violations for coaching are always judgment calls left to the chair umpire's discretion. A different chair umpire might have glimpsed Mouratoglou's hand gestures and done nothing—might have thought, *This is a Grand Slam final, a historic one, perhaps, let them just keep playing.* A different chair umpire might have reasoned, *Serena Williams is not one to avail herself of coaching, even in matches where it is permitted.* A different chair umpire might have concluded, *Mouratoglou is not so much coaching as praying,* given that Williams had never been one to rush the net and volley and was not about to begin now. Or a different chair umpire might simply have said to Williams, quietly, as the players changed ends of the court, as they do after the conclusion of every odd-numbered game, *Tell your coach to cut it out*—that is, might have given her what's called a soft warning. Ramos had a reputation for punctiliousness, however; he issued the warning and the code violation that came with it.

That Mouratoglou was gesturing in a manner that signaled coaching was obvious to TV viewers (ESPN had captured him during its telecast). Whether Williams was looking his way was not clear (though that is not a factor in a code violation for coaching).

What exactly *was* transpiring on court between Ramos and Williams was not clear to the more than twenty-three thousand ticketholders inside Arthur Ashe, the largest tennis arena on earth—tennis umpires, unlike, say, football referees, make no attempt to communicate directly to those in the stands, except to quiet them occasionally. The crowd was already disheartened by the way the match was unfolding—these were Serena fans, in the main, or, as is often enough the case in New York, men (mostly) and women who'd paid hundreds or even thousands of dollars for a last-minute ticket on StubHub to witness (the hope was) a bit of sports history, Williams securing her twenty-fourth Slam. They were growing confused, unsettled.

Williams was already beyond unsettled. She did not wait for the next changeover to let Ramos know what she thought. She approached the chair and said, her words picked up by his microphone, "I don't cheat to win. I'd rather lose. I'm just letting you know." And, like *that*, a narrative that had been building for weeks, that had been reinforced to overdetermination and embraced by fans of tennis but not only by fans of tennis—the narrative of Williams winning her twenty-fourth major championship, as a working mom—was about to be supplanted by another. During the change of ends that followed, Williams holding her serve once more to go up, 2–1, Williams told Ramos, again, "Just know I've never cheated." Ramos said he understood her feelings.

Might Williams have left it at that? A first code violation carried no penalty, no loss of a point or such that figured into the score of a match. Williams did not leave it at that. She broke Osaka's serve in the next game, and Osaka, to judge from her body language, was growing discomposed by the remarks Williams was making to Ramos, and by the crowd's derisive murmuring and, from time to time, un-tennis-like booing—of Ramos and, Osaka had to feel, if only by implication, of her. But Williams could not consolidate the break by holding her own serve. She double-faulted twice and was soon enough broken back. In frustration, she smashed her racquet on the court. Racquet abuse is an automatic code violation in any professional tennis match. Now Williams had two, which meant, by the rules of pro tennis, that she would be penalized a point. Accordingly, Osaka would begin serving the next game, after the changeover, leading 15–0. Could Williams, having played hundreds of professional matches, not understand this? Walking to her bench during the changeover, she was, perhaps, by this point, beyond understanding.

Control, as in being in control, was something Williams strove for. But she seemed unable, at times, to control her anger—especially when it surfaced when she was losing and could not glimpse a path to victory. (In the Williams family, this angriest on-court side of Serena is referred to as Taquanda: *Here comes Taquanda, Taquanda just got loose.*) She was always invested in winning; she was especially invested in winning this match, and the narrative that winning it would fulfill. She said to Ramos, "This is unbelievable." She said, "You owe me an apology." She said, "I have a daughter and I stand for what is right for her." She said, "You will never do another one of my matches."

Osaka held her serve. Then she broke Williams again. The match, for all intents and purposes, was over, but Williams was not finished with Ramos. Before Osaka, now leading 4–3, could step to the baseline and serve again, Williams used the changing of ends to approach Ramos one more time. She called him a "thief." She called him a "liar." The crowd was by now something of a well-dressed mob. Ramos, having his character and fairness questioned, issued Williams a third code violation. That meant, by the rules, that Osaka would not have to serve, would not have to hold her serve under the pressure of the moment (though she had been broken only once), but would directly be granted the game by default. She now led 5–3. Williams was done with Ramos. She demanded to speak with the tournament referee, Brian Earley, and the WTA supervisor, Donna Kelso. When they arrived at the umpire's chair, Williams argued that she was being treated unfairly as a woman. She said male players "do a lot worse." Earley told her he could not and would not overrule any of Ramos's decisions. Williams then held her serve easily, but Osaka held hers, too, and won the set, 6–4, and the match in straight sets. (Williams was fined $17,000 for her actions. She earned $1.85 million as the US Open's women's runner-up.)

Later, in a press conference, Williams seemed calm enough at first. She said Ramos had always been a great chair umpire. She praised Osaka for her consistency and said she deserved to win. Williams expressed her displeasure, as she had on court during the postmatch award ceremony, with the crowd's booing. But as the press conference drew to a close, she was asked, If she could go back and change how she'd behaved on court, would she? Her eyes welling, her voice thickening, she replied:

I can't sit here and say I wouldn't say he's a thief, because I thought he took a game from me. But I've seen other men call other umpires several things. I'm here fighting for women's rights and for women's equality and for all kinds of stuff. For me to say "thief" and for him to take a game, it made me feel like it was a sexist remark. He's never taken a game from a man because they said "thief."

For me it blows my mind. But I'm going to continue to fight for women. . . .

I just feel like the fact that I have to go through this is just an example for the next person that has emotions, and that want to express themselves, and want to be a strong woman. They're going to be allowed to do that because of today. Maybe it didn't work out for me, but it's going to work out for the next person.

There was no evidence that any player on the men's tour had ever called Ramos a thief, or that any player at any time over the years had ever impugned his character. There was, however, plenty of evidence, in tennis as in all aspects of life, of a double standard for men and women. Here was Williams, provocative and impellent, seizing a moment, amplifying and redirecting, speaking out for and to others and in the same breath self-valorizing, rousing herself and looking to rouse others. Several reporters in the room actually applauded her. An understanding that what had happened to her in the US Open final was sexist would take hold. Articles were written about the way men's and women's angry outbursts were treated differently by tennis umpires. Sports columnists weighed in. WTA officials and Billie Jean King came to Williams's defense.

Brought to wider attention by what had transpired during the Open final was an existing discourse devoted to why and how Black women express anger, and how that anger is often mischaracterized, or worse. Michelle Obama had been described, during the 2008 presidential campaign, as threatening, emasculating, and, on Fox News, as exhibiting "militant anger." Dissertations have been written on the anger of Black female characters in Toni Morrison's novels, characters such as the protagonist of Morrison's first novel, *The Bluest Eye*, an eleven-year-old unloved and lonely Black girl named Pecola Breedlove, who thinks to herself, "Anger is better. There is a sense of being in anger. An awareness of worth. It is a lovely surging."

Morrison herself, in a *Paris Review* interview, said, "Anger is a very intense but tiny emotion, you know. It doesn't last. It doesn't produce anything." The poet Claudia Rankine, in her 2014 book, *Citizen: An American Lyric*—a mélange of free verse, anecdote, and reflection—writes at some length about Williams's on-court outbursts, glimpsing in them something of herself, of every Black woman, discriminated against and maltreated:

"For Serena, the daily diminishment is a low flame, a constant drip. Every look, every comment, every bad call blossoms out of history, through her, onto you. To understand is to see Serena as hemmed in as any other Black body thrown against an American background."

Brittney Cooper, a professor of Women's and Gender Studies and Africana Studies at Rutgers University, had, only months before the US Open began, published a book, *Eloquent Rage*, in which she suggested, among other things, that Black women "have the right to be mad as hell," and that rage was a legitimate "political emotion," while acknowledging that her own anger could use more focus. She cited Serena Williams as a hero, as a Black woman whose rage was focused, whose greatness on court "belongs to all of us."

It wasn't that everyone thought what had happened between Williams and Ramos was race-suffused or sexist, or that Williams's rage was justified. Martina Navratilova, an outspoken women's champion herself in the 1980s who went on to be a voice for feminism in her role as a tennis commentator and a human-rights activist, wrote in a *Times* op-ed titled "What Serena Got Wrong," "This is the sort of behavior that no one should be engaging in on the court." There was a sense, too, and it would grow, as Osaka made the rounds on television in the days after the final, charming Ellen DeGeneres and others with her shyness and her quiet, gnomic pronouncements on pop culture and the vagaries of a tennis life, that Williams had hijacked a moment that was due the victor, who was also a woman of color. Williams had comforted Osaka on court after the match as she wept, the boos loud and implacable, as they'd never been at any other Grand Slam final that anyone could recall. Williams, as the post-match ceremony began, had demanded the crowd stop booing. But wasn't it—and this was getting said now—wasn't it Williams who had started the whole thing? Wasn't the booing her fault in the first place? Wasn't this not only on Ramos, the chair umpire, but on *her*, too?

Athletes find neither comfort nor advantage in *what has happened*. They move on. They live in the moment, the now and the near future: today's match, tomorrow's. If Williams's rage at Ramos was an example for other women, she wasn't going to be referring to it as that again. She wasn't going to be talking about that match again much at all, if she could help it. When discussions that fall about a possible *60 Minutes* interview took place, they foundered, it was said, because there were to be no questions, Williams's camp insisted, about the US Open final. When Williams once again flew to Abu Dhabi at the end of the year to play an exhibition match—this time against her sister Venus—reporters, according to one of them there, were instructed to ask no questions about the US Open final. And when, a month later, after Williams's first-round victory over Tatjana Maria at the Australian Open, a reporter sitting behind me brought up the controversial Osaka match with her—even as he took note that "you kind of parked what happened at the US Open"—she glared in his direction and said firmly, "I, like, literally have no comment."

7

"I don't think she was ready," Patrick Mouratoglou was saying. "I mean, she was ready to reach a final, but there is a big difference between reaching a final and winning it. I don't think she was ready." He was talking about Williams and the US Open final. He paused, then went on, "I didn't want to say it when she lost because it sounds like an excuse. But you cannot buy time. Things take time. To get back in shape after a baby . . . I mean, the *story* said it was too early. That's it."

It was late one night during the first week of the Australian Open, a couple of days after Williams's first-round win over Tatjana Maria, and Mouratoglou was in the main pressroom on the fourth floor of the nearly empty media center, talking with a handful of reporters. He had a Continental presence—tanned and trim, at forty-eight, with his hair and salt-and-pepper beard carefully groomed. His mind had a searching, even philosophical cast; he thought for a moment before answering questions, and those answers often unspooled toward broad-ranging considerations of tennis's essence and standing. (He believed, for example, that the game needed to do more, much more, to attract younger fans; perhaps that is why he had just released *Tennis Manager 2019*, a mobile game.) His lightly French-accented English was superb, and alluring. The son of a highly successful Greek-born businessman and a French mother, he grew up playing tennis until, at fifteen and at his parents' request, he abandoned the game to concentrate on his schooling. He was being readied to take over his father's company—one of the largest renewable-energy concerns in France—but informed his parents, at the age of twenty-six, that he had one passion in life, tennis, and, instead, planned to open a tennis academy outside Paris. He turned out to be a good coach, and within a few years he was guiding the Greek Cypriot Marcos Baghdatis into the top ten. Mouratoglou turned out to be a good businessman, too, developing what would become one of the largest and best-thought-of tennis academies in Europe, eventually relocating, several years ago, to the more weather-friendly south of France, near Nice. Recently, he had been taken on by Stefanos Tsitsipas, a twenty-year-old Greek comer. Mouratoglou also had a burgeoning international career as a tennis commentator. On TV, he favored slim-cut suits and the top buttons of his dress shirts unfastened. He came across as tennis's answer to Bernard-Henri Lévy.

Mouratoglou and Williams had met in June of 2012. Williams had just crashed out of the French Open in the first round, losing to Virginie Razzano, a Frenchwoman ranked No. 111. Williams had never before lost in the first round of a Grand Slam. It was a new low in a stretch of them, beginning shortly after she won Wimbledon in the summer of 2010. A few days after her Wimbledon victory, she was leaving a restaurant in Munich when she stepped on a piece of broken glass. She was wearing sandals, and a tendon in her right foot was gashed. Surgery followed, then a second surgery; and then, in February of 2011, she was hospitalized in Los Angeles for a pulmonary embolism that might have been a result of being immobilized by the foot surgeries. While in the hospital, she also required emergency treatment for a hematoma, a pocket of blood that had swelled under her skin. She was prescribed anticoagulants—the blood thinners that, years later, she was taken off while giving birth to Olympia, resulting in myriad health complications. She returned to tennis, but struggled with ankle and back injuries. Her upset loss at Roland-Garros would make it nearly two years since she had won a Grand Slam. She had reached her thirties and, along with the injuries, seemed to lack confidence and focus.

Williams had an apartment in Paris, and after her French Open loss, she stuck around and arranged to practice at Mouratoglou's academy. By the end of that summer, he'd become her coach—supplanting the only coach she had ever had, her father. Mouratoglou and Williams became something more than coach and player. They were photographed walking with their arms around each other, Williams's hand tucked inside the back pocket of Mouratoglou's jeans, and not long after that, Mouratoglou's wife, Clarisse, an interior designer with whom he had three children, filed for divorce. The affair apparently ended in the summer of 2014, but

Mouratoglou continued as Williams's coach. He had restored her on-court intensity, Williams said, and the results showed it: she had won four Grand Slam titles in their first two years working together. He talked back then of how he understood her—understood her drive, her stubbornness, her way of hoping you'd understand what she *wasn't* saying. She would win six more majors with him as her coach before beginning her thirteen-month-long maternity leave from the tour in February 2017. Some perspective: that's a total of ten major championships in fewer than five years. Only seven women have won ten or more majors in their entire careers.

A relaxed smile crossed Mouratoglou's face when he was asked if he'd worried that Williams would fire him for his coaching gestures at the US Open. "No, I didn't worry about that at all," he said. "First of all, I hope that every time a coach gets a code violation for coaching he doesn't get fired, otherwise there will be guys fired every two days, a problem." He went on to talk about how Williams always takes the blame on herself, completely, after a loss; about her strong sense of loyalty; about how she doesn't tend to make snap, emotional decisions about anything. He said, "It's not a reason for taking a decision that would have an impact on your future. And I think she's smart enough to think like that."

I asked him about her fitness—about whether she needed more time in the gym than on the practice court since returning to play after giving birth to her daughter. I knew he worried about the weight she continued to carry after giving birth to her daughter, as she herself did, and about her regaining her elite fitness level. (And I knew, too, that relating this conversation with Mouratoglou—two men discussing a woman's fitness after she'd given birth—would strike some as inappropriate. But athletes, their work lives, come down to physical performance, and their fitness is crucial, and, matter-of-factly and in detail, regularly discussed by those around them and by reporters.) He'd urged Williams to stop nursing when she arrived in

France to train for the French Open in May of 2018, believing that nursing was taking time and focus from her practice regimen—as difficult a conversation as they'd had, Williams would later say.

Replying to my question, Mouratoglou said, "I think the transformation of the body for a woman when she has a baby is huge, and to get back to what it was before, you need time and you need a lot of exercise. But not exercise for two months—it's a long process. And more than that: for months, you can't do what you want to do because the body is not able to do it. So you have to go, really, step by step. So you can't practice."

He continued, "And then there is the emotional part also, and the transformation between—I mean, yeah, she's a professional tennis player and she's become a mother and it's a big transformation in her life, and I don't think it's something that you deal with easily."

That said, he was confident, or said he was, that she would win another Grand Slam. Champions have a different mind-set from other players—this he had discovered coaching Williams. "There are guys who win one tournament and they celebrate for fifteen years," he said, and laughed. Everybody laughed. It didn't have to do with her fitness, ultimately; he believed that would come. It had to do, he suggested, with having a champion's experience of winning and winning again, with having a tireless work ethic, with an undiminished hunger to prevail. He said, "There is only one Serena in terms of mind-set."

8

Williams was making news during the first week of the Australian Open on the days she wasn't playing—with her off-day practice sessions. She and Mouratoglou had decided that to sharpen her game and raise her intensity level she should practice with players on the men's tour. For sure, none of her female opponents in the early rounds in Melbourne were giving her much of a challenge. After her first-round flattening of Tatjana Maria, she'd gone on to crush Canada's Eugenie Bouchard, 6–2, 6–2. In the third round, against eighteen-year-old Dayana Yastremska of Ukraine, Williams sliced or blasted eight aces, Yastremska scattered or netted eight double faults, and the 6–2, 6–1, pummeling left the teenager in tears.

"It seemed very simple before the match," Yastremska said afterward. "But when I entered the arena, I felt the crowds. I felt: I was here with Serena. I could feel her energy." Yastremska searched for the right word, but couldn't find it. The word was *intimidated*. She said that when Williams found her after the match, crying in the locker room, she comforted her: "She told me, 'Don't cry, you're still young, you don't have to cry.'"

One of the men Williams hit with in practice was Frances Tiafoe, an American, twenty-one, rising in the ranks, with a compelling backstory. He'd gotten interested in tennis at the United States Tennis Association's training center in Maryland, where his father, an immigrant from Sierra Leone, worked as the head of maintenance. Tiafoe spoke after his practice with Williams about how flat and hard her ground strokes were, so flat and hard that he'd been forced to adjust the timing of his shots to absorb them.

A couple of weeks earlier, Tiafoe had partnered with Williams in a mixed-doubles match against a Swiss team, Belinda Bencic and Roger Federer. This was in Perth, in western Australia, at the Hopman Cup, a thirty-years-running exhibition tourney and Australian Open lead-up named for the legendary Australian tennis coach Harry Hopman. It was designed as a team competition: eight countries each year are invited to send a team, one female player and one male; each team played a series of matchups, on an indoor hard court, that was decided by one men's singles match, one women's singles match, and one match of mixed doubles. The

Hopman Cup, always popular with TV viewers in Australia, signaling for them the beginning of the Aussie summer and the tennis season, was drawing more international attention than usual with the promise that Serena and Roger would, for the first time in their storied careers, meet across the net from each other, even if with doubles partners and in a quick-set, first-to-four-games format. Once their match began, Williams had little problem with Federer's pace; she took his ground strokes early and returned his serve, too, once she got used to reading it. (Federer and Bencic won the mixed-doubles match 4–2, 4–3, their stronger net play providing the difference.) Williams displayed her own power. On court after the match, Williams at his side, Federer said of her serve, "I was nervous returning!" They laughed. They took a selfie together. (As it happened, this was the final Hopman Cup to be held.)

That match, and her practice sessions with men's-tour players, brought to mind Williams's first trip to the Australian Open, as a sixteen-year-old, in 1998. She was ranked No. 99. She and her sister Venus (ranked No. 22, and also playing her first Australian Open) had concluded that both of them were capable of beating any player on the men's tour ranked outside the world's top two hundred. One male player stepped forward: Karsten Braasch, a German ranked No. 203 in singles, and only in Melbourne because he was in the top forty in doubles. Two things distinguished Braasch's game: his service motion, which, convulsively rushed, looked like something he'd learned from a windup toy; and his habits during the pause as players changed ends, habits that included a quick smoke and, occasionally, a lager. It was said that by the time he met the Williams sisters to play on an outer court on the Open grounds—the arrangement was he'd play a set against each of them—he'd already completed a round of golf and quenched his thirst with two shandies. He beat Serena 6–1 before beating Venus 6–2.

The difference between the men's game and the women's game, now even more than twenty years ago, is not a matter of power. Women pulverize the ball. Madison Keys, a top-twenty-five American for a number of years now—and another woman of color drawn to the game by the example of the Williams sisters— hits her forehand with more pace, on average, than lots of men. Serena Williams has a first serve that can, at times, be harder than either Novak Djokovic's or Rafael Nadal's. Women in this era hit with more oomph than men did back in the time of McEnroe and Borg, and it is not just about new racquet and string technology. Women players today are bigger and stronger than they once were and are trained in technical ways and through fitness regimens to strike the ball viciously. They crush it.

The chief difference between men's and women's tennis is that men tend to run faster. In particular, they exhibit greater lateral speed—the quickness to run down, and to get back with zip, balls hit to the corners of the baseline and balls angled far off the court. Not every male player can run, but those who can *really* can. No player currently on the women's tour can match that speed. Scientists offer various theories for why men's bodies lend themselves to faster running: narrower hips that more closely align to the quads and make running more efficient; greater lung capacity; larger fast-twitch muscle fibers. But men thirty years ago didn't run like the quickest men today. Men have been nurtured better, too, for quickness.

Williams understands this. Back in 2013, Andy Murray joked about playing her—warmly joked; Murray, throughout his career, has been a vocal supporter of women and the women's game. Asked about playing Murray by David Letterman during an appearance she made on his late-night show, Williams laughed and said, "I'm like, 'Andy, seriously, are you kidding me?'" She went on, "For me, men's tennis and women's tennis are, completely, almost, two separate sports. If I were to play Andy Murray, I would lose six–love, six–love in five to six minutes, maybe ten minutes. No, it's true. It's a completely different sport. The men are a lot faster." Williams wasn't practicing with male players in 2019 to measure herself, as she had been years before—wasn't much at all intrigued by the topic of men's tennis versus women's tennis. She and Mouratoglou wanted the workout that speedier male players might provide.

Gender is a topic in tennis as in no other professional sport of its reach: Where else do you get men and women competing for glory and prize money in the same tournaments? This makes for a distinctive crowd vibe, and for a different sort of sports conversation, not always inspiriting. The issue for Williams had long been and had, to a stunning degree, remained the insults, often buttressed by racism, that she had the body, the heft, and the muscularity of a man—*was* a man, somehow, in a women's game. In September 2017, shortly after giving birth to her daughter, Williams published an essay on Reddit, the website cofounded by her husband, Alexis Ohanian. In the form of a letter to her mother, she wrote about her baby having arms and legs like her own, and how she hoped her daughter wouldn't have to go through "what I've gone through since I was 15-years-old and even to this day." She wrote about being called a man, being accused of taking drugs to bulk up, being told she belongs in men's sports. "I just work hard and I was born with this badass body, and proud of it."

Not long before Williams arrived at the 2019 Australian Open, a photograph surfaced of two Australian-football players, members of the Penguin Football Club in Tasmania, bewigged with black curls, in white outfits with white sun visors, holding tennis racquets. They were also in blackface: "Venus and Serena." The "Serena" had what appeared to be stuffing around his midriff. They were dressed for Mad Monday, a traditional celebration of the end of the football season. The whites (British convicts and free settlers) who colonized Australia in the nineteenth century did not enslave Black Africans (though they did coerce Pacific Islanders into working on sugar plantations; blackbirding, it came to be called). Few Black Africans are to be found in Australia today. But here was that peculiarly American and enduringly popular expression of racial bigotry and insult, traceable to pre–Civil War minstrelsy: whites blackening their faces, and costuming, to mockingly depict Blacks as freakish grotesques. Here, too, was misogyny along with racism, especially in the case of the footballer masquerading as Serena—filled out to be bigger, more "manly," than the male athlete derisively portraying her.

This trope of Serena Williams as unwomanly, as unnaturally big and strong, as masculine, as *hyper*masculine, could crop up, or seem to, in surprising places. As I made my daylong way from New York to Melbourne in mid-January, on the airport newsstands rested stacks of the year-end issue of *GQ* magazine, with its annual choices of Men of the Year. Henry Golding was on some *GQ* covers, Michael B. Jordan on others. There was Jonah Hill. And there was . . . Serena Williams, in a black bodysuit with a vintage Chanel belt dangling from her waist. Not one of the Men of the Year, exactly. The word *Men* had an *X* drawn through it on the cover she appeared on. Above the crossed-out *Men* was handprinted the word *"Woman"*—just like that, in quotation marks. Scare quotes? I didn't get it. Neither did a lot of other folks. A Twitter storm had erupted about the cover presentation:

"@GQMagazine out here thinkin they slick by putting Woman of the year (as it relates to Serena Williams) in quotation marks. The thought of a Black woman with muscles really disturbs [*sic*] this country so much that you'll call em a man at every chance. Even when they identify as woman."

Was *GQ*, a sophisticated men's magazine, actually saying, with those quotation marks, that Serena Williams wasn't exactly a woman?

It was not. But that took some explaining. The handwritten *"Woman"* had been done by Virgil Abloh. He was a friend of Williams's. He was an American street-wear designer, the son of Ghanaian immigrants. He'd collaborated with Kanye West. He had his own fashion label, Off-White, and had recently been appointed artistic director of Louis Vuitton's menswear collection. He'd designed the one-bare-shoulder black tennis dress that Williams had worn at the 2018 US Open. If you looked closely at that dress, you could see that the Nike swoosh had quotation marks around it. Quotation marks are Abloh's signature logo, sort of like Ralph Lauren's polo player. The cover was, or was meant to be, a fashion statement, not a gender statement.

The connection between a word and its meaning, the signifier and what's signified, could get slippery for a multihyphenated popular icon such as Serena Williams—an icon, in part, for the body she had, for what she had achieved with it, but also as a result of the projections made upon it by those who cared about her, cared to love her or cared to detest her or cared because she was interesting, *interestingness* being what we seemed to ask most of all now from our pop icons. There was no debating Serena Williams's interestingness.

9

Rennae Stubbs is among the most attentive and deep-thinking observers of the women's game. She played on the tour for nearly twenty years, most successfully in women's doubles, winning sixty titles, four of them Grand Slam championships, and reaching No. 1 in 2000—the best women's doubles player Australia has ever had. Six years later, she did the rarest of things in tennis, in sports in general: she came out to an Australian newspaper interviewer, while still an active player, identifying herself as a lesbian. She retired from the game in 2011. She works now as a coach on the tour, and as a tennis commentator for Australian TV and ESPN.

We met for coffee one afternoon, in the Australian Open's media lounge, the air-conditioning humming conspicuously; the temperature outside had reached 107 degrees. Stubbs was soon to turn forty-eight; she looked match-ready still. She recalled the first time she'd seen Serena Williams play. "I remember it clearly, she was eleven years old, Baltimore, Maryland," she began, speaking genially but concisely, without hesitations or filler words, the way those who spend a good deal of time on television do. Stubbs was in Baltimore for a 1993 charity event organized by Pam Shriver, who lived there and was, in the early 1990s, still a top-ten doubles player, though no longer the commanding competitor she'd been in the mid-1980s. "Pam had invited these two young kids from LA to play in the event, and she asked me, 'You want to come hit with these kids?' I said sure. We hit, and when we walked off the court, Pam turned to me and asked, 'What do you think?' And I said, 'Yeah, not bad.'" Stubbs laughed and shook her head. "You don't know—at ten or eleven, you just don't know where they could go or will go. The other thing I said to Pam, and I remember this clearly: 'The young one, the little one, she's better.'" More laughter. "Serena was more athletic, even then. And her technique was better. Would continue to be. Still is. Doesn't break down technically late in tight matches. Venus can be up and down in those situations. Forehand can break down, serve can break down. Not so with Serena. Not technically. That was the way they were as kids. It's the way they are today."

Stubbs recalled facing Serena and Venus in doubles at a number of Grand Slams. (The Williams sisters played doubles together for many years, but only at Grand Slams and in the Olympics.) The last such time was in 2009, Stubbs partnering with her fellow Australian Samantha Stosur: the Wimbledon women's doubles final. The Williamses won in straight sets. Stubbs talked, as all players do, about the power and unreadability of Serena's serve. But there was more to Serena's game on that afternoon and so many afternoons, Stubbs explained. "Her depth of shot, returning your shots consistently within a foot or two of the baseline. Lots of players hit hard. Not many can do that. She doesn't get enough credit for staying in points. When she wants to. And then there's her presence. *Presence*. Can't explain it, exactly. But it's unmistakable."

Stubbs was currently coaching Karolína Plíšková, in her prime at twenty-six and in the top five for the previous few years (she'd reached No. 1 in the summer of 2017). Plíšková was a six-feet-one Czech powerhouse with an aggressive baseline game. What advice would Stubbs give her should she find herself confronting Williams in the coming days in Melbourne—a genuine possibility, given the draw?

Stubbs didn't hesitate: "I think the way to beat Serena is to hope she is having a bit of an off day emotionally. Her being a bit more nervous. Now that she's getting older, she understands the enormity of these moments. How many more Slam opportunities will she have?"

Stubbs continued, "She's looked vulnerable in big matches, those Slam finals at Wimbledon and in New York. Now, does that have something—not sure what, but something—to do with being a mother? An openness to the enormity of the moment, which you don't want to be feeling in a Slam final, because she is now so much more open in her life, as you have to be as a mother to your child? Serena used to be *so* much about herself at big events. And now it is so clear she loves being a mom. She's still tough. She's still Serena. But more vulnerable.

"She wants a Slam as a mom," Stubbs said before running off to ESPN's makeshift quarters, tucked in among the myriad other international broadcasters, all their Potemkin sets and office trailers on the edge of the Open's grounds, near an exit to a light-rail station. "Yes, she wants to beat Margaret Court, have that record number of Slams. But winning as a mom—*that's* what's driving her. So she loves being a mom, and I'm sure she wants another kid. But she's not getting any younger. And there are only those four Slam opportunities a year. Try having all *that* on your mind as you try to win a major."

10

In 2003 the Australian Open renamed its Show Court One the Margaret Court Arena, and for good reason: Margaret Court was the greatest women's tennis player Australia had known. Court completed an in-year singles Grand Slam, winning all four major titles in a calendar year, in 1970, and her record of sixty-four major titles, singles and doubles and mixed doubles combined, is unlikely to be eclipsed. Her total of twenty-four Grand Slam women's singles titles was the record that Serena Williams was currently chasing. But now there were people, lots of them, in Australia and around the world, who wanted Margaret Court's name removed from the arena. This new sort of issue came down to this: Had the public's sense of Margaret Court, as a tennis legend, been overtaken by a different identity, that of an antigay zealot? Was the name Margaret Court, even affixed to a tennis arena, no longer mostly associated with a great athlete but with someone who, to many, was a relentless, hurtful bigot?

Court came to voice her homophobic views after she put down her tennis racquet. She showed no signs, as times changed, of altering or even softening them. Court maintained she was doing nothing more than drawing on Scripture, expressing her religious beliefs. She came to her particular faith, she'd said, while attending Bible school, in 1982, five years after she retired from tennis. She said that her newfound faith got her through postpartum depression and believed that it cured some heart trouble she was having. Soon after, she founded a Pentecostal church of her own, in Perth, and began making her biblically attributed denunciations of gays and lesbians. By the early nineties, she was declaring that lesbians were ruining women's tennis, and that Martina Navratilova, in particular, was "a great player" but that she, Court, would "like someone at the top who the younger players can look up to. It's very sad for children to be exposed to homosexuality." When, in 2011, the call for reforms that would legalize gay marriage began to grow louder in Australia, Court's views became even harsher, and she began voicing them more loudly and frequently. By the time same-sex marriage was put to a national referendum, in the fall of 2017, she was a prominent and tireless opponent.

She claimed gay marriage was corrupting countries where it had been legalized, by which she mostly meant she saw gay marriage as increasing LGBT tendencies in children. "That's what Hitler did," she said. "That's what communism did, get in the minds of the children. There's a whole plot in our nation and in the nations of the world to get in the minds of the children." When the CEO of Qantas Airlines voiced support for the referendum, Court announced that she was boycotting the airline. On the eve of the ballot measure, she said a yes vote would lead to the end of Christmas and Easter being celebrated in Australia. She remained worried now that, with gay marriage the law of the land in Australia, she would not be able to express her religious views. In a formal submission in 2018 to a government panel established to assess the implications marriage equality would have for religious organizations, Court warned that Australia was "forsaking foundational truths and the blessings that have made Australia great."

Numerous Australian players, active and retired, have criticized Court's views. Casey Dellacqua retired in 2018, having broken into the top twenty-five as a singles player and, in 2016, reached world No. 3 in doubles. When Dellacqua and her partner, Amanda Judd, announced the birth of their first child, Court wrote of her "sadness that the baby has seemingly been deprived of a father." During the run-up to the marriage referendum, in 2017, Dellacqua, who knew Court personally and as a teenager played tennis with her in Perth, told reporters that she was "very conscious of the fact that everyone is allowed their opinion, but when you start singling out my family especially, that's when it's not okay."

Billie Jean King, who, in 1981, became the first prominent female athlete to come out, after her partner filed a palimony suit against her, had in 2003 enthusiastically supported the arena being named for Court. King raised no public objections for years, even as other players denounced Court; as gay rights activists in Melbourne protested a speech that Court gave; and as musicians who played concerts at the arena condemned Court's views from the stage. However, when King attended the 2018 Australian Open to receive its Woman of the Year award, meant to call attention to the tournament's commitment to diversity, equality, and inclusion, she took the opportunity of having the spotlight at Australia's biggest international sporting event to say that she'd changed her mind. Seated on a podium next to the tournament's director, Craig Tiley, she said, "I think it's really important if you're going to have your name on anything that you're hospitable, you're inclusive, you're 'open arms' to everyone that comes. It's a public facility." She added, "I personally don't think she should have her name anymore. I think if you were talking about indigenous people, Jews, or any other people, I can't imagine the public would want somebody to have their name on something. Maybe because of our community, the LGBTIQ community, people might feel differently. But we're all God's children. We are all God's children, so I probably don't think it's appropriate to have her name."

Rennae Stubbs told me that Margaret Court's determination to continue to publicly denounce gay rights, after the passage of the referendum and same-sex marriage legislation, was a sign that an antigay fanatic is who Margaret Court was—*that* is whose name is on the arena now. Stubbs would like to see the name changed. "She had an opportunity after gay marriage passed," Stubbs said. "You know, 'I don't agree but so be it.' Instead, she went on the attack. Gay players know that. Gay fans walking in that arena know that."

Stubbs was confident that the change would come at some point. Discussing names that might replace Court's, she brought up, as others had, that of Evonne Goolagong Cawley, who was from an aboriginal family, as few Australian tennis players are, and who, following Court's retirement, rose to become Australia's leading women's player and a world No. 1. Another, perhaps more likely, possibility was that someday Australian tennis officials would announce that they'd sold the arena's naming rights to a corporate sponsor—nothing personal or political, just business. It had been the intention of tennis officials in Melbourne, having named the Australian Open's main venue for the men's great Rod Laver, to do the right thing by naming Show Court One for a woman. History can get complicated.

Serena Williams, meanwhile, was adding a new cohort to her fan base: gay tennis fans, along with members of the LGBT community who never gave a thought to sports, were rooting for Williams to break Court's record.

11

The top opponents Serena Williams faced over the years were in large measure determined historically, if not directly, by Mikhail Gorbachev and Boris Yeltsin. Thirty-one Americans were in the women's top fifty as the tennis season drew to a close in 1980, the year before Williams was born. Six players were from what were then the Soviet Union and the Warsaw Pact nations. Perestroika and then the collapse of the Soviet Union in 1991 changed all that. (The reintroduction of tennis as an Olympic sport in Seoul in 1988 played a role, too.) Young teenagers from Russia and Eastern Europe were soon flocking to tennis academies in Western Europe and Florida, and tennis federations in the Czech Republic and elsewhere began modernizing their facilities and training programs. Of the thirty-two women seeded in the 2019 Australian Open, sixteen were from countries that once constituted the Eastern Bloc. There were three Americans. (Two of these women— Sloane Stephens and Serena Williams—were Black, and the third, Madison Keys, a woman of color, another striking change from 1980.) The balance had more or less been trending that way for twenty years, an era of the Russians, Belarusians, Ukrainians, Romanians, Latvians, Estonians, Serbs, Croats, Czechs, and on— an era of the Williams sisters versus the "ovas" (Daniela Hantuchová, Ekaterina Makarova, Maria Sharapova, and on).

Serena Williams's fourth-round opponent as the second week of the Australian Open got underway was Romania's Simona Halep. She was currently No. 1 in the world. Of the original 128 women who'd begun the tournament, 16 were left (hence the designation of the fourth round at a Grand Slam tournament as the Round of 16). Halep, the tourney's top seed, was arguably the best all-around defensive player in the women's game and had over the previous few years improved her only glaring weakness, a tendency to suddenly grow dark and self-punishing in tough stretches of matches. That said, she had to fight through three sets to win each of her first two matches in Melbourne before beating Venus Williams handily, 6–2, 6–3, in the third round. Serena, Halep knew, had never been a good matchup for her. Halep was five foot six and wiry, with a modest first serve and a second serve that, when she was brooding, could arrive at a pace better suited to suburban-club play. Halep had beaten Williams just once and lost to her eight times.

The evening was warm and humid as the match got underway, and Williams, serving first, could not find her range, losing four straight points, the last a double fault, to be broken. She figured things out quickly enough, though: she'd take the first set 6–1 in twenty minutes. Those six games she ran off after dropping the opening game may have been her best tennis overall since returning to the tour after her daughter was born. Afterward, Halep would say of the first set, "I felt like I'd been hit by a train."

Halep took the second set, extending the rallies and winning most of them, and as the third set began, Williams looked fatigued. Halep had a look at three break points as Williams served in the sixth game, with Halep up 3–2. It was the game of the match, pivotal but also full of tremendous shotmaking under pressure: a rocket of a Williams serve up the T (formed by the intersection of the center and service lines) that glanced off Halep's racquet frame and saved Williams one break point; a Halep down-the-line forehand winner that earned her a second break-point opportunity; a Williams inside-out backhand winner down the line—a risky shot that few players other than Williams would even *think* of attempting—that secured her the game, finally, and appeared to deflate Halep's energy and will. Williams broke Halep in the game that followed and took the set, 6–4, and the match.

After the match, Williams seemed satisfied. She seemed, too, more responsive to questions about her tennis, her comeback, than she had been during the first week of the tournament. "I feel like each day, each match, and each tournament, I'm learning something," she said, learning again that "I can, I have to fight for titles. Fight for matches." She went on to say, "I have been working really hard, and I haven't played that many tournaments on my road back, but I am just trying to do the best that I can do, and I think I will get there. I don't know when, but I know I will get there."

12

Anna Wintour was in Williams's courtside player's box for the Halep match and had been for Williams's previous matches. Player's boxes, or guest boxes, as they are sometimes called, have grown to a dozen seats or more on the main show courts of Grand Slams, as players have increased the size of their entourages to include physical trainers, nutritionists, and massage therapists, along with their coaches and parents, their agents and clothing representatives. The players like having their friends on hand, too, and if those friends are famous, and TV cameras find them during a match, between points or during changeovers, that works for all involved. Wintour was famous, the longtime editor of *Vogue* and a global "influencer" not only in fashion but in all that touched fashion: art, film, women's issues, politics. Sport, too: Wintour was an avid and informed tennis fan (and a serious recreational player). She'd been a fixture for years in Roger Federer's player's box at the US Open, Wimbledon, and the French Open. More recently, she'd been noticed sitting in Williams's box.

This was Wintour's first time at the Australian Open. Williams said that she and Federer had coaxed her to make the trip. Wintour was close to Williams—she'd attended her wedding in New

Orleans and helped her to choose her wedding dress. Williams was as passionate about fashion as Wintour was about tennis. Williams cared about how she looked, even and perhaps especially when she played. "I like to look my best on court," Williams said in her 2009 as-told-to autobiography, *On the Line*. "It goes to self-esteem. . . . If you put your best effort into how you look, you'll put your best effort into whatever it is you do. . . . Appearances *do* count. I believe this."

As a girl she'd liked shopping, fashion magazines, having her older sisters dress her up, "the fuss and attention." She liked that her first clothing sponsor, Puma, and later Nike, sought her input on the outfits she'd wear on court. In 1999, she'd enrolled at the Art Institute of Fort Lauderdale at the urging of her sister Venus, with whom she was sharing a house, and who was already taking classes there during the fall-winter quarter when no tournaments were played. Serena drew and sewed and learned about garment construction and manufacture. Back on tour, she sketched on plane trips and in her hotel room. She designed clothing items for the Home Shopping Network.

In the spring of 2018, she launched her own fashion line. She described the new label, Serena, with its *S* logo, as one in which she was "fully creative." The Serena line is not the sort featured in photo spreads in magazines such as *Vogue*. The clothes are mostly street wear, and many of the items cost less than $100. Some carry motivational messages such as I AM BEAUTIFUL, I AM STRONG. Williams was also seeking, she said, to reimagine clothes for women referred to in retail as plus-size. Among the models she had wearing her clothes, in photographs on the Serena-line website and on Instagram, were women whose body mass indexes were not those of women typically photographed in fashion shoots.

In the weeks following her loss in the US Open final in 2018, Williams had skipped the WTA tour's Asia swing—she'd routinely been bypassing tournaments in China and Japan in recent years—and focused instead on her clothing business. She opened her first pop-up shops in Dallas and at Miami's Art Basel. When I asked her, during the first week of the Australian Open, about how she found time to run her business when she had tennis matches to prepare for and play, she replied, "Yeah, you know, it's way more demanding. Even today I was replying to emails about our next collection with my brand, where we want to see it. So it's different.

"I'm very hands on. I feel like my business with my brand, what I do on the tennis court, is exactly the same. I'm really involved. I'm really opinionated but open to suggestions. I always want to hear what other people have to say because I don't want to be that kind of a boss or person or CEO that have really myopic views. I think it's important to understand and see what everybody else thinks, then take a decision from that."

Over the years, Williams had received advice from Wintour about the fashion business. Recently, Wintour had asked Williams to cochair (along with two singers-cum-actors, Lady Gaga and Harry Styles) her annual Costume Institute Gala, a fundraiser for the Metropolitan Museum's fashion exhibitions that had grown to become the most exclusive and paparazzied event on Manhattan's social calendar. "She's always believed in me," Williams said in a video tribute to Wintour that was shown before Wintour addressed a luncheon at the Australian Open held to honor her, and to highlight the power of women in tennis and beyond.

Asked by a woman after her talk what Wintour thought the "look" would be for the coming year, Wintour deadpanned, "Sneakers, and more sneakers." This was an allusion to the rise of what has come to be called athleisure. In the world's most fashion-conscious precincts, women were walking around in yoga leggings or track pants, hoodies, and running shoes. The look was meant to convey health and fitness, and increasingly, the look was deigned just fine for work as well as the weekends. Lululemon, a Vancouver-based company devoted to yoga clothing that was not just for practicing yoga, was one of the fashion brands of the moment—a Lululemon shop was even set up on the grounds of the Australian Open. Williams's contract with Nike meant she couldn't offer athleisure in her own line. Still, women, fashionable women, wanted to look the way Williams looked when she was headed to the practice court.

13

Tennis is a game designed to thwart inevitability. You may have a dominant serve that delivers steady aces, but after you've hit four aces in a row, the game will end, and your opponent gets a turn. You may win the first six games, but if you do, there is no seventh: you are awarded a set, and the next set begins at 0–0, giving your opponent another chance. If you are a professional tennis player, and your opponent has just taken a set from you and has the crowd chanting her name, deepening her confidence and determination, you can ask for a bathroom break and head to the locker room for what may seem to fans like an eternity, and there you can search for *something*—focus? steadier nerves?—and hope that the passing minutes get to the player left idling out there on court.

Still, Serena Williams, up a double break, leading 5–1 in the third set, and serving for the match—a quarterfinal match, in a Grand Slam? The ending is inevitable, and at hand. Except it wasn't: Williams double-faulted, had her serve broken soon after, and never won another game. Karolína Plíšková, of the Czech Republic, won instead, 6–4, 4–6, 7–5, and advanced to the semi-finals. Williams would jet home without a twenty-fourth Grand Slam singles title, which would have tied her with Margaret Court for the most ever. If Williams had ever lost a match in such a fashion in a major before, after being so far ahead and so close to victory, no one I spoke to or heard from could remember it.

Williams was moving sluggishly as the match began, lunging for balls that she couldn't get her feet under, and, several times, finding herself out of position: too far back behind the baseline, where she seldom roams, or caught inside the court near the service line, "no-man's-land," as it is referred to. You never want to be there—unless you're Serena Williams and you're bolting forward to take a ball out of the air and swat a swinging volley, which is what she did when Plíšková was serving to close out the first set. But in that case, Williams got to the ball *just* late, as it dropped below net height. She buried the ball in the bottom of the net, threw up her hands, and screamed. Soon enough, she was aced, and the first set was Plíšková's.

Williams's court coverage had not been all that great in the four matches she'd won in Melbourne to reach the quarterfinals. You could see that at times she looked winded, and you could hear it during rallies in her ball-strike grunt. But Williams had never won big matches because she could scramble. She'd won by having the best serve in the women's game—hitting big *and* hitting her spots. (Her slider, when she hits it out wide, often arcs and spins irretrievably. She's powerful, yes, but she's more than that.) She'd won by getting herself a foot, or even two, inside the baseline to take an opponent's second serve and send it back so flat and hard and deep that her opponent simply had no time to do anything with the incoming ball. And perhaps most important, she'd won because she brings it on the big points, the ones that matter—the deuce point that gains an advantage, say, and then the ad point that wins a break or secures a service hold. That's who she'd been. That's what got her up a double break and serving for the match at 5–1.

But she got called for a foot fault on her first serve, a serve that might well have won the match. A *foot fault*? *Again* in a big moment? Williams did not yell at the line judge who made the call, not this time. After serving again, however, and putting the ball in play, she appeared to roll her left ankle and lost the point. Then she double-faulted. A right-handed server lands hard on her left foot as she completes her service motion. Was the ankle affecting her serve—which would, in turn, gnaw at her focus and confidence? It wasn't possible to tell. Adrenaline can often mask the severity of a sprain, initially. Williams never called a trainer. What was clear was that, instead of closing out the match, she'd had her serve broken.

Plíšková then held her serve. Williams then had another chance to serve out the match, but quickly went down 0–40 and, just like that, was broken again. Her lead was down to 5–4, with Plíšková to serve. But Plíšková didn't do so with much steadiness or conviction, and Williams quickly had two more match points. However, Williams couldn't find a way to win them—even when she was offered a second serve that didn't reach seventy-five mph. Then Williams got to see yet one more match point and watch her forehand fail to clear the net. Two points later, it was five games all.

Williams, with the serve now hers, did not win a point, nor did she win any of the first three points as Plíšková served for the match. That was ten points in a row, over three games, that Williams lost, if you're counting—and I *was* counting, having never seen her on the losing end of so many consecutive crucial points. She would find a way to stave off two match points, and the crowd stood and roared. They knew what she was capable of, knew that when a match was on the line, she could will her way to the win. They were still standing, somewhat stunned and murmuring, as she packed her racquet bag and made her way slowly to the tunnel, and out of the tournament.

In her on-court interview after the match, Plíšková couldn't quite believe she'd won. Down 1–5 in the third set, facing match point on Williams's serve, her mind, she said, was already "in the locker room." In the time it took Williams to change and get to a pressroom packed with reporters, she had arrived at the abrupt conviction that Plíšková had actually lifted her game at the end of the match. Williams said her ankle had not been injured, or not injured seriously enough to be a factor in her late-match undoing, though, by summer, in conversation, she would be referring to her ankle injury in Australia. (Williams was not one to call attention to an injury if she lost, even if she knew the injury had been a factor.) She also said, unbidden, "I cannot say I choked on those match points." That hung in the room for a moment.

Before she left the room, and Melbourne, Williams smiled a forced smile and said, "I mean, the big picture for me is always winning. I'm not going to sit here and lie about that. It hasn't happened yet, but I feel like it's going to happen."

14

Naomi Osaka won the Australian Open women's final, defeating Petra Kvitová, 7–6 (2), 5–7, 6–4, in what was the best women's match—power packed, fevered, fraught—of the tournament. Osaka had won the US Open in September, her first major championship, and now this: no one on the women's tour had won her first Grand Slam and followed it up by winning her next since Jennifer Capriati did it in 2001. Osaka was still only twenty-one, but no longer the promising newcomer (ranked No. 72) she'd been a year before. She'd arrived. The tennis grounds were swarming with Japanese TV crews; the broadcast of the final had been watched by more than 20 million viewers in Japan, one of the largest audiences for a telecast there in recent memory. Social liberals in Japan believed that Osaka's being a *hafu*—half Japanese, with a Japanese mother and a Haitian father—could lead their nation, finally, to more warmly embrace its mixed-race citizens, who often faced discrimination. The WTA believed the path to growth in women's tennis ran east, through Asia, and Osaka came as an answered prayer. Sponsors believed her mixed-race heritage, along with her wry-sweet, pop-attuned persona, could make her a global sports icon for the millennial generation. She'd just signed an $8.5 million endorsement deal with Adidas, the most the company had ever offered a female athlete. It was not the $40 million contract Nike was said to have with Serena Williams, but this was just the start—if Osaka kept winning.

Osaka had the winner's game—the thunderous ground strokes and cannon of a serve; the steadily improving movement; the growing confidence and court savvy. Craig Tiley, the Australian Open's director, who knows his tennis, said after Osaka's win in the final that she was only going to grow more difficult for her opponents: "Get her now. It's going to be harder in a year or two." Kvitová had a game, too. The Czech Republic had produced a remarkable generation of world-class female players, and Kvitová, at twenty-eight, was arguably the best, having won twenty-six tour titles, including Wimbledon twice. She had been attacked in her apartment just before Christmas in 2016, in the Czech city of Prostějov, by a knife-wielding assailant who slashed her left hand, her hitting hand; it was not clear that she would ever be able to play again. But after surgery and a lengthy struggle to regain her form, she'd won five titles in 2018, and there she was, in the final of the first major of 2019, striking the ball with outstanding pace and accuracy. She would leave Melbourne back in the top five for the first time since 2014. Osaka would be the new world No. 1.

Together, they would, among other things, be perceived as two of the more daunting roadblocks Williams would face in 2019 in her quest for one more Grand Slam. Tennis, like many other sports, is a game of matchups and moments. With their power, their ability to absorb pace as well as produce it, and their gathering self-assurance, Osaka and Kvitová were two players very different from Simona Halep, who'd entered the Australian Open ranked No. 1, or Caroline Wozniacki, the tournament's defending champion. Here, for Williams, was what looked like trouble.

15

Before I left Melbourne, I had a quick lunch with Craig O'Shannessy. He refers to himself as a tennis strategy coach, a role he more or less invented, and pretty much had to himself. He'd grown up playing tennis three hours from Melbourne and went on to Baylor University, in Texas, and played there. But when it didn't work out for him on the men's tour, he turned to coaching, and then to fine-grain data of the sort tennis had yet to show much interest in. O'Shannessy became the game's *Moneyball* guy. He studied probabilities of players' patterns of play. He came to work for Novak Djokovic, the men's No. 1, who loved all things technological and statistical, and was eager to know what the data said about where an opponent was likely to hit a ball and when, and what the data said as well about what was working best in his own game. When I met O'Shannessy, he had just signed on with Sloane Stephens, too, and had ideas about the women's game.

O'Shannessy told me, without hesitation, that Serena Williams would, to his mind, remain a favorite to win any tournament she entered. One of his stat-steeped conclusions was that the vast majority of points in tennis were over in four shots or fewer. We, as fans, tended to think of short-point tennis as something deep in the serve-and-volley past of the last quarter of the twentieth century. In the current era, with most players situated on or near the baseline for a match's entirety, what we thought mostly happened in matches, because they stood out in our memories, were long and glorious rallies. We thus believed the best players, the top players, won by winning, for the most part, those rallies. But long and glorious rallies were, in fact, few. O'Shannessy had crunched the numbers. A long rally was five shots. Most points had fewer shots than that.

He liked Williams's odds because Williams had a game designed to win points in four shots or fewer. "Serena Williams plays an incredibly efficient game style." He took a big bite of his wrap and held up a finger to signal a pause. "She tries to end the point before it starts. More than any other player on the tour, men's or women's, she wants to win a point before a rally can begin. She doesn't want her serve coming back. She wants her return of an opponent's serve to finish things. Ultimate aggression."

If he was the strategy coach for an opponent of Williams's? His advice?

"Try to weather the storm of her serve and her return. Keep it in the middle of the court. Don't try to go for angles, change direction, on those first shots of hers. Players want to get Serena on the run. Sure. But you aren't going to do that off her serve or her return. And don't serve into her body—you see that. I get the idea: don't let her extend her arms. But if you miss by an inch, you wind up putting it right on her racquet. Goodbye."

He smiled. "You know, I've actually done that—been hired to advise an opponent of hers. Maria Sharapova. Here in Melbourne. The final four years ago. Close, but Serena prevailed. She had . . . what, *fourteen* aces second set? Not much strategy against that."

And if he was advising Williams?

"I'd tell her, 'Go to the practice court. Hit tons of serves. Hit tons of returns. Do not spend time trying to make your rally backhand better.' As for her game: 'Don't evolve it. As big a first serve as you can. Go for it. And deep returns down the middle.'"

In the weeks after the Australian Open, what, or if, Williams was thinking about her tennis game was unclear. There she was, on Instagram, boarding a private jet. There she was, in an ad during the Super Bowl, promoting Bumble, the female-centric dating app. There she was, onstage at the Academy Award ceremonies, introducing a clip of *A Star Is Born*. There she was, making a cameo on the cable show *Lip Sync Battle*, reprising the role she'd had in the video for Beyoncé's "Sorry," before mouthing the lyrics to the Cardi B section of Bruno Mars's "Finesse," all the while busting moves with abandon.

Part Two

Indian Wells

1

No place to watch professional tennis in the United States is more alluring than the Indian Wells Tennis Garden. It's a two-and-a-half-hour drive east from Los Angeles, and sixteen miles southeast of Palm Springs, amid the desert resorts and retirement communities of the Coachella Valley. In the early 1980s, two former tour pros, Charlie Pasarell and Raymond Moore, founded a tournament in Indian Wells that grew and grew to become a sort of fifth major, with both men and women playing there during the same two weeks at the beginning of March each year, and with prize money, attendance, and prestige second only to the four Grand Slams. It is one of only four so-called Premier Mandatory tournaments on the women's tour—tournaments offering a lot of ranking points for winning matches, and tournaments that players face fines for skipping. Williams had routinely skipped such tournaments in Madrid and Beijing in recent years, unconcerned about her ranking or potential fines. Only the Grand Slam events mattered to her now. But she needed to play matches to be ready to play majors. She needed to find again that frame of mind that comes with winning a tournament. And Indian Wells wasn't all that far from one of her homes, in Beverly Hills.

Indian Wells was bought in 2009 by Larry Ellison, cofounder of Oracle and a tennis devotee, and is called the BNP Paribas

Open, after the French bank that is its chief sponsor. Ellison poured his resources and technological acumen into creating a tournament atmosphere—call it Luxe Country Fair—that has made it a worldwide favorite among fans and players alike. Among its innovations, since adopted by other tournaments, was to turn players' practice sessions into fan experiences. The number of practice courts was increased, and bleacher seats erected around them. Electronic signs were installed at the entrances to the tennis garden, displaying which players were practicing on what court and when. Spectators flocked—often enough forgoing the matches they'd paid to watch. Here was a way to be as close to marquee players as to a tennis team in action at your local high school. Here, tennis-viewing etiquette—silence, please, and no coming or going except during changeovers—was unnecessary. Wander in or out, talk with your friends, stand and take a selfie with your favorite player in the background somewhere doing crosscourt drills.

Or, if you're lucky enough and care enough, sit almost by yourself and watch what an elite tennis player does, day in and day out, to maintain her form. It can be entrancing and illuminating. It becomes available at Indian Wells toward dusk, when most of the day's matches are completed, and people head home, and the sun setting behind the Santa Rosa Mountains has a way of pinking and purpling the gathering quiet of the valley floor. And it can happen in the morning, before ticketholders begin crowding the grounds, when the sun has just peeked above the Little San Bernardino Mountains, and the air is still fleece-jacket crisp. That's when Serena Williams preferred to practice, if *preferred* is the right word. She'd made a point in recent years of talking about how much she didn't like to practice. "When I stop playing," she'd told an interviewer in *Rolling Stone*, "it's not going to be because I'm sick of playing. It's going to be because I'm sick of practicing."

She was out one morning, as the tournament got underway,

on Practice Court 9, on the eastern edge of the grounds, in black leggings and a white pullover, a visor tugged down against the low, slanting sun. It had rained (a rarity) overnight; the drying desert beyond the practice courts exuded petrichor. Williams was standing a foot or so inside the service line. Her coach, Patrick Mouratoglou, was crouched a couple of yards to her left, gently but briskly feeding her balls—balls whose bounces would not rise higher than Williams's knees. She was bending to strike them, backhands and forehands, again and again. These shots required enough brushing up the back of the ball to lift it over the net and have it come down, on the other side, inside the court. (Tennis balls tend to sail in the dry desert air of Indian Wells.) But these shots also had to be struck with force: you were supplying all the pace (the balls you were hitting had none of their own to absorb and use); and in a match, if presented with such a ball, you were going to have to do something aggressive with it, smack it deep toward a corner of the baseline, or else wind up providing your opponent with an easy next ball to hit—to hit past you as you stood stranded at the net.

Any player with a coach—recreational player, college player, pro—has done this drill. Williams had done it since she was a child, done it so many times, for so many years. Tennis practice is essentially repetition. You learn to do something that has to be done just so to be successful, then practice it again and again, day in and day out, so that it will be done just so unthinkingly, late in a match, when you are tired or under duress. That's what amounts to muscle memory. The development and maintenance of it is why a tennis player comes to hate practice. It's not the kind of practicing other performers do—it's not learning new lines in a Shakespeare tragedy you've been cast in, or memorizing a piano sonata you've never played before. It's rote.

Practice can, on the right morning, renew. It can remind you how good you are. Williams was blistering the ball. During the drill, she paused and had an exchange with Mouratoglou that I was out of earshot of. I could see a smile spread broadly across Williams's face. It seemed clear that she was, for this practice, anyway, where she wanted to be.

2

The park in the East Rancho Dominguez neighborhood of Compton where Williams trained to play tennis is no longer an open-air drug market, the pair of courts her father worked to fix up no longer strewn with shards of glass. I'd spent an overcast afternoon wandering around Compton on my drive from LAX to Indian Wells. The plague of murderous gang violence had abated. Like much of South-Central Los Angeles, Compton remained home largely to the lower middle class and the working poor. The windows of the small houses I saw, built for the most part in the 1950s, had barred windows and little or nothing growing in the tiny garden plots out front. But there were few signs of the poverty and despair still so apparent in nearby Watts.

Another big transformation was that Compton was no longer a Black-majority city, as it had been when Williams was a child, and before that, going back to the 1970s. Compton's population (estimated at ninety-six thousand) was now mainly Latino, immigrants from Mexico or Central America. The signage on storefronts along Long Beach Boulevard, a main shopping street, was nearly all in Spanish. Flyers pasted to lampposts along East Stockton Street, where the Williamses had lived, advertised LOS SERVICIOS DE PASAPORTES.

I'd easily enough found the small postwar bungalow at 1117 East Stockton that the Williamses moved into in March of 1983:

Richard Williams; his wife, Oracene Price; the three daughters—Yetunde, Lyndrea, and Isha—she'd had with her first husband, Yusef Rasheed, who'd died in 1979; and Venus (about to turn three) and Serena (one and a half). Oracene may not have moved to Compton happily. As Richard recalled in his 2014 as-told-to autobiography, *Black and White: The Way I See It*, Oracene told him, "I'm not gonna move to Compton. There's a limit, Richard!" The stucco facing was beige now, no longer painted mint green, or graffitied, as it had been in the early 1990s, when sports reporters and TV crews began making their pilgrimages here to see for themselves just how extraordinarily good the two youngest girls were at playing the game of tennis. For sure, the living room was no longer dominated by a ball machine or strewn with racquet covers and tennis magazines, as it was when Sonja Steptoe visited for *Sports Illustrated*.

The Williamses had been living in a house in Long Beach, not far from the ocean, that Richard had purchased not long after he and Oracene were married in 1980. She'd come to Los Angeles from Michigan, having grown up in Saginaw and graduated from Western Michigan University. She was working as a nurse when she met Richard, who was ten years older than she was. His route to LA was longer and more fraught. He'd been born in Shreveport, Louisiana, in 1942, one of five children his mother would have with the same man, who would never live under the same roof with her or their children or acknowledge them as his own. The neighborhood, Cedar Grove, was poor and Black, the family home three rooms, the South in the last vicious throes of unchallenged segregation and Jim Crow. Richard recounted, in his book, being chased by white boys and beaten by a local sheriff. He began stealing when he was eight—berries, nuts, melons, cotton—and fencing what he stole. A friend he'd made, a fellow small-time thief, stole a pig from a farmer who was a Klansman.

The friend's lifeless young body was found hanging from a tree. Richard Williams spent his youth in a rage. He got into fights and had thoughts of doing terrible things. "I had a lot of hate in me in those days," he judged of himself in his book.

Not long after he arrived in Los Angeles, in his early twenties, he met and, in 1965, married Betty Johnson, with whom he is believed to have had four or five children (the record is unclear) before they divorced in 1973. (This period of Richard Williams's life is only mentioned in passing, in one sentence, in his autobiography; and in that sentence, he relates only that he had one son with Johnson.) Seven years after splitting up with Johnson, and now newly married to Oracene and watching TV one Sunday afternoon in September with her and her daughters, Richard, in his telling, had what can only be called his satori. The story has no doubt been smoothed and embellished over the years, as Serena herself has acknowledged: Richard could be a boaster and exaggerator, a mythologizer and fabulist, amusingly as well as annoyingly, in the service of convincing himself, perhaps, no less than others, of his worth and his mission. He was also a Booker T. Washington bootstrapper, a man who wisely reckoned how America worked (and didn't), and how it could, through hard work and fortitude, be coaxed to work for him. Flipping through the channels that afternoon, according to his recounting, he'd happened upon a postmatch awards ceremony. It was a tournament, now defunct, in Salt Lake City, and the winner of the championship, a twenty-seven-year-old Romanian player named Virginia Ruzici, was being handed a check for $40,000. He had thought tennis was a "sissy" sport. No more. Now he saw it as something a daughter of his, and maybe more than one of them, could make a career of, perhaps grow rich doing.

In his late thirties at this point, Richard was managing a small security business he'd established in South-Central. "It was natural," he reasoned in his book, "for someone who knew as much about stealing as I did." The job gave him time during the day, and he began using that time to learn how to play tennis. He'd been athletic as a youth, or liked to say he'd been—played basketball, football—and was tall and well-built and still in good shape. First, he bought a used racquet and taught himself, acquiring the basics from books, magazines, and videos, and hitting against a wall for hours on end. Then he found a coach to take lessons from in a park in Watts. Richard taught what he knew to Oracene, who like him was tall and fit and had played volleyball and other sports back in Michigan. He also began developing or adapting theories about how to fashion a future tennis star: tossing a football would build up the arm and shoulder strength required for a proper, powerful service motion; practicing with old, flat tennis balls would necessitate increased racquet-head speed.

Richard Williams had always explained his decision to move the family from Long Beach to Compton as one steeped in his belief that the "ghetto" (his word) forged greatness. He had in mind Muhammad Ali, and Malcolm X. Oracene thought Compton was a dangerous place to raise girls; he thought it would be a testing ground: "They'd be used to combat. And how much easier would it be to play in front of thousands of white people if they had already learned to play in front of scores of armed gang members?" Compton would make tough fighters of his young daughters. So went the reasoning, or the lore. It would also, as he noted in his book, lower his mortgage payments from more than $1,000 a month to $135—which meant less time spent drumming up security-business clients and even more time for tennis.

The older girls—Yetunde, Lyndrea, Isha—played at first. Yetunde was the least athletic of the girls, it's been said; Lyndrea got good enough to play college tennis; Isha had talent but also a balky back. Maybe none of them began playing early enough to reach the levels Venus and Serena would. Maybe they weren't born with the athleticism. Maybe they were not where Richard Williams's focus lay. He'd read enough to know that those who got to be very good at tennis, who got to be good enough to reach the pro tour—to be among the best fifty or one hundred women at the game in the world—had been inculcated before they lost their primary teeth. By the time Venus and Serena were born, he had honed his game competing on public courts in and around Compton and was eager to make players of the two.

Serena can recall seeing a photograph of Venus pushing her in a stroller on a tennis court and has heard enough times that her father first put a racquet in her hand, positioned her near the net, and softly tossed balls to her when she was three. By the time Serena was six, she was doing drills most every day, in Compton, or on a court in nearby Lynwood, or from time to time somewhere else, she and her sisters taking turns hitting. It wasn't all tennis all the time: Richard and Oracene put an emphasis on education, and both Venus and Serena got top grades in elementary school. Richard read, then had the girls read, a book about the New York City playground-basketball legend Lloyd Daniels. "He didn't go to class and then drugs took him," Richard told a reporter back then. "That will never happen with my kids."

Mornings before school, tennis instruction started at 6:00 a.m., with more tennis in the late afternoon after school, and more on weekends. Richard would load the whole family and all the equipment into his battered VW bus. Venus, though, got most of Richard's attention those first years. Serena mostly hit with her mother on an adjacent court. (She would later say her mother was the more demanding coach of the two.) When it grew too dark to play, the girls would collect the near-lifeless balls they'd been practicing with and pack them in the crates Richard kept in his VW bus. He'd often leave behind the shopping cart he used on court to hold the balls, chaining it to a net post. He'd come to leave up, too, at times, in the park the signs he'd made and then fastened to the chain-link fence at the back of the courts, signs to inspire and urge on his daughters:

When You Have Failed to Plan Properly You Fail
Venus <u>You</u> Must Take Control of Your Future
Serena <u>You</u> Must Learn to Listen

The little house they returned to together at day's end cannot be more than a thousand square feet, or so I reckoned, standing before it that gray afternoon. Seven of them, two bedrooms, and all female, save for Richard. In her 2009 autobiography, *On the Line*, Serena summoned a home life of discipline, chores, school-work, and sisterly whining. Two sets of bunks were in the girls' bedroom, which meant Serena had to crawl into bed with one of her sisters each night. "Instead of feeling like I didn't quite belong anywhere, I felt like I belonged everywhere," she says she concluded. As she got older, she mostly chose Venus's bed. Later, when Yetunde moved out on her own, and Serena finally had her own bunk, she'd often as not, come bedtime, still crawl in with Venus.

The Williamses, it would seem from their autobiographical accounts, and from what they've told reporters over the years, did not spend all that much time hanging around inside. Talking on the phone and watching television were strictly limited. There was all that time spent on the tennis courts. Every Sunday, and every Tuesday and Thursday evening, too, there were meetings or Bible study at the local Kingdom Hall, the place of worship of Jehovah's

Witnesses. Oracene had become intrigued when a few Jehovah's Witnesses knocked on the door one morning—she'd been raised in a churchgoing household back in Saginaw. (Richard never did become a Witness.) Soon enough, she had the girls heading with her to the Kingdom Hall. "We weren't allowed to miss a meeting—for *anything*" is how Serena remembers it in her book.

Her religion, her parents and sisters, her schoolwork, her tennis: that, more or less, was Serena's Compton. She was just nine when the family left for Florida. Only Yetunde, nine years older than Serena, remained behind in California, where she eventually worked as a nurse, opened a hair salon, and had three children before she was shot dead in Compton at the age of thirty-one. (Serena and Venus opened and support the Yetunde Price Resource Center in Compton, which puts women and families at risk from violence in touch with other nonprofit organizations that can help them find housing and services.)

In 2006, Serena purchased a six-thousand-square-foot home in one of the wealthiest neighborhoods in Los Angeles, Bel Air, for $6.6 million. In the fall of 2017, in the weeks before she got married, she bought a new place in LA: a five-bedroom, seven-bath contemporary Spanish-style mansion in the guarded and gated Summit estates enclave in Beverly Hills—an hour north of Compton, and worlds away. We are all, eventually, set adrift from our past, self-exiles, ever renegotiating our distance from it, and what distance entails. I would ask Serena, later at Indian Wells, if, with a daughter just a couple of years from reaching pre-K age, she'd thought about whether she'd choose her Florida house or the place in Beverly Hills—or somewhere else, such as the Bay Area, where she'd spent a lot of time after giving birth—to settle in and call home.

"Well, I'm still on tour and very much involved in tennis, so not really thinking about that yet." After pausing, she said, "I actually feel ashamed I haven't really thought about that. Yeah, I thought about that I *didn't* think about that a couple of weeks ago." She shook her head and raised her eyebrows and smiled that big smile of hers. "And I was getting nervous because I understand a lot of these schools are filled up, like, when your baby is in your belly. I'm like, 'Oh, my God, what am I going to do?' I don't know what I'm going to do. I really am kind of nervous that I'm not nervous more about it." That particular sort of anxious maternal concern, a concern today especially among affluent new mothers such as her, is, you could say, a measure, too, no less than her stately residence in Beverly Hills, of the distance she has traveled from the bungalow in Compton.

It was approaching dusk in Compton when I got back in my rental car, which I'd parked a block from the Williamses' old place. Minutes later, I was driving slowly along Long Beach Boulevard, looking for the freeway entrance that Waze promised would begin my route to Indian Wells, when I spotted Serena across the street from a 99 Cents & Up store. There she was, much bigger than life, but a child, following through on a backhand in a summer-print skirt and blouse: a Nike billboard ad. GIRLS FROM COMPTON DON'T PLAY TENNIS, it reminded the locals, in assertive English. THEY OWN IT.

3

Stadium 1 at the Indian Wells Tennis Garden holds sixteen thousand spectators, making it the second-largest tennis-specific arena in the world. (Only the US Open's Arthur Ashe Stadium seats more people.) It was close to filled by the time Serena Williams and Victoria Azarenka were midway through their first set—an enormous crowd, a championship-final-size crowd, for a second-round match on a chilly night, albeit a Friday night. The turnout had nearly everything to do with the presence of Williams, seeded tenth and playing her first match after a first-round bye. It's what she could do, and no other woman on the tour could do, and what only a few men in tennis—Roger Federer, Rafael Nadal, and, more recently, Novak Djokovic—could do. Fans come out to see tennis, but more of them come out to see a star.

It was also a compelling matchup. Williams had played Azarenka twenty-one times since the Belarusian had emerged on the WTA tour back in 2006; the only player Williams had met more times was her sister Venus. To call it a rivalry would be a stretch: Azarenka, over the years, had only beaten Williams four times. But a lot of those matches had been semifinals and finals, including the US Open finals in 2012 and 2013, the most rousing matches they'd had, both of them three-setters won by Williams. The last time they'd squared off, in the final at Indian Wells in 2016, Azarenka had prevailed, 6–4, 6–4. They were both power baseliners, and the shotmaking tended to be ferocious. They were fervid on court, glaring and grunting, shouting and fist-pumping. Williams always had a marked respect for a player who'd won majors and reached No. 1, as Azarenka had. You accomplished those things, you had her attention.

One more aspect to their twenty-second meeting made it unique. Since they'd last met, they'd both become mothers. Azarenka had faced none of the medical dilemmas Williams had, but she had had complications of her own. She'd given birth to her son, Leo, in December 2016. The father was Billy McKeague, a onetime hockey player from Missouri who was working as a golf pro at a resort in Hawaii when Azarenka met him. They broke up the summer after Leo was born and commenced an international custody battle over where, first of all, a custody decision should be made. (Leo was born in California, where Azarenka had lived for a number of years, but Azarenka and McKeague had traveled with Leo to Belarus a few months later, and Azarenka took actions then to establish the baby's legal residency as Minsk.) Court dates and travel restrictions on where Leo could be taken kept Azarenka off the tour for a significant stretch, and that, along with injuries, had caused her ranking to fall from No. 5 to outside the top one hundred.

One thing Azarenka had accomplished recently off the court, as a member of the WTA's players' council, was to help bring about a rule change to ease comebacks to the tour for mothers. For her, as for Williams, taking maternity leave had meant watching her ranking tumble, as matches went unplayed, and ranking points went unearned. That meant that she, like Williams, would no longer have the benefit of being seeded when she first returned to action—would no longer be guaranteed that her first matches would be against players ranked outside the top thirty-two. This is what happens when a player, say, suffers a stress fracture or has to skip a tournament or two because of an infection. Pregnancy and caring for a newborn were not injuries or illnesses. (Male players could become fathers during their playing careers and keep right on playing, as Federer and Djokovic had.) Beginning in 2019, however, thanks to the new WTA rule, maternity leave would no longer penalize women players in this way. A new mother with a ranking that, when she began her leave, would have earned her a seeding would now be granted special status as an "additional" seed in the first eight tournaments she played upon her return.

Azarenka, approaching her thirtieth birthday, was ranked No. 42 and unseeded as she took the court to face Williams. (The new WTA rule only applied to maternity leaves going forward.) She'd been playing well the past month and had comfortably won her opening-round match at Indian Wells against a younger fellow Belarusian, Vera Lapko. Azarenka broke Williams's serve in the third game, and that pretty much set the tone of the match. They would pounce on each other's second serves, and each break the other *three* times in the first set. They'd belt flat forehands in extraordinary extended rallies, but bury easy sitters in the net. They'd hit high-risk down-the-line backhand winners at some crucial moments, but double-fault at others. This close-fought, tense, and punishing battle was exciting in the way tennis can be even when the play is inconsistent and error strewn. Williams prevailed, 7–5, 6–3, closing out the match in the final game with an ace after saving four break points that Azarenka had earned. The two had an extended embrace at the net. The jumbotron reminded us it was International Women's Day. The crowd, standing and applauding, applauded some more.

Afterward, Williams seemed satisfied but emotionally drained. It was as if the match with Azarenka had reminded her (as if she needed reminding) that the times, not that long ago, had been easier times, easier than now, anyway, and there would be no recapturing those times, that particular sense of herself and her game. "I would say we're pretty close," she said of Azarenka, her voice subdued, her breathing still audibly heavy nearly an hour after the end of the match. "We're both moms, and we know how hard it is and how hard it's been for us to come back, you know, and starting literally from scratch and fighting our way back. It's been an arduous road."

4

Tracy Austin was a product of a different Los Angeles than Williams, and of a different time. Austin came from a tennis family: her mother and uncle were serious players. She'd grown up in the 1960s in suburban Rolling Hills Estates, south of the city on

the Palos Verdes Peninsula, where two of the foundational pil-
lars of American tennis, Jack Kramer and Vic Braden, had a club.
She was coached there by Robert Lansdorp, considered by many
to be the greatest ground-stroke maestro of his time. (He would
go on to instruct, among others, Lindsay Davenport and Maria
Sharapova.) A photograph of Austin, blond bangs and white tennis skirt, appeared on the cover of *World Tennis* magazine when
she was four. She was just sixteen in September 1979 when she
won her first major, defeating Chris Evert in the final of the US
Open—from the baseline, patiently, and almost daintily. She was
slender and not quite five feet five.

Austin had retired from tennis and was back in Rolling Hills
starting a family by the time the Williams sisters were starting
to gain attention. "You heard the rumblings of these two girls
from Compton," she recalled. We were sitting and talking late one
morning in the media center at Indian Wells. Austin, now fifty-six,
was working at the tournament as a commentator for the Tennis
Channel. She had on a sun-shielding straw hat and was spoon-
ing brunch out of a take-out acai bowl; she was due, in forty-five
minutes, for her on-air hair and makeup. She recalled how the Los
Angeles area was known for the quality and depth of its junior-
tennis circuit, in her era and later, too, when the Williamses were
beginning to play competitive tennis in the late 1980s. The Williams sisters, though, rarely got challenged playing girls their age
in and around Los Angeles. Venus never lost a junior match in
California (63-0), and Serena was bringing it, too (49-2).

"The talent they showed at a very young age was just tremendous," Austin told me. "Their serves were weapons you hadn't
seen before—they could hold serve so easily. And they were
the first ones who could hit offensively from a defensive position. You know, most players in a pickle—off-balance, on the run,
stretched—they'll just try to simply get the ball back: hit a neu-

tral ball, reset, stay in the point. Venus and Serena in those situations . . . they were so strong, so physical, that they could hit an *offensive* shot. It hadn't been seen before. It would change the level of the women's game."

The Williams sisters, Venus especially, were beginning to get the attention of the tennis industry. Agents, coaches, representatives from sports-clothing manufacturers, began trekking to Compton. In the fall of 1990, at a charity tennis event hosted by Nancy Reagan at the exclusive Riviera Country Club in Pacific Palisades to promote her Say No to Drugs campaign, the sisters played as a doubles team. They met former president Reagan and talked with Zina Garrison, the rare African American on the women's tour, who that summer had reached the Wimbledon final. The sisters wowed LA's glitterati with their play, and soon the *Today* show and reporters from national news outlets were streaming west to interview them, write about them, and film them. Richard Williams was thrilled, but also worried that things might be going too far, too fast, for two girls not yet out of elementary school.

Austin and her husband, Scott Holt, a businessman, have three sons. The middle one, Brandon, a twenty-year-old, had recently turned pro and won his first title on the lowest-rung Futures circuit after playing tennis at USC. Austin had spent a lot of time thinking about how important, and how tricky, it can be to mesh a tennis life with family life. "Oracene and Richard did a great job in somehow managing to place family first," Austin said. "You saw that right from the beginning. They were very respectful little girls, Venus and Serena. I remember that clearly. Maybe it's their religion. Maybe it's just the closeness that comes with spending so much time together. Venus and Serena were *always* together. And then competing against one another. But no jealousy. No bitterness. And the two of them so different. Venus is—what's the word?—reserved. Serena? Big personality. And what has Serena said? 'Venus takes care of me.' I mean, that's unique. And it's gone on so long—if it weren't genuine, there were too many places you'd get a glimpse of something. There's nothing at the net even after one has beaten the other in a Grand Slam final!"

Austin paused, then said, "They had each other. I don't think Serena would have made it without Venus, or Venus without Serena. All those hours on those courts in Compton—you need somebody to hit against. Maybe Serena had a brighter, burning fire because she was always trying to catch up to Venus. That gap at that age—not even a full two years—that can be a catalyst." Another pause. "Tennis is tennis. But family is family."

Before Austin headed off for an afternoon in the broadcast booth, we talked about the girls of color who, as a result of the Williams sisters' example, had taken up tennis and trained to play at an elite level. Austin suggested, "It's not just girls of color. It's little girls who don't belong to country clubs. It's not even just tennis, I think, but track and field, or swimming, or playing the piano. It's a recognition that 'I can pave my own way. Even with things stacked against me.' That's their impact."

5

It could be argued that Serena Williams *became* Serena Williams, the one we came to recognize—self-willed, unbending, imposing, overpowering, and with a focus at once icy and blazing—at Indian Wells on the afternoon of March 17, 2001. She was nineteen years old and had entered the year ranked No. 6 in the world. It was the women's final. The newly built Stadium 1 that Saturday had few empty seats. Her opponent was a teenage Kim Clijsters, two years younger than Williams, but already a top-twenty player and an impregnable ball-chasing defender who had beaten the then

No. 1, Martina Hingis, to reach the final. No one doubted Clijsters deserved to be in the championship match. It was Williams's presence that was being questioned—being protested loudly by thousands of those on hand, with the boos resounding through the chasmal arena when Serena was introduced before play began, and continuing, at various times and decibels, throughout the match.

The booing, and worse, grew most raucous when the crowd glimpsed Richard and Venus Williams, just as the match was set to begin, making their way down the stairs to Serena's player's box. Venus had been scheduled to play a semifinal against Serena the previous Thursday night, but had withdrawn minutes before the match was to start, citing a flare-up of tendinitis in her right knee. Injured players are urged to report any injury that will keep them from playing hours, not minutes, before a match, especially a big match late in a tournament such as a semifinal, so that a substitute match (a doubles match, usually) can be put on the program. In a recounting of the events surrounding the Serena-Clijsters final written by Joel Drucker, a longtime tennis writer and a historian-at-large at the International Tennis Hall of Fame, Charlie Pasarell, the tournament director, maintained he only heard of Venus's withdrawal when it was announced over the public-address system to spectators settling in that night at the stadium. Serena, in her autobiography, insisted her sister had been trying to convince the tournament trainer all day that she was not able to play, but the trainer "kept telling her to hold off on making any kind of final decision." American tennis—fans, tournament sponsors, TV—had been waiting for this match: sister versus sister, both of them in the top ten now. Pasarell: "I only wish she had at least gone out and given it a try. . . . This hurts the game of tennis more than the individual tournament."

Venus held that she had injured her knee in a match the afternoon before the scheduled semifinal, a match in which she'd dispatched easily enough another young up-and-comer, the Russian Elena Dementieva, 6–0, 6–3. Asked at her press conference following the match which of the Williams sisters Dementieva thought would prevail the following night, she remarked, "I mean, I don't know what Richard thinks about it. I think he will decide who's going to win tomorrow." She mentioned the first tour final in which Venus and Serena had met, two years before, in Key Biscayne. "If you saw the match, it was so funny." Venus had won that match, in three sets, defending her title there. No published account of the match related anything but a hard-fought, if patchy, match. (And there were many such accounts; the two teenage sisters were going head to head in a tour final for the first time, and the *New York Times* and the *Washington Post* both sent reporters.) Dementieva might or might not have read or heard about a just-published story in the *National Enquirer* claiming Richard Williams had fixed the previous summer's Wimbledon semifinal, in which Venus defeated Serena 6–2, 7–6. The source was said to be an unnamed family member who alleged that since Serena had already won a major (the 1999 US Open) it was, Richard had decided, Venus's turn. The story was getting a lot of play.

This story informed the booing and would seem to have informed accounts of the Serena-Clijsters match published in the days to follow. This from Bill Dwyre, award-winning sports columnist of the *Los Angeles Times*: "If . . . Venus' knee truly did get sore just in time for her match with Serena; if all this is just the product of a bunch of jealous competitors on the women's tour and a bunch of dopes with overactive curiosity glands, then why don't the Williamses set the record straight?" This from Selena Roberts, a sports columnist for the *New York Times*: "Revealing no sign of a limp, no wrap on her controversial right knee, Venus Williams kept her head down as she slipped into her row. . . . Few wanted to forgive Venus Williams for pulling out of her semifinal against her sister four minutes before the match on Thursday night. Few wanted to believe that her exit was not part of a fix conjured up by their father. His string of wild tales over the years had left his denials hollow."

Richard Williams, from the player's box, raised his fist, Black Power–style, at those in the crowd, an almost completely white crowd, jeering him. The ridicule grew louder. He maintained he was called a "nigger," and more than once. He got on his cell phone and requested security around the box where he and Venus were sitting. He watched as the match got underway, and the derision turned toward Serena. Cheers could be heard when she double-faulted, catcalls while she waited to smash an overhead. No one would associate this behavior—loud, scornful, and rude— with tennis. Richard Williams, in the account of that afternoon he provides in his autobiography, raises rather succinctly a question at once rhetorical and heartrending: "Would another family have been treated as mine was?"

He had in mind a white family. Roll your eyes at his tendency (acknowledged by his own daughters) to obfuscate and even fabricate; take seriously, if distrust suffuses your outlook, rumors about his covertly manipulating the matches of two emerging tennis stars who, nonetheless, somehow showed, when they were on court, nothing if not a relentless desire to win. But taunt and boo a teenager trying to win a championship match? Richard understood—and raised his daughters to understand—that the racial divide was not like other divides, that it was profound and perhaps, at its deepest levels, insurmountable, as that between rich and poor was not. He'd been born into a South where slavery was no more, but where the racial injustice of its wretched essence continued to pervade almost every aspect of life. He wanted family to be the bulwark against racism, and it had been and would be, but not on that particular sunlit afternoon at Indian Wells. No white girl on the tour had ever been subjected to anything like what Serena was hearing. There could be no debating that. And he could do nothing for her. In tennis, you're on your own.

Serena was clearly shaken, at first. That's the sense I had watching a tape of the match nearly twenty years later. Her timing was off, and the errors came in batches. She lost the first set. "I didn't think I had it in me to keep going," she'd say later. "The booing was just wearing me out." During a changeover early in the second set, she buried her face in a towel and wept. She reasoned the crowd was protesting Venus's withdrawal from the semifinal, but believed, too, "there was some racial component" to it. She thought about her father and sister. She thought, she'd later say, about Althea Gibson, the pioneering Black tennis great, and how she had to sleep in her car after matches because the nearby hotels were whites only. Serena prayed. Before she got out of her chair and went back on court, this came to her, and here, I'd maintain, was Serena becoming Serena: "I'm not out there busting my butt for the blue-haired Palm Springs jet-setter. No, I'm out there for me. People need to understand that."

The level of Williams's play began to rise. Clijsters's rose to meet it. Match on. The second set was marked by long rallies, tremendous athleticism, and a fair amount of thoughtful point construction. The crowd hadn't let up on Williams much—disconcertingly baffling, to hear it in the background, watching a tape nearly twenty years later. But now Williams seemed to be defiantly absorbing energy from it. She'd win the second set, then go on a tear in the deciding third. As the match neared its end, and Williams was increasingly staggering Clijsters with big first serves and concussive crosscourt forehands, scattered cheers came for her. But the booing returned, loud and sustained, after one more unreachable crosscourt forehand secured Williams the match, 4–6, 6–4, 6–2. This, the most determined and mighty victory of her young career, appeared to forge her, show her fullest capabilities to herself. She raised a fist as her father had earlier, then waved, then circled the court with her racquet raised, smiling broadly but at the same time fighting back tears in the face of all of it. She walked to her player's box and hugged Venus and their father. The boos pealed. It remains as arresting an us-against-them moment as sports TV has ever captured.

The following year, first Venus (in February), and then Serena (in July), would achieve a world No. 1 ranking. But neither returned to Indian Wells that year, or for many years after that. Serena would not end her boycott until 2015, Venus the year after. They eventually faced off against each other at Indian Wells in 2018, Serena's first tournament back after giving birth to her daughter. Richard did not attend. He had become less and less a courtside presence after he and Oracene divorced in 2002, following allegations of domestic violence. He'd remarried and, with his third wife, had another baby, a son, before they, too, divorced in 2017. He had suffered a debilitating stroke and hardly traveled from his home in Florida.

That 2018 meeting at Indian Wells between Serena and Venus was a third-round match. (They hadn't met that early in a tournament since they'd first played each other on tour at the Australian Open twenty years before: two girls with beads in their braids.) The crowd on hand on a cool Monday evening was large, appreciative, and animated. No one believed any longer that a match Serena and Venus played was fixed. Venus won in straight sets. There wasn't a heckler to be heard.

6

Serena's win over Victoria Azarenka that began her quest for a title at Indian Wells—a *title*, something she'd yet to claim since returning to tennis after giving birth to Olympia—had lit up social media. There was talk that she had never moved better since returning to the tour a year earlier or looked more vehement. Two nights after defeating Azarenka, Williams was back on court in Stadium 1 in a third-round match and was quickly up a break and leading 3–0 before most of the spectators found their seats. Her opponent was Garbiñe Muguruza of Spain. The two had met in two Grand Slam finals when Muguruza, a tall and an aggressive ball-striker, emerged a few years back as a possible Serena heir. She'd lost to Williams in the 2015 Wimbledon final, but turned around and defeated her the following summer on clay in the French Open final. In 2017, Muguruza rose briefly to world No. 1. But struggles with injuries and what appeared, at times, to be a lack of commitment, soon sent her down the rankings. Now twenty-five, she'd arrived at the 2019 Paribas Open ranked No. 20.

Those first three games, it would turn out, were the only games Williams would win. Muguruza would hold her serve in the fourth game, then break Williams in the next—even though Williams had quickly gone up 40–0. From then on, Williams struggled to win a stray point. The velocity of her serves plunged. Her way of walking on court—from side to side when serving or returning, to her chair during changeovers—had long been an I'm-cool-and-in-control saunter. But her walk to the umpire's chair after losing the first set 6–3 was that of someone trying to stay on her feet. The trainer was summoned. Williams sat and stared with a faraway look as the trainer questioned her. She returned to the court for the start of set two, lost four straight points and the game, returned to her chair, and soon enough retired from the match. Later that night, a statement was released that Williams was suffering from a viral illness.

7

The 2019 women's title at Indian Wells would be won by a Canadian teenager, Bianca Andreescu. She had visualized winning it the morning of the match. She was into creative visualization. It had been her mother's idea, and her mother, Andreescu told me, had showed her a website where she could learn, through a course, all about it: "image generation" and "image maintenance," "image inspection," and "image transformation." Not that she wanted to get into all that. "It's also a secret of mine," she said. She first started doing it at age thirteen and used to do it for hours and hours, but she had so much else to do these days, such as going online at night to do the assignments and take the tests required to finish up high school.

The final took place on Sunday afternoon, one of those cloudless and gentle March afternoons that keep retirees from the Midwest flocking to the Coachella Valley. Andreescu defeated Angelique Kerber of Germany, a shrewd veteran, outstanding defender, and former No. 1 who, the previous summer, had defeated Williams in the Wimbledon final. The Indian Wells final was some match, a three-setter: 6–4, 3–6, 6–4. Andreescu was all of eighteen years old. Not since Williams, twenty years before, in her notorious match against Kim Clijsters, had someone that young won at Indian Wells—or won any of the other Premier Mandatory events. If that's not remarkable enough, Andreescu only got into the tournament by way of a wild card, awarded to a player at the discretion of the tournament organizers. At the beginning of 2019, Andreescu was ranked No. 152.

Her game was not the first-strike power game Williams had mastered. Andreescu was an all-court player. She could drive her two-hand backhand, roll it with topspin at acute angles toward the sideline when presented with a short ball, or slice it with one hand on an unwavering glide path, as if on a frozen rope. She had a deft drop shot. Her topspin lob was well disguised and deadly. Her second serve was not a sixty-five-mile-per-hour rec-league-like spinner (all too common in women's tennis), but the kind of ninety-mile-an-hour dare, slid out wide or blasted flat up the T, that you seldom saw from any woman on the tour without a last name of Williams. And Andreescu's forehand, or better, forehands—she could hit it flat, sliced, or loopily arced with heavy topspin—was like watching the Dodgers' Clayton Kershaw pitch. Andreescu seldom puts two shots in a row to her opponent in the same hitting zone, at the same pace.

If you were an older fan of tennis, this was tennis as it had once been. This style of play was thinky, crafty, and often enough as lovely as tennis could get. Andreescu had befuddled a number of power players with this kind of tennis—she'd defeated Muguruza in the quarterfinals. But this style of tennis, twenty years ago, could not get you far against Serena Williams. She and her sister, along with injuries, more or less chased Martina Hingis, who'd possessed a game not unlike that of Andreescu's, from singles tennis and all-court tennis, by and large, from the women's game. But that was twenty years ago, when Williams was not a woman in her late thirties, and the all-court players were small and lithe. Andreescu was neither. Here was someone else, and something else, that Williams would have to contend with if she was going to win another Grand Slam.

Part Three
Miami

1

With a big year that included winning five Association of Tennis Professionals (ATP) titles and losing a tough final at Indian Wells to Roger Federer, James Blake ended the year 2006 ranked No. 4 in the world—the first men's tennis player of African American heritage (his father is Black, his mother a white Englishwoman) to enter the top five since Arthur Ashe in the mid-1970s. It was a long drought. Another ensued. One sign of it was that Blake, who'd retired in 2013, remained the most recognizable Black male in American tennis. He was a commentator on Tennis Channel. He was also standing in front of the Grand Hyatt in New York on the morning of September 9, 2015, when a plainclothes police officer named James Frascatore did not recognize him, rushed toward him, tackled him to the sidewalk facedown, put a knee in his back, and handcuffed him. Frascatore later said that he and his unit had mistaken Blake for the ringleader of a fraud conspiracy they were after.

Blake, along with his tennis commentating, was now the tournament director of the Miami Open, which moved in 2019 from Key Biscayne north to Hard Rock Stadium, home of the Miami Dolphins. (Professional tennis and its broadcasters were comfortable with tournament directors working as commentators, active coaches, too. Tennis was rife with conflicts of interest, or potential ones, or the optics of what looked like ones. But that was another story.) That made Blake among the few Black executives in tennis. I caught up with him one morning, during the first days of the Miami Open, after he'd finished up a lengthy meeting devoted to scheduling the following day's matches—a three-dimensional-chess-like undertaking that had to take into account, among other things, which tennis stars were left in the draw to potentially fill the stands in the big Stadium Court; the desires of international TV channels, which wanted their marquee players on court in their countries' respective prime times; and the necessary rest periods of players still competing in both the singles and doubles draws. "I think players, when they complain about the schedule, I don't think they realize what goes into it," Blake said, as he settled in at a cafeteria table in the stadium's executive suite. "I know I didn't."

Blake, looking trim and fit enough to still be lashing forehands as he once did, had no ready answer on how to increase the number of African American men playing tennis. At that moment, only three American Black men were in the ATP top two hundred: Frances Tiafoe (No. 34), Michael Mmoh (No. 115), and Christopher Eubanks (No. 150). Disadvantaged Black neighborhoods and towns produced a disproportionate share of America's elite athletes. But boys growing up in these places preferred other sports, especially basketball, which made sense. Basketball was inexpensive to play; was taught and coached in public schools; was all over television eight months a year; and was a means to higher education, and perhaps to wealth, if you were that rare player who made it to the NBA. It had become a part of the very fabric of African American life. Many of the Black male college basketball players dominating sports coverage during March Madness, which coincided with the Miami Open, were hoping to make the kind of money in the NBA, even as a bench player, that only the very top tennis players in the men's game earned.

For athletic women, Blake pointed out, it was another story. No other sport offered the money that tennis potentially did. Playing basketball in the WNBA, which was dominated by African American women, was no path to wealth. A rookie entering the league in 2019 was paid around $50,000; and even a WNBA star earned a base salary of no more than $120,000 and, to earn more, was probably spending her off-season playing in the EuroLeague. Meanwhile, according to *Forbes*, eight of the top-ten-earning female athletes in the world were tennis players. (The other two? Race-car driver Danica Patrick and India's badminton megastar, P. V. Sindhu.) Serena Williams had made enough to make the *Forbes* list of wealthiest self-made women. "You lose first round at the US Open," Blake told me, "you get more than fifty grand. It's a lucrative sport."

Blake called attention to the obvious: a lot more African American women than men can be found throughout the tennis rankings, from the top down through the juniors. This he attributed to two factors, Venus and Serena Williams. Black girls, or their parents, knew the story of the Williams sisters. "People talk about their amazing abilities," he said, "but their longevity has been unbelievable. They've inspired two whole generations." He mentioned Sloane Stephens and Madison Keys, and also a pair of girls of color a cohort younger: Coco Gauff, who had just turned fifteen ("She's going to be a superstar"), and Whitney Osuigwe, soon to be seventeen, whom he'd watched recently and noticed, he judged, a significant improvement in her game. Venus and Serena Williams, Blake said, "encouraged African American girls to go out and get a racquet instead of a basketball."

I'd brought up Gauff with Serena a couple of days earlier. "I love her!" she'd exclaimed. "I love her game. She's just fun. She seems supercool." I mentioned how Gauff has spoken of being inspired by her. "That's what we play for ultimately," Williams said. "It's to not only be remembered but to inspire other people to want to play, not as good as you but better. Be better than me."

It was too soon to know just how good Gauff would turn out to be. She'd earned a wild card into the Miami Open, and I'd watched her first match out on tiny Court 2. Like all the other outer courts in Miami, this one, with its few rows of aluminum bleachers, had been set up in what most weeks of the year was a stadium parking area. The main Stadium Court was a fourteen-thousand-seat arena constructed within the sixty-four-thousand-seat Hard Rock Stadium itself. Hard Rock was the kind of mammoth arena that worked for football. Football can legitimately be watched from high up and far away, not least because feeling part of the crowd, roaring continuously with it for the home team, wherever your seat happens to be, is a big part of being there. Tennis? Not so much. The Stadium Court was too big, with too many seats too far away or with poor sight lines, for a sport that demands close observation, mostly in silence. The stadium-within-a-stadium also *felt* indoors, atmospherically. Who wanted to be inside in Miami in March? Lots of fans with main-stadium tickets, especially during the first week of the tournament, joined folks with ground passes in the bleachers on the overflowing outer courts. There, they not only got close-up views of the players, but could repair to nearby salsa-pulsing tented lounges for margaritas or mojitos. This was tennis, Miami-style: a Latin American Open.

As the Gauff match was set to begin, the afternoon sky like the Caribbean ones Winslow Homer painted, blue-blue with tall cumulus clouds on the horizon, more people were hovering around Court 2, wanting to get in if someone left and a space opened up, than were crammed in the bleachers inside. This was Gauff's first-ever WTA tour–level match. She was thought by tennis insiders to be the best next-*next*-generation tennis product to be found in Florida. Florida was where elite tennis players got manufactured. Florida was where the United States Tennis Association had its national training center; where the famous tennis academies were; where the big-name private coaches were; where the top junior tournaments were held; where the top youths to compete against were. The year-round tennis weather was in Florida, too. Parents, often enough today onetime elite athletes of some sort themselves, uproot their families and move here, homeschooling their would-be prodigy during the few hours a day she or he is not on a tennis court, repeating strokes and drills—and being scrutinized. Ten- and twelve- and fourteen-year-olds got evaluated like yearlings on a Kentucky horse farm. They developed or, more often than not, stalled, got injured, burned out. This expensive process was neither as pretty nor as clean as the ground strokes we fans gathered in tennis stadiums to admire.

The talk of the Miami Open, as it got underway, was a story in South Florida's *Sun Sentinel* about Naomi Osaka's years in the area as a tennis star in the making. The story was of Osaka's father, Leonard François, originally from Haiti, having seen the Williams sisters on TV playing in the 1999 French Open, two years after Naomi was born. The story was of a family leaving Long Island for Florida and its promise of better tennis when Naomi was eight and her older sister, Mari, was ten. The story was of their mother, who was Japanese, working an office job to house her family while her husband pursued his dream of doing for his daughters what Richard Williams had done for Venus and Serena. And the story was of coaches who reportedly went unpaid, one of whom had filed a lawsuit over a contract he said Osaka's father had signed, granting him 20 percent of any future earnings of Naomi and Mari, in return for two years of free coaching in Pompano Beach. Reporters had gathered around Osaka the morning the Miami

Open began, questioning her about the lawsuit. She'd replied she couldn't talk about it and seemed even more uncomfortable than she tended to be in front of the press. She would crash out of the tournament a few days later, in the third round.

Gauff's parents decided to move to Florida from Atlanta when Gauff was in the second grade. Not long after, at the age of eight, she was attracting attention—winning the Little Mo Internationals (named for Maureen "Little Mo" Connolly Brinker, who won nine Grand Slam singles titles in the early 1950s) in Palm Beach Gardens, where Serena Williams has had a home for years. In 2017, Gauff became the youngest player to ever reach the US Open girls' final for junior players. Last summer, she'd won the French Open girls' championship. She was coached by her father, Corey, who grew up in South Florida and played basketball for Georgia State. He was there in the first row of bleachers on Court 2 to watch his daughter play, as was her mother, Candi, who'd run track for Florida State. Patrick Mouratoglou, Williams's coach, sat with them. Gauff had trained a bit with him at his academy in the south of France, and the time would come, if things unfolded as they often did for young tennis hopefuls, when Gauff's father would bring on a seasoned coach of a proven champion to round out his daughter's development.

Gauff was still ranked far from the top one hundred, as was her opponent, another young American prospect and wild-card entry, seventeen-year-old Caty McNally. McNally was not African American and did not train in Florida but in Cincinnati, where her mother, who'd played at Northwestern, was a coach. McNally's parents were on hand, too, as the match got underway, and they, along with the couple hundred spectators in the stands behind them, got quite a show. Gauff was broad shouldered, athletic, and a fierce competitor. She was disinclined to leave the baseline, from where she pounded balls with the kind of topspin that drives an opponent back, then back some more. She had talked in interviews of copying Serena's service motion and was already clearly producing a reasonable facsimile of Serena's stare-down and deeply growled "Come on!" when she blasted a winner. McNally, who had lost to Gauff in last year's French Open girls' final, had a more all-court game. Her volleys were remarkable—WTA remarkable. It would come as no surprise to see her on tour one day as a top doubles player if she failed to make it in singles. (Small world, tennis: she and Gauff had partnered to win the 2018 US Open girls' doubles championship.)

Both Gauff and McNally were nervous and tight as the match began. Both made errors they wouldn't make in practice. Both went on to play stretches where they were seeing and feeling the ball and confidently constructing points. Both hit patches where little seemed to go right. That's what tennis is like when it's being played by those of high school age. Gauff eventually outlasted McNally, 3–6, 6–3, 6–4. They hugged at the net, without a whole lot of feeling, and, worn-out by the heat and each other, made their way back to the locker room, largely unnoticed by the ticket-holders crowding the grounds.

Later, speaking with reporters, Gauff sounded like a seasoned pro, discussing how she worked to stay positive and to control what she can control. She also sounded precisely fifteen: "I hit with Kyrgios this week." That would be Nick Kyrgios, age twenty-three and six feet four, the controversial, moody, and, when the mood strikes, brilliant Australian player. "We didn't play a practice match, obviously, because I would have lost. But I hit with him, and he told me that 'You're going to go far in this tournament.' I was like, 'All right, that's basic.' He's like, 'No, you're really going to go far.' I was like, 'Okay.'"

She lost her second-round match the following afternoon and returned soon enough to the daily practice-court toil of becoming.

2

The Williams family arrived in Florida in the summer of 1991, lured east, in the end, by Rick Macci, who ran a tennis academy at the Grenelefe Golf and Tennis Resort in the central Florida town of Haines City. Macci, like many illustrious tennis coaches, had never been an exceptional player himself. But he had an eye for talent, and a way of developing it, especially in promising girls. He'd coached Mary Pierce, who'd win her first tour title in the summer of 1991, as a sixteen-year-old, and would go on win two Grand Slams and reach No. 3 in the world. He'd gotten even more attention, including that of Richard Williams, with his grooming of Jennifer Capriati, who, in the fall of 1990, had entered the top ten at the bewilderingly young age of fourteen. Richard phoned Macci and invited him to Compton to have a look at Venus and Serena.

"My first impression, honestly? Watching the girls on court—I'm thinking, 'This is a waste of my time,'" Macci was telling me. We were sitting at a canopied picnic table near a clutch of courts at his academy, which is now located in Boca Raton. I'd driven up from the Miami Open one drizzly afternoon. Macci, sixty-four, had the sun-weathered visage of a man who'd spent countless afternoons on a tennis court. His academy, like many academies, was no longer turning out would-be champions at the rate it once did, though Sofia Kenin, a promising twenty-year-old, Russian-born American currently on the tour, worked with him early on. Tennis parents and their boy or girl wonders had other options today: doing it yourself or taking advantage, if you were a talented teenage American, of the USTA's coaches and facilities. Macci exuded not a hint of bitterness about this. He clearly enjoyed his work, enjoyed, too, his memories of the Williams sisters, and was more than happy to spend a couple of hours sharing them.

Macci, before heading west to Compton, had never before gotten on a plane to see prospective recruits to his academy. But he'd been hearing so much about Venus Williams from agents and other coaches he'd run into at junior tournaments; there was, as well, the fact that Capriati, on the verge of turning pro, had left Macci (her father's decision) for the Hopman Academy at the Saddlebrook Resort up near Tampa. "Richard [Williams] was a pretty funny guy on the phone," Macci recalled. "It's May of 1991, I think. He's interested in having his girls attend a tennis academy and is shopping around. He says he'd like to meet me, have me come out. I knew the girls were beating everybody in juniors, but when a girl is good in the tens and twelves, it means something but doesn't necessarily mean a lot. Then at some point in the conversation he says, 'I guarantee one thing: if you come out, you won't get shot.' And I crack up and think, 'I got to meet this guy.'"

Macci recounted how Richard picked him up at his hotel in Los Angeles, just after dawn on a Saturday morning. He climbed into Richard's beat-up VW bus—"McDonald's wrappers all over the floor of the thing; this spring in the seat harpooning me"—and, with Venus and Serena in the back, was driven to what Richard referred to as the East Compton Hills Country Club. "There's these guys on the grass still passed out from drinking the night before, other guys playing basketball who clearly knew Richard and the girls and acknowledge them—'Hi, King Richard,' that's what they called him, 'Hi, V, hi, Meeka'" (Serena's middle name, affectionately shortened, which is what Richard called her, at least at practice in Compton). "Richard takes ten minutes to get all the chains off the shopping cart he uses to hold those dead balls of his and has locked to the net post. He starts hitting with the girls. Lots of technical flaws. They were just improvising. Venus? I'm thinking she should be running track. Serena? Seemed like she didn't want to be there."

Macci related how he eventually suggested to Richard that rather than just hitting, the girls play some points. Richard, Macci said, was not comfortable with Venus and Serena competing against each other in front of him, so instead they paired up for doubles: Macci and Venus, Richard and Serena. "Immediately, their level *soared*!" Macci told me, growing animated. "It was crazy! The preparation got better, the footwork got better, I saw the adjustment steps were enhanced. Keeping score was the whole thing! The *competitiveness* of the girls. The thirst to get to balls. Hard to teach that. Hard to teach internal qualities. They were running, arguing. Just so intense. On the outside, their games needed reconstructive surgery. Inside, they had it. And they were going to grow, get big." Macci chuckled a little and sighed. "I left those courts in Compton thinking one thing: *contract*. These were going to be the best two female tennis players someday in the world."

Macci got the Williamses an RV to drive themselves to Florida, housing once they arrived, scholarships to the academy for Venus (age eleven) and Serena (age nine). The plan Macci and Richard devised was for the girls to be on court four to five hours a day, six days a week. They were to hit only with young men, players who had tried to make the pro tour but couldn't climb the rankings. Both sisters had Macci's attention for technical development, though he told me that among the things *he* learned, from the Williams sisters, was to leave well enough alone. Serena was soon hitting more with her dad than she had in Compton, hitting, she'd say years later, "a ton of balls." Neither Venus nor Serena would play any more junior matches or tournaments, not one, while they trained with Macci. Richard thought traveling the junior circuit a waste of time and a preteen stress machine—the sisters had proved themselves in juniors already. Not that Venus and Serena disappeared, exactly: reporters and TV crews showed up from time to time at the academy to watch and film and look on, lost for words.

Macci moved from Grenelefe to Pompano Beach in 1993, and the Williams family followed him there. Oracene, with the help of tutors, began homeschooling the girls, and there were gymnastics and ballet and karate along with the tennis. Richard continued to manage his security business back in Compton by phone. Serena recalled, in her autobiography, a period about two years after the family had settled in Florida when she grew to hate the courts and didn't want to play. Macci told me this story about eleven-year-old Serena: "She didn't want to practice one afternoon. Richard wasn't around—he was off doing something. I remember telling her, 'You got to move your feet.' And she says, 'I am.' And I say, 'I mean, *faster* than that.' And she says, 'What will you give me?' And I'm like, 'What do you *mean*, what will I give you?'"

It turned out that she was hungry or bored, and something to eat was a way to cure either. "She's a child, you have to understand that, they are children we are coaching," Macci said with a sudden firmness. "So when I ask what she wants, she says she wants curly fries, a Snickers bar, and a Pepsi. Oh, and a Green Day T-shirt. There was a guy she'd passed in the car earlier that morning selling Green Day T-shirts on a corner. She was into Green Day." Macci sent an assistant coach off to get the food and the T-shirt. "For the next hour, one to two in the afternoon, hot, no breaks for water, she moved like she was running on coals, just ripping balls." Macci paused. "Richard understood this. Would talk crazy stuff at times, but he was a great dad. He'd sense the girls needed a break, and like *that*, they were off to the beach for a day, or off to Disney World in Orlando for a few days. Family first, Richard."

I asked Macci to compare Venus and Serena, their games as girls.

"Venus was a year and a half older, had the legs then, the speed.

Serena had this natural throwing motion. The serve is essentially a throwing motion, and Serena—the arm, the hips, the weight transfer—looked like a pitcher already at nine. Venus's serve mechanics had too much arm and wrist, still do, too much wiggle. After practice they would each get a cart filled with balls and have to serve all those balls before they could go home. Richard believed in repetition. Serena, even then, had that serve. Venus used to tell Serena that she'd never beat her. That turned out not to be true."

Serena, Macci went on to say, also had a competitive fire he'd never before seen in a girl he was coaching. She *hated* to lose. "She had to be first at everything, even if it was running to the water fountain." He believed that her fight would win her matches even on days she couldn't summon her A game. "We had this giant sandpit. I'd get the kids running around in it to build up leg strength and nimbleness. They would play tag. Serena? Only kid I ever saw, all those years, would tag with a closed fist. A *fist*. Bang!"

Richard Williams had a timetable, he would tell people back then, for when he thought his daughters would be ready to turn pro. For years, the WTA rule was that you could join the tour officially in the month you turned fourteen, but Richard thought parents of teen phenoms who were okay with that "ought to be shot." He had in mind the case of Capriati, who had made her professional debut at the age of thirteen years, eleven months. The WTA was thinking about Capriati, too, when it announced in 1994 that, beginning the following year, girls under eighteen who turned pro would be limited to playing just a handful of events each year. Capriati, approaching her eighteenth birthday at the time the WTA made public its new rule, was on a fourteen-month hiatus from the tour and finishing up a stint at a Miami drug-rehab center. Her young life had gone off the rails.

Venus Williams was to turn fourteen in 1994, and Macci was

advising Richard to get her into a tournament before the year was out or she'd be in a professional limbo of sorts, playing sporadically, for the next four years. Richard eventually agreed, and on Halloween, at a tournament indoors at the Oakland Coliseum Arena, on a quick-playing carpeted court, dressed in a homemade, sponsor-free outfit and with blue beads in her cornrows, Venus Williams—having played not even a junior tournament during the previous three and a half years—played her first WTA tour match. It attracted Wimbledon-final-level media attention: 252 press credentials were issued, up from 24 the year before. "It was almost like Elvis arriving," Macci said. Her opponent was fifty-ninth-ranked Shaun Stafford, whom Venus dispatched in straight sets. That set up a second-round match against twenty-two-year-old Arantxa Sánchez Vicario of Spain, then the world No. 1. Venus took the first set against her, then went up a break, 3–1, in the second. Was this going to be the biggest upset in the history of the women's game? Sánchez Vicario took a ten-minute bathroom break a bit later in set two that allowed her to regroup—and threw Venus off. She didn't know what she was supposed to do: sit, stand, warm-up. Sánchez Vicario returned and won nine straight games and the match. But the big winner was Venus. She, or rather, Richard, would soon after secure a multimillion-dollar deal with Reebok.

That changed everything, Macci said. "Richard comes to me. He's won the lottery with Reebok, and he says, 'Forget the academy, coach Venus and Serena exclusively. A million dollars a year.'" Macci paused, shook his head. "We go back and forth for two years, meeting and discussing it." Meanwhile, Richard was beginning to mix up the girls' training. Fewer sessions were at the academy, with additional ones on public courts near where they were living, then on the court he had built next to a house he'd bought, with hitting partners he'd lured from Macci's place. Venus was now a part of the tour, but playing only occasionally, which had been

Richard's plan. Serena played her first match in October 1995 (the loss in Canada), under the new rules limiting tournament appearances. Macci decided he didn't want to give up his academy and reached a financial settlement with Richard. "Stupidest decision I ever made," Macci told me, and laughed a little. "It'll sound corny, but they were like family to me. Really were."

Before I drove back to Miami, I asked Macci what he thought about the Williams sisters' still playing, so many years later.

"Never would have predicted that. No one would have." He paused once more for a moment. "Serena, she still wants to knock you out. It's about competing, not making another mil or two. She loves to compete. And if you do, it's so hard to give it up. When she *does* give it up, it'll be the hardest thing she'll ever do."

3

As you get older as a pro tennis player, it becomes more and more important to win efficiently in the early rounds of a tournament, to conserve energy and build confidence. That's what Serena had done at the Australian Open in January. That's what she needed to do in her first match at the 2019 Miami Open. Her opponent was Rebecca Peterson, a twenty-three-year-old Swede of Estonian descent who had never cracked the top fifty, and whose only tour title had been earned four years before, playing doubles. On paper, she represented for Williams no more than an hour or so of workaday effort.

It was a cloudless late afternoon, but the high reaches of the Hard Rock Stadium's upper tiers were brimming shadows on the Stadium Court as play got underway. Swaths of seats sat empty; those who'd decided to sneak off from work for some tennis this Friday were crowding the outer courts. Williams, serving, quickly won the first three points, then lost the next five and—like *that*—was broken. Williams broke back the following game, began to hold her own serve with little struggle, gained one more break, and struck three aces to serve out the set: 6–3, thirty-three minutes, just right.

Then, in set two, her first serve took a walk. She could manage to place just more than a third of them in and was routed 6–1. In the third-set decider, Peterson's serve failed her, and Williams turned things around, winning the set 6–1 and the match, a fitful one that gave her little satisfaction, as was clear from her press conference that followed. "I wasn't really happy with my performance," she said. She mentioned the darkness the shadows produced, and her being distracted the previous week by matters she wasn't going to get into. She was grumpy—at one point she asked the tournament official choosing reporters who raised their hands with questions for her how much longer she had to stay. Before leaving, she said, "I'm not really thinking about this match. I need to just move on and really focus on playing better or not being in the tournament much longer."

4

Qai Qai made it to Miami. I'd seen a photograph of her on Instagram, seated in an Adirondack chair with what looked to be, behind her, a big floor-to-ceiling mural of Biscayne Bay. Qai Qai went everywhere Serena, her husband, and their daughter went, or seemed to. *Seemed* to because Qai Qai was and wasn't actual, depending.

Qai Qai was Serena Williams's granddaughter—that's how Williams had referred to her when she spoke of her, one afternoon back in January at the Australian Open. Which was how lots of parents referred to a doll their child was attached to. Qai Qai had brown skin, a hairless head, not uncommon with babies, and that look on her face that dolls have that must work some kind of magic for a toddler, but which, to a grown-up's eye, can come across as chilly indifference.

The first glimpse the world got of Qai Qai was in a brief video that Williams had posted and narrated the previous summer, just before the 2018 US Open began. The camera roamed what appeared to be a playroom before settling on a tricycle with one of its wheels yanked off, and Qai Qai, bent over in a stroller nearby, being accused by Williams, in her voice-over, of "vandalism." Williams explained that she was documenting the scene for Olympia's "insurance." But all turned out okay for everyone in the end, with Qai Qai in one high chair and Olympia in another. Olympia, who was nearing her first birthday, was having her breakfast and could not have been less concerned with a vandalized tricycle or, as the video reached its end, with Qai Qai.

Here was something echt twenty-first century: parenting as performance art, distributed digitally. Since the video dropped, Qai Qai had taken on a life of her own. Or *lives* of her own. She was a Twitter user. She was an animated character photoshopped into photographs. She was still a favorite plaything of Olympia's, except when she wasn't. (You know how kids are.) And she was a sensation, with more than one hundred thousand Instagram followers by the time Williams talked a little about her in Melbourne. Williams said she'd wanted her daughter's first doll to be Black, and that her nephew had come up with the resonant plaything name of Qai Qai (pronounced *kway kway*). Not long after the Australian Open ended, an interview with Qai Qai appeared in *Oprah Magazine*. She would seem to have arrived for the interview prepared. Among the Oprah-esque quotes attributed to her was "When I make enough space to focus on myself and what I love, I no longer have room for self-doubt or comparisons."

Olympia often appeared in Qai Qai's postings. But costarring with her doll was not Olympia's only outlet on social media. She had her own Instagram account, with more than half a million followers, the posts composed by "Mama" and "Papa." She had her own Twitter account. She had cameos in both her father's and her mother's Instagram and Twitter feeds. She is an adorable child, with lovingly engaged parents. She was part of a much larger social-media phenomenon, celebrity "sharenting," itself an outgrowth of a trend that began in magazines such as *People*, and on reality TV shows. Here were celebrities performing, on social media, their identities as new mothers (and, in fewer numbers, fathers). The photographs of mothers with their babies conveyed, simultaneously, that they were new moms like everyone else, and—how *did* they do it?—new moms who continued to deliver an allure of otherworldly glamour. In the contemporary Instagram gallery of Madonnas with child, Serena thrived as few athletes did. It was a realm of Kourtney Kardashian and Jessica Alba and Kylie Jenner. Ivanka Trump was an eager poster on Instagram of staged photos with her three children until the Trump administration's policy at the Mexican border of separating undocumented parents from *their* little boys and girls became news in the summer of 2018. Williams and the others found this realm enticing as not every celebrity who happened to be a mother did. Some celebrity mothers—Serena's friend Beyoncé among them—spent considerable energy shielding their children from public view.

Right about the time that Williams was battling her way to the final of the 2018 US Open, the Cambridge scholar and popular historian Mary Beard published a book, *How Do We Look: The Body, the Divine, and the Question of Civilization*. It approaches art history as essentially the relationship between images and how viewers understand them. The *New York Times* had the clever idea of talking with Beard about Instagram, which was now our chief contemporary image repository: it's currently used by some 35 percent of American adults. A book-review editor showed Beard a posted photo portrait of Kylie Jenner (130 million Instagram followers), whom America first came to know on the reality-TV show *Keeping Up with the Kardashians*, and who now was a media personality with a thriving cosmetics line. Jenner, in the Instagram portrait, is dressed in a fashionable, foliage-patterned tracksuit and is standing tastefully in front of white garage doors, holding her baby. Her hair and makeup are perfect. The baby she's cradling, lost in a hooded onesie, appears to be asleep. Beard:

> Isn't that just amazing? She could be the Virgin Mary, couldn't she? One of the roles of these celebrities is to convince us that we can do this. That maybe—for those of us who know that in real life motherhood means not losing weight very quickly or being frightfully messy or never having a chance to do your hair like this—this is our fantasy. Maybe we need a fantasy of what it's like to be a mother. Because otherwise, I just want to kick her.

Williams, like other celebrity mothers on Instagram, often attached captions to her photographs that told of how unglamorous mothering could be: Olympia not sleeping, or throwing up on her. Or she wrote in an inspirational vein of how mothers needed to be strong and lift one another up and share their stories at #ThisMama. She identified as a working mom, though this working mom—like all celebrity moms—was not posting photos on Instagram with a nanny (or two) in it. Some photographs posted, too, seemed to blur home life and work life in ways meant not to depict working-mother stresses but to enhance a brand, including hers. How else to understand a photograph of a custom baby-shoe-size pair of high-tops sent to Olympia by Nike?

How long this Instagram-mom craze would last was not clear, or, anyway, how long it would be before some broader cultural questions began to be raised, questions like the ones that were already being raised about the threat social media poses to privacy. How okay was it for a toddler to have hundreds of thousands of adult followers on Instagram? Or for parents to be posting pictures and texts in the name of someone too young to understand them, let alone approve them? Stacey Steinberg, a law professor at the University of Florida's Levin College of Law, and an expert in family and children's law, had recently warned that parents "haven't considered the potential reach or longevity of what is happening with information we're posting." One nation had: a French law now allows a child to later sue her or his parents for posting images of her or him as a child if the images have distressed or shamed her or him.

Meanwhile, Serena and Olympia would soon star together in a new ad for Pampers, promoting a diaper designed to stay on an active, ever-on-the-move "wild" child.

5

Williams withdrew from the Miami Open the afternoon after defeating Rebecca Peterson. "I am disappointed to withdraw from the Miami Open due to a left knee injury," she stated in a release. (Qai Qai weighed in with an Instagram post shortly thereafter, raising a foam finger from a luxury seat in the Stadium Court: "Foam fingers in the air for a speedy recovery!") Was the knee injury related to her turning her left ankle in Melbourne two months earlier? Williams's left knee had given her problems before. She'd first seriously injured it not playing tennis, but on a dance floor at a Los Angeles nightclub in the summer of 2003.

115

She tried a spin move, her left quad detached from the knee, and the surgery subsequently required kept her off the court for the remainder of the year. She'd also withdrawn from both Indian Wells and the Miami Open in 2017 citing an injured left knee. Later, she revealed she hadn't played those tournaments because she was pregnant. Players in all sports masked injuries, cited injuries when the real reason they weren't playing was something otherwise, and played on with injuries despite being racked with pain.

This is all to say that, with regard to injuries, as with so much else, we don't ever really know athletes, even the ones whom we've watched regularly for years and established such emotional proximity to, thanks, among other things, to television and social media. We truly know, in the end, the outcomes of their competitions and their *presentations*, little more.

It would turn out that Williams did, in fact, have an injured left knee. Injuries were likely to visit her more frequently now. Williams's body was that of a thirty-seven-year-old. All the training in the world could not make it the body of someone who was twenty, or even thirty. Like everyone else approaching forty, her lung capacity was in decline. She had fewer fast-twitch muscle fibers now to provide power and explosive speed. Her sight and other senses were gradually diminishing, and her brain's prefrontal cortex—the engine of focus and decision-making—was shrinking. Her balance, too, might not be what it once was. Which is to say that the aging body was more prone to injury. Macci had told me that down through the years he had watched Williams win any number of big matches by simply "*athlete-ing* it out"—winning with endurance and power, even when her shotmaking was off. It would seem, biologically, that such a path to victory—and especially the two weeks of victories required to win the Grand Slam championship she coveted—was less and less available to her.

6

Ashleigh Barty of Australia won the Miami Open women's championship. Her journey to the upper ranks of the WTA tour was a world away from the tennis hothouse of Florida. She'd begun taking lessons, at the age of four, in Brisbane, a forty-minute drive from her suburban home in Ipswich, and still talked about her first coach, Jim Joyce, who coached her into her teens. She developed into a junior star. Then, as a sixteen-year-old, with the penetrating backhand slice and firm volleying technique Joyce had taught her, and with her fellow Australian Casey Dellacqua as a partner, she went on a tear as a doubles player: the pair reached the finals in 2013 at both the Australian Open and Wimbledon. But Barty was understanding that it was all coming too quickly for her. At the end of 2014, she announced she was taking a break from tennis. "I wanted to experience life as a normal teenaged girl," she said then, "and have some normal experiences."

She returned home. She helped Joyce run clinics at the club where he coached. She played pro-level cricket. She returned to the WTA tour in 2016, still playing doubles but focusing more on singles. And now, in 2019, still only twenty-two, she was flourishing, reaching the final at a WTA tournament in Sydney (at which she defeated World No. 1 Simona Halep) as the season began, and then the quarterfinals at the Australian Open that followed. She arrived in Miami as one of the hottest players on the tour, and on the verge of entering the top ten.

At five feet five inches, Barty was a smallish player. She didn't lack for power, though: the way she got her racquet head around the ball on her forehand provided it with snap. Still, the shots and skills she'd honed as a doubles player were her keenest assets. She had an on-court clairvoyance, anticipating shots and patterns, and thinking through points. Her slice backhand was among the best in tennis—*all* of tennis. She could hit it deep with bite; it seldom floated. She also had remarkable hands and was not afraid of coming to the net, a rarity in the women's game.

Barty beat the Czech Karolína Plíšková in the final, 7–6, 6–3. The three-month-long hard-court season that begins each pro-tennis year was over. Hard courts were what Serena Williams learned on, developed on, and had done most of her winning on throughout her long career. She'd won the Miami Open *eight* times, the most she'd won anywhere, though not since 2015. She left Miami not yet having come close to winning a championship in 2019, and now it was on to clay, a surface she'd won on (she *could* win *anywhere*), but one that was slow, less suited to her first-strike game, and one—with its slipperiness, and with the longer rallies its slowness engendered—that could tax and drain an aging player's body. Her body.

Part Four

Rome

1

Not even two complete matches at Indian Wells. Just one match in Miami. Williams needed more match play. She couldn't simply practice and wait for the French Open to begin, in Paris late in May. That had been the plan as the season began. That kind of plan had worked for much of her career: play as few tournaments as necessary, concentrate on the majors. But the plan had figured on her making deep runs at Indian Wells and in Miami—playing, perhaps, six or seven or more matches in all, not six sets. To wait now until Paris, a layoff of nearly two months, would be to bet that she could manage to play her way into the tournament—defeat the low-ranked opponents she was likely to face at least in her first two matches and be rounding into Grand Slam form by the third or fourth round, when stiffer competition would begin. Still, having completed just two matches since January; seven, officially, since the start of the year; and fewer than thirty, in all, since returning to the WTA tour after giving birth to Olympia? Simona Halep, to take but one example, had played more than double that number of matches during that time, and so had many, if not most, of the top women's players. To stay match-ready, match play was crucial. Rust was every bit the encumbrance in tennis that an injury was.

Williams decided last-minute, past the entry deadline, to play the Italian Open, held each year in Rome just before the French Open. Any player in the women's game who has won a Grand Slam tournament can request and will receive a late wild-card entry into an international WTA event and be seeded, depending more or less on her ranking. Williams (along with her sister Venus, Victoria Azarenka, and several others) secured a wild-card entry into the Rome event and, with a ranking of No. 11, was seeded tenth. She looked forward to getting back to competing. And she liked Rome—the city, the food, the tournament. She'd won the Italian Open four times, with three of those championships coming in the four years before spending the 2017 clay season away from tennis, pregnant.

In 2015, she had withdrawn before her scheduled third-round match, citing a right-elbow injury. That trip to Rome would prove significant in another way. It was there, in the second week of May, at the hilltop Cavalieri Hotel, with its Bond-movie sixties grandeur and panoramic views of the city, that Williams met, by chance, Alexis Ohanian.

She was staying at the hotel with her team. He was attending a tech conference there he'd been invited to speak at. They met one morning, alongside one of the hotel's three outdoor pools. Both had been late for the buffet breakfast, and poolside was where you could still get coffee and something to eat. Ohanian took a seat at a table next to one where Williams and members of her team had gathered. The meet-cute, which Ohanian and Williams relayed to *Vanity Fair* and other magazines, unfolded this way: (a) Williams and her team inform Ohanian they need his table, as others in her entourage were on the way, and point out to him other tables where he could sit; (b) Ohanian, with his laptop and headphones, and a little hungover, is unmoved; (c) a member of Williams's team claims she has seen a rat near his table; (d) Ohanian replies that he was born in Brooklyn and is not afraid of rats; (e) Williams, with a certain Williamsesque firmness, repeats the request that he find another table; (f) the conversation about rats continues, during which Williams begins to find the whole thing hilarious and Ohanian comes to understand that he is, in fact, talking with Serena Williams; (g) she invites him to join them for breakfast.

Ohanian, two years younger than Williams, had just turned thirty-two. He'd been born in Brooklyn, but grew up in Columbia, Maryland, the small-town-feel planned suburb, and went on to attend the University of Virginia. Several weeks after graduating, in 2005, Ohanian, with Steve Huffman, a college roommate of his, founded Reddit, a news-aggregation-and-discussion site that they imagined might one day grow to be "the front page of the Internet." They sold it the following year to Condé Nast, the media company best known for the magazines it published, for between $10 million and $20 million—too soon and for too little, went the judgment in Silicon Valley. The site's traffic grew. It also became increasingly toxic, with "subreddit" forums devoted to alt-right conspiracies, racial demonizing, and other topics festering along the darker contours of the American psyche. Ohanian remained on the company's board but was no longer involved day to day. (He'd said he'd accepted the offer from Condé Nast, in part, because his mother was dying of brain cancer.) He journeyed to Armenia, where his father had been born; he helped along a couple of start-ups; he cofounded a venture-capital firm, Initialized Capital; he wrote a book, a sort of internet-utopia manifesto, *Without Their Permission: How the 21st Century Will Be Made, Not Managed*, and promoted it on a bus tour of seventy-seven colleges. By the time he arrived for breakfast at the Cavalieri, he had become a tech-world personality: tall (six feet five inches), 2.0-savvy, boyishly charming, wealthy, if not Serena wealthy (his estimated net worth: $10 million), and a frequent presence at conferences and on business-news shows.

He would not seem Williams's type—she had, at one time or another, been romantically linked with Common, Drake, and the NBA power forward Amar'e Stoudemire. Ohanian had never watched a tennis match. But he wound up attending Williams's first-round match later that day they met in Rome. When she withdrew from the tournament a couple of days later, citing an injured elbow, she invited him to come watch her at the French Open. A year and a half later, Ohanian proposed to Williams at the Cavalieri, at the table where they had met, he having arranged the whole thing—with her friends, with the hotel, with her—as a rom-com-style surprise that was less a surprise in the end than a display of how much she meant to him. It was also the harbinger of romantic extravagances to come, extravagances he would readily share on social media. When she returned to tennis, at Indian Wells in March of 2018, six months after giving birth, he professed his adoration for her by renting billboards, along a road leading to the tennis gardens, that declared her THE GREATEST MOMMA OF ALL TIME. When she had a hankering for Italian food, he flew her to Venice and posted a photo of her on Instagram finishing up a glass of wine.

2

Williams might have gotten back on the tour earlier than Rome—in Madrid, for example, where a prominent tournament begins each year the first week of May. She'd played there many times, winning in 2012 and 2013. Perhaps her injured knee hadn't been quite ready for competition. But even if the knee was no longer hobbling her, she would not have been in Madrid the first week of May. The first Monday night of the month she was cohosting the Met Gala, Anna Wintour's annual fundraiser for the museum's

Costume Institute, with a star-studded cast of invitation-only attendees and a red carpet like that of the Oscars. There was tennis, and increasingly, there was fashion and pop celebrity, and this was a Slam-like commitment to the latter.

The gala, as it normally did, coincided with the opening of a big annual exhibition conceived and organized by the curator of the Costume Institute, Andrew Bolton. The show, called *Camp: Notes on Fashion*, was inspired by a famous essay Susan Sontag wrote in 1964, "Notes on 'Camp.'" It's an untypical Sontag essay, both in form—fifty-eight numbered entries, many just a couple of sentences long—and in voice: it doesn't muster the commanding sense of authority she tended to bring to the cultural subjects she chose to write about. Camp was a sensibility, an elusive one, informing expression but, more, interpretive taste. Theatrical, epicene, extravagant; embracing failed seriousness and a certain vulgarity: Sontag viewed camp as multifaceted, and shifting. Near the end of her list of notes, she raised the "affinity" she perceived between camp taste and homosexual taste: "Homosexuals, by and large, constitute the vanguard—and the most articulate audience—of Camp." They imbued modern sensibility, she suggested, with aestheticism and irony. In 1964, gays and lesbians remained marginalized and victimized, ghettoized or (like Sontag herself) closeted. One sign of how all that had changed was that camp sensibility was now a mainstream American sensibility. One of Serena Williams's cohosts of the gala was Lady Gaga.

The Met's show, being devoted, by and large, to fashion garments, highlighted most effectively the aspects of camp associated with extravagance. It had become a tradition of the evening gala for participants to dress in accord with the show's theme, and luxury and excess were on full display on the red carpet—a pink-carpeted staircase, actually, lined with roses and, behind them, scores of photographers—as guests made their way inside the museum for the dinner. Williams wore a Hi-Liter-yellow gown, designed by Atelier Versace, to which pink-fabric leaves, hundreds of them, were delicately attached and appeared to float. Beneath the gown could be glimpsed Williams's neon-lemon sneakers, the product of a collaboration between Nike and Off-White, the brand of her designer friend Virgil Abloh. Ohanian wore a white dinner jacket and stood by on the pink-carpeted stairs as the cameras whirred and Williams posed.

It struck me that nothing about Serena's look was particularly campy—the sneakers were "street," not camp, and sometimes extravagance was just extravagance. It struck me, too, that off the tennis court, Williams was something else. Ohanian himself had said that the woman he watches play tennis was not the woman he married. There were lots of ways to understand that. One way, perhaps, was that the woman on the court maintained a visage forged by frightful determination. Much was made of this; along with her size, it was a component of what was discussed as her "unconventional" beauty, which, in turn, she'd incorporated as a facet of what had come to be called her brand. But to see not her game face but her carefully tended celebrity face—a mask of sorts, too, for the photographers' cameras—was to see a woman with striking, regal-high cheekbones; expressive almond-shaped dark eyes; and a relaxed smile that widened unequivocally (she enjoyed the attention). Williams was beautiful in conventional ways, too.

3

A couple of days after the gala, I dropped by the *New York Times* offices to talk with Vanessa Friedman, the paper's fashion director and chief fashion critic. I was coming from the Met Museum, where I'd seen the Costume Institute's camp show, and Friedman had just finished writing about it, so we discussed that a bit—how it was refreshing to see a museum show of any kind based on an idea, and how the show managed to stay with you, made you think. When I brought up Serena Williams, the reason I'd come by to talk with Friedman, the first thing she said was "I don't think of Serena as a fashion person. She has a clothing line, but so do a lot of people. A fashion line is a trendy way to diversify your personal brand. It's an effective way today, a pop-culture way, to reach people."

So how did Friedman see her?

"I think Serena is much more interested in her power as a cultural figure. She's such a complicated figure. She's a great athlete. She's clearly interested in celebrity—look at her friendships. And then you have all these worlds colliding: sports, celebrity, film and television, fashion. You saw that at the Met Gala. You see that on social media. It's all pop culture. Serena has moved from tennis into this world. She's interested in her power there."

Friedman brought up the 2016 Pirelli calendar. The calendar was an annual, limited-edition "art item" released by the Italian tire company. It had typically featured twelve photographs, one for each month, of nude or almost nude models. But for the 2016 calendar, shot by Annie Leibovitz, the preeminent celebrity photographer of her time, the portraits were of women from various realms notable for their abilities and power. Agnus Gund, the philanthropist, for instance. Patti Smith. Both of them were photographed fully clothed. And Serena Williams: topless, but shot from behind, her muscular back and shoulders displaying the years of fitness training that helped to make her serve and groundstrokes what they were. "It was a statement about achievement," Friedman said. "Serena was slowly coming to embrace her status and role as a symbol."

Friedman wasn't sure—and wasn't sure Williams was sure—where she would take this. She had developed a role for herself as a celebrity working mom, relaying stories on social media and offering advice and inspiration. Then there was the careful portrayal, online and elsewhere, of her marriage as a modern partnership of equals. (Ohanian, too, was projecting this in his appearances and his posts, advocating, among other things, paternity leave to deepen spousal equality and the at-home responsibilities of fathers.) And there was her emergence as an entrepreneur and investor—a woman with money who was interested in using it to help other women build their businesses. Friedman talked about Rihanna, whose cosmetics line, Fenty Beauty, launched in 2017, was an instant success, with its diversity-informed range of blushers, compacts, bronzers, and on, all available online and in stores in more than a hundred countries. The luxury-fashion group LVMH had just announced the creation of a Fenty fashion label, making Rihanna the first woman of color from the pop world to have a clothing and accessories line backed by a global luxury-brand conglomerate. "What this is saying is that you no longer have to fit into a mold created for and by little white women fifty years ago," Friedman said. She smiled knowingly. She was a fashionably slim white woman.

A fashion line was not the only path, Friedman went on to suggest. A few weeks earlier, Williams had announced the founding of Serena Ventures. She'd already made investments, most of them early stage, in thirty-four start-ups, chiefly in fashion, cosmetics, and e-commerce. Ohanian was helping her with this, as was her friend Sheryl Sandberg, Facebook's chief operating officer, who was also a member of the board, with Williams, of the software company SurveyMonkey. Only the smallest percentage of venture capital flowed to start-ups run by women or people of color. Williams understood this and wanted to be a force for change: 60 percent of the investments she'd made, according to *Forbes*, were to woman- or minority-run young companies.

"It's a moment—the woke, Black superwoman," Friedman suggested. "Oprah, Gayle King. It's Rihanna, it's Beyoncé. It's body positivity—the rapper Lizzo. It's be authentically yourself. Stand up for who you are—the old molds are breaking down. If you're smart, or your manager or agent is smart, you're like, 'I have a place in this. *I can own this.*' It will burnish your brand, draw more people to you, increase your power. That's where I see Serena now."

4

The Italian Open is held at Rome's Foro Italico, a sports complex in the affluent residential neighborhood of Vittoria, along a northern curve of the Tiber River. It was constructed in the 1930s as the Foro Mussolini, with the purpose of attracting the Olympics to Italy in 1940. (The 1940 Games were eventually awarded to Helsinki, but never held: war got in the way.) The Foro, with its parade-grounds piazza and colossal statuary inspired by a hazy, heroic appreciation of imperial Rome, remains a distinguished example of Fascist architecture. Its newer tennis courts attract thousands of fans each year, who are among the most attentive and engaged on the pro tour. Campo Centrale, the Foro's main show court, was filled on an overcast and unseasonably cool Monday afternoon, as Williams's first match was set to begin.

In this second-round match—Williams being seeded and receiving a first-round bye—her opponent was Rebecca Peterson, the Swede whom Williams had squared off against in Miami seven weeks before, in the last match she'd played. Peterson, who'd battled her way into the Italian Open draw as a qualifier, looked sharp in the opening minutes, and broke Williams's serve in the fourth game to go up 3–1. But already she was not getting Williams on the move enough and was too often putting the ball on

Williams's forehand: tactical lapses she would soon enough pay for. Williams broke Peterson right back, and Williams's serves and ground strokes were beginning to arrive with more heaviness and pace. Peterson called her coach (and father), Mart Peterson, on the court—as is permitted on the women's tour in non-Slam tournaments—but whatever he told her, it failed to adjust the timing of her backhand, which was too often meeting the incoming ball too late. Williams won the first set 6–4, and then the second more quickly and decisively, 6–2. She hit twenty-eight winners, struck nine aces, and looked to be moving well enough.

Afterward, Williams seemed upbeat, even when talking about how difficult it was for a player to remain match-ready during a nearly two-month layoff. The sore knee, she explained, had limited her time on court and her time in the gym. "I did everything I could to stay fit and keep my cardio up," she said. "I've just been on this diet basically. It's been awful. When you're sedentary, it becomes hard to manage your body. So it's basically you have to eat grass."

Next up for her was a familiar opponent, her sister Venus. But the following day Serena released a statement: "I must withdraw from the Italian Open, due to pain in my left knee. I will miss the fans and competition at one of my favorite tournaments. I will be concentrating on rehab and look forward to seeing you all at the French Open."

The Rome Open would be won by Karolína Plíšková, the Czech who'd defeated Williams in Australia in January—the only time Williams had been beaten, so far this season, in a completed match. It was also true, glaringly true, that, since then, she had won only three matches in three months.

Part Five

Paris

1

Chris Evert won the French Open women's singles title seven times. No woman then, in the 1970s and 1980s, and no woman now could dominate on a surface of red clay like Evert. She came up in an era when three of the Grand Slam tournaments, not just Wimbledon but the Australian Open and US Open, too, were played on grass, and the players—the women and the men—served and volleyed, chipped and charged: got to the net, and fast, to end points with volleys. The bounces on grass were too low and too erratic, especially as tournaments wore on. No one wanted to stay back at the baseline and get into lengthy ground-stroke rallies.

Evert had other ideas. She had practiced and practiced her ground strokes with her father in Florida. She brought a consistency to forehands and backhands that the women's game hadn't seen. Her accuracy in placing and angling these shots from back at the baseline was uncanny. She was a master of the passing shot, leaving net rushers with little to do but watch the ball they'd hoped to volley hurry by. Her topspin befuddled net chargers, too: the ball passed high over the net, then plunged, forcing volleyers to hit weakly and up, floating the ball back. She won plenty on every surface, won eighteen major titles overall and a higher percentage of matches than any other woman, or man, in the Open era. But her winning percentage on clay was preposterous, nearly *95* percent. At one point in the 1970s, she won 125 straight matches on clay. She'd perfected a steady, grinding game, building the points she'd mostly win from the back of the court, tactically and methodically. The clay (actually, crushed red brick) that coated the surface of the courts in Paris and elsewhere slowed a ball down and increased the height and (on topspin shots) depth of bounces, and she brought a game designed for it. For most of two decades, she reigned as the Queen of Clay.

There would never be another player on the women's side who was as dominant a clay-court specialist. Put still another way: How did Serena Williams—with a game designed to win points quickly, with power, and, as she grew older, with as little athletic movement as possible—how had she managed to win three French Opens, more than any other active player on the women's tour? I phoned Evert one afternoon to ask her. I reached her at her home, in Boca Raton. In her midsixties, she continued to instruct there at the Evert Academy (which she founded with her brother John), when she wasn't traveling to a Grand Slam to work as a commentator. She was about to leave for Paris, where she'd be on air for Eurosport.

She preferred, she said, to be called Chrissie. She then began to discuss the *King* of Clay: "Oh, God . . . well, Rafa Nadal. I mean, there's no woman in tennis like him. No other man, either." She paused. "Okay. So, for starters, let's just say Nadal is, like, the outlier. He has the quickness to play so far behind the baseline and chase down balls. And he has that topspin."

The topspin that Nadal lathered on the ball was not the topspin of Chrissie Evert or, for that matter, Björn Borg, who was the King of Clay in his time. The ball coming off Nadal's racquet when he hit a forehand would spin, on average, at a rate of thirty-two hundred revolutions per minute, and as high as four thousand. This was simply impossible with the small wooden racquets and, specifically, the gut strings used by professionals back in Evert's day. Today's polyester and "co-poly" (polyester with other softer plastics) strings were more slippery, and as they absorbed an incoming ball and launched it back, they slid toward and away from one another, significantly increasing the spin generated by a player's topspin stroke.

The spin on Nadal's forehand did a number of things for his clay-court game, and Evert talked them through. It allowed him to hit with blistering pace and still keep the ball in the court: the ball looped up and over the net, then down without sailing long. This "shaped ball" took longer to land, and thus longer to get returned, than a flat shot did, and Nadal used this time to establish the court position he wanted. On clay, especially, Nadal's heavy topspin created a bounce that sent the ball high up and angled deeply in whichever direction it was heading. It was hard, Evert noted, not to be pushed back from the baseline by it—back so far that his opponents found it nearly impossible to find angles with their shots and too often left their own ground strokes vulnerably short. Slugging an arriving ball loaded with Nadalian topspin also tired the arm. In the parlance of tennis coaches and insiders such as Evert, Nadal's heavy topspin wore down an opponent's "shot tolerance."

Nadal didn't invent this shot; after spin-inducing polyester strings came along, in the late nineties, Brazil's Gustavo "Guga" Kuerten began using them, brushing the back of the ball violently upward with his forehand and creating unprecedented topspin. (He won three French Opens.) But Nadal perfected it. He arrived in Paris, as the French Open began in 2019, having won the championship *eleven* times. He was dominating a Grand Slam tournament as no player had ever dominated any tournament, with that topspin of his.

So why, I asked Evert, wasn't there a woman generating Nadal-like forehand topspin with *her* poly strings?

"Women for the most part can't," she said. Women tend to struggle with the grip required for maximum topspin on the forehand side—what's called an extreme-Western grip, with the palm essentially underneath the racquet. Nadal's vehement brush up the back of the ball, and his lariat-like "reverse" follow-through—not across his body but with his thick left wrist straining far forward before his hitting arm whips nearly straight up—requires tremendous arm strength. "It's the same with serving big: most women just don't have the shoulder. I mean, we're different. We have hips for childbearing." Evert laughed a little.

So, I suggested, we should just expect women with power-baseline games, built for hard courts, to continue to win French Opens, whether or not they have the particular skills associated with clay? Serena Williams had, in this decade, won the championship twice in Paris, in her *thirties*; Maria Sharapova had won the French twice, too. Neither would be mistaken for a clay-court specialist. Spain's Garbiñe Muguruza, with her flat strokes and attack game, had won in 2016 (defeating Williams). Then, Jeļena Ostapenko, of Latvia, who was nineteen years old and had never won a title on the women's tour, won the French Open in 2017 by blasting nearly every ball she could put her racquet on as hard as she could, errors be damned. Her opponent in the final, Simona Halep, was arguably the player on the women's tour with the strengths best suited to clay. She was a quick and agile scrambler and a discerning reader of her opponent's patterns and weaknesses. Halep was up a set, and 3–0 in the second, but was overpowered and undone by Ostapenko's big-strike, high-risk, go-for-broke game.

The following year, 2018, Halep did win the French Open, her first Grand Slam title, defeating American Sloane Stephens in the final. Evert liked Halep and her game and thought she had a number of Grand Slam wins in her if she could maintain her composure and not get so down on herself when she hit rough patches in big matches. But Evert doubted the emergence of any woman dominating on clay. "Back when I played, there were a couple of baseliners like me, relying on consistent ground strokes, and there were the women who served and volleyed," she said. "That was it. We didn't have to contend with the power."

Power came to claim all the surfaces in the women's game as Evert neared retirement in the late 1980s. Steffi Graf won the French Open six times. Monica Seles won it three times in the early 1990s before being stabbed in the back on court in Hamburg by a deranged Graf fan, an attack that would thwart her career. Then came more power players, Serena Williams the most powerful among them. "It is hard to play defense again and again, point after point, against that power. You have to get these big girls on the run, move them from the center of the baseline." Evert allowed how difficult it was to redirect the incoming ball or to hit drop shots from the backcourt—the kinds of shots that get opponents moving—when that incoming ball from a powerful opponent had been (1) taken early, on the rise or short hop, to take time away from you, which was Williams' approach; and then (2) sent back at you at eighty miles per hour or more, flat, deep in the corner, which Williams could bring off with her forehand.

Is it possible, I asked, that, in the not too distant future, there would be bigger players on the women's tour, as there were now on the men's tour, who could move like the Halep-size players but hit hard and offensively, like Williams, once they reach the ball?

"I think that will happen," Evert said. "The game is always evolving."

Evert wasn't sure that Williams herself had another French Open title in her. She moved uneasily on the often slippery crushed brick, and this uneasiness was becoming more pronounced as she aged. Evert also thought the field in the women's game was stronger down through the rankings now than at any other point in Williams's career—breezing through the early rounds was no longer a given. More generally, she had the off-court distractions of being a mother, and being Serena. Evert herself had her children, three sons, with the Alpine ski-racer Andy Mills, in the 1990s, after she retired. It changed her, she said, and she was sure it had changed Williams, made compartmentalizing, something Williams could do so well, more difficult. Evert had been a celebrity, too, in her time, and in a way that no player in the women's game in America had been before her—not Maureen Connolly or even Billie Jean King. Evert was a sort of American Darling, riding and encouraging the so-called Tennis Boom of the 1970s, when the middle class, or anyway an increasingly educated, professional aspect of it, took to tennis, playing and watching, as never before (and never since). It wasn't only Evert's game that drew attention: the monitoring of her love life was more or less constant. Still, she said, it was nothing like today: the money and media and social media. It was nothing like Serena Williams's life.

2

The photograph popped up in my Twitter feed, posted by an all-but-unheard-of Belgian tennis player, Ysaline Bonaventure: Serena Williams in a wheelchair. It was just days before Williams was to play her first-round match at the French Open. She was visiting Disneyland Paris. What first came to my mind was a scene in a documentary, *Serena* (it aired on cable TV in 2016), that showed Williams celebrating her victory in the French Open final the summer before, celebrating alone in front of her laptop, eating Chinese food and watching *The Little Mermaid* for the umpteenth time. Williams had a long-standing thing for Disney. Richard Williams would take his daughters to Disneyland and, later in Florida, Disney World when he believed they needed a break from tennis. "Under the Sea" remained a go-to karaoke song for Serena (and karaoke a go-to diversion). She had recently spoken, with a mother-of-a-toddler eye roll, of how many times she and Olympia had watched *The Little Mermaid* together.

Olympia was in Williams's lap as Ohanian pushed the wheelchair at Disneyland Paris. What is it about seeing a star athlete in a wheelchair or on crutches or, as is not uncommon now with social media, photographed postsurgery in a hospital bed? What, if you are a fan of sports, made it so unsettling? There was this: Athletes' selves (to us, anyway) resided in their bodies, or to a great extent in their bodies, as was not the case (to us, anyway) with, say, authors or pop singers or TV actors. When great athletes broke down, it tore at the bond we'd made with them. And more: It hobbled an unfolding narrative we'd constructed from their expectations, and from ours. It revealed their vulnerability, and our vulnerability to a relationship we'd conjured of their physical *invulnerability*. This was especially true of those athletes we associated with toughness and power—athletes such as Serena Williams.

As it turned out, Williams was simply being cautious about her left knee, which continued to bother her, though whether she remained injured and in pain or was feeling okay but was wary of reinjuring the knee remained unclear. She was out practicing at Roland-Garros the following day. And she was not going to discuss the wheelchair. When a reporter brought it up, she snapped, "I'm fine, I'm here, aren't I? It's a personal matter that I will not go into."

Williams looked as if she wasn't ready to be up and around in the first set of her opening-round match. Her opponent was a Russian journeywoman, a lanky twenty-eight-year-old who had spent most of her career outside the top one hundred, Vitalia Diatchenko. In their only prior meeting, Diatchenko had failed to win a game. But here was Williams, beating herself, finding little rhythm on her serves, shanking balls off her frame. She lost the first set, and quickly, 2–6, but she soon enough gathered herself and breezed through the next two sets to win 2–6, 6–1, 6–0. After, she talked about feeling off at first and, once again, about needing more match play. She spoke, too, as she usually did now after her first match of a major, about the outfit that her friend Virgil Abloh had designed with Nike for her. The skirt and crop top were striped, sort of zebra-style, with what looked to be a stenciled botanical print here and there, and on her similarly patterned warm-up jacket were the words, in French, for "queen," "champion," "mom," and "goddess."

"Déesse," a reporter said to Williams. "Goddess." "That's a lot to carry, isn't it?"

"Yeah, it's a lot to carry," she replied evenly. "So is being Serena Williams."

3

Williams, nearing the end of her long career, had no rivalry with another formidable player, no opponent at the top of the women's game that she'd squared off against repeatedly in big finals across a significant stretch of time. There hadn't been a star who, over the years, presented a contrasting style of play to hers, who challenged her to adjust or enhance her game. There was nothing to compare to Federer versus Nadal, or Federer versus Djokovic— or Chris Evert versus Martina Navratilova, the greatest rivalry in women's tennis, and arguably the greatest rivalry in any sport of the past fifty years. Evert versus Navratilova: baseline steadiness versus power and speed; righty versus lefty; eighty matches (sixty of them tournament finals!); one or the other usually ranked No. 1

(playing one or the other not far from No. 1). Evert versus Navratilova seemed to go on forever—tournament after tournament for fifteen years, more or less, not far from forever in tennis—and somehow never got old.

Martina Hingis looked to be a rival in Williams's first years on tour. Both she and Williams turned pro in the mid-1990s. Hingis, a year older than Williams, had had a racquet placed in her hands at age two, her parents, both among the best tennis players in Czechoslovakia in the 1970s, determined to mold her for tennis greatness. They divorced, and Hingis's mother defected to Switzerland with her when she was six. If anything, Hingis's development grew more focused and determined. She honed a unique game, an all-court game based ultimately on tireless athleticism and an unrivaled ability to think under pressure on court and to adapt on the fly. This was augmented by the shot variety she possessed: she seemed to have them all. A few months after she turned sixteen, she won the 1997 Australian Open, becoming the youngest Grand Slam winner of the Open era and, soon enough, the youngest world No. 1. Over the next six years, Hingis and Williams would meet thirteen times, always late in tournaments. They played a lot of rousing tennis against each other, and Hingis managed to thwart Williams's power and defeat her six times—most memorably in a 2001 Australian Open quarterfinal that went to three sets and lasted nearly two and a half hours before Hingis prevailed 8–6 in the third. Williams didn't like to talk much now about losses such as that one, but she would allow she made a point of learning from them and could never forget them.

Williams did win the only Slam final she and Hingis played, at the 1999 US Open, and would go on to hold a seven-to-six edge in her matches against her. And after that Australian Open match, Hingis never beat her again. (By the end of 2002, still only twenty-two, Hingis was sidelined with ligament injuries in both ankles that would require surgeries and years of recovery, effectively ending her run as a top singles player. She would, with her guile and exactitude, remain a formidable doubles player until her retirement in 2017.) So it would go with other would-be rivals Williams faced in her early years: Jennifer Capriati, Lindsay Davenport, sister Venus. Serena would come to prevail, and especially in big finals. These players were older than Hingis, established at or near the top when Serena broke through, and were power baseliners who provided none of the contrast that colored Williams's square-offs with Hingis.

Matches between the Williams sisters (there had been thirty of them by 2019) were for many years the most anticipated in the women's game, and a number of times—in the 2003 Australian Open and Wimbledon finals especially—they played hard-fought matches; tight, dramatic matches. But they seldom brought out great tennis in each other, and it was understandable: their games were too similar, and too familiar to each other from all those years of practicing together. And neither Serena nor Venus could contain with consistency the emotions stirred by facing your sister across the net in a consequential match. The tennis tended to get patchy. And then, over the years, the results grew lopsided. In majors, Serena came to dominate. She'd won eleven of their sixteen matches at Grand Slams, seven of their nine Slam finals.

The only player to truly merit the appellation *Serena rival*— if only for five years or so—was a lithe but doggedly combative Belgian, months younger than Williams but, it could seem, older souled. Justine Henin, or, as she was at the time of her fiercest matches with Williams, Justine Henin-Hardenne, had, like Hingis, an all-court game. Her footwork was impeccable. Her shotmaking was precise. Her one-handed drive backhand, a rarity in the women's game, was as effective as it was elegant. And she could summon power in moments that Hingis couldn't, despite her relative (to Williams, for sure) slightness and average (five-feet-six) height. And to clay, on which Henin played her finest tennis, she brought the unyielding focus and resolute consistency that winning on the surface (without overwhelming power) tends to require. She was, before retiring suddenly in the spring of 2008—only twenty-five and ranked No. 1 but burned out from the tour grind, and burdened by a recent divorce and a soured relationship with her domineering father—the player who *got* to Williams, who, as Williams once put it, "gave me a world of trouble."

Williams had crushed Henin, 6–2, 6–0, in Miami, in the last match they played before Henin's announcement that she was calling it quits. (She would come out of retirement eighteen months later and play for a couple more years before developing a chronic elbow injury, but would never again find the level she'd earlier achieved.) Williams, at that time, was leading overall in wins in their matchup, seven to six. *No* player, except for a few veterans who played her once or twice when she first joined the tour in her teens, left tennis with a winning record against Williams. Henin, however, did have a winning record against Williams on clay (4-1) and, more nettlesome to Williams, a winning record against her in Grand Slam tournaments (4-2), and not just on the *terre battue* of Roland-Garros. Moreover, in the years when Henin battled Williams most vehemently—in 2003 and then in 2007; they never met in the three years in between—Henin defeated Williams *five* out of seven times, the last three of those at the French Open, Wimbledon, and the US Open. And those wins of Henin's in 2003 came at a time when Williams was playing the greatest tennis, month in, month out, she would ever play.

In 2002, Williams had gone 56-5 and won eight titles, including the French Open, Wimbledon, and the US Open. She was beating her sister, and every other top player, consistently. She rose to world No. 1. She began 2003 by winning the Australian Open, beating Venus in the final, as she had, the previous spring and summer, at the French Open, Wimbledon, and the US Open. Serena now held all four major titles: not titles won in the same calendar year, a so-called Grand Slam, but nevertheless a rare feat, a Serena Slam, as it came to be known. She went on, after Australia, to win twenty-one matches in a row. She seemed as invincible as any tennis player in memory. In Charleston that April, at what was then called the Family Circle Cup, played as it would continue to be on green-gray Har-Tru clay (made from crushed metabasalt, and slightly faster-playing than red clay), Henin ended Williams's win streak, 6–3, 6–4. Six weeks later, they faced each other again in a semifinal match at Roland-Garros that would prove their most memorable meeting.

A number of long highlight reels of the match are available on YouTube, and I spent a *gris* morning in Paris during the first week of the French Open watching and rewatching them. How *young* Williams was—objectively, of course (she was twenty-one), but youthful, too, in her daring and indefatigability. She chased each ball as if it were the last point in the match, got to balls that drew her into the doubles alleys, hit ground strokes on the run and sliding on the stretch. She played breathtaking tennis without needing to catch her breath.

Henin, with her plain-Jane kit and white cap tugged broodingly low, was cool and homed in. Defender that she essentially was, she showed, from the start, great anticipation and preternatural preparation, getting her racquet back and taking her first explosive steps toward the ball before it left Williams's strings, or so it appeared. Henin forced long rallies and stayed in them with sharp slices, changes of pace, deep forehands and backhands, deft drop shots, and adamant retrieving. What Henin failed to produce, because she didn't have it, was a serve that she could confidently hold, never mind use to win free points with a few aces and service winners. Williams took the first set 6–2, and was up 4–2 in the second, and serving, ahead in the game 30–0, when it all took a turn.

The point that had brought the game to 30–0 had initially been awarded to Henin—a deep ball Williams failed to return. But Williams challenged, maintaining the ball was out. The chair umpire, Jorge Dias, came down from his seat, walked to where the ball had landed, looked down, pointed to a pock in the clay, and ruled that the ball was, in fact, out. (Hawk-Eye did not yet exist; and still, in 2019, it was not used on clay courts, the reasoning going that the ball left a mark the eye could see.) The crowd began booing and whistling. Maybe some French fans were still smarting from Williams's trouncing (6–1, 6–2) of Frenchwoman Amélie Mauresmo in the quarterfinals. Maybe some Belgians had driven hours to see and cheer on Henin. Maybe some weren't happy with this big African American girl winning and winning and winning.

As Williams was in her service motion, Henin stretched an arm before her and called time, signaling that she, Henin, wasn't yet prepared to play. Williams saw this as she followed through on her serve—which landed in the net, a fault. Williams explained to the chair umpire that Henin had raised her hand and called time, and that, as a result, Williams should get to repeat her first serve. The chair umpire said he didn't see it and turned to Henin. Henin said nothing. This, for a tennis player, was unsportsmanlike. Meanwhile, the crowd, unaware of what was transpiring, but seeing Williams speaking with the chair ump, raised the volume of their boos and whistles. Rattled, Williams lost the next four points and the game. Now the crowd understood its own effectiveness. Williams's faults and misses were cheered, her winners scorned. She lost the set. Her composure, then her game, evaporated. She'd eventually lose the third set, too. She met Henin at the net, barely touched her outstretched hand, and never glanced anywhere but away.

Henin would go on to rout Kim Clijsters in the final. Years later, Henin would tell a Belgian TV interviewer that her behavior in that semifinal match with Williams was "not my best memory." Not long after, Williams would tweet, "Question. I keep hearing about an admittance to someone cheating me & lying about it after the French Open? Did she confess finally?"

What lingered that morning after rewatching those highlights of the match was the look on Williams's face, in a close-up, as she stood at the baseline that afternoon years ago, the jeers cascading; as she prepared—tried to prepare her*self*—to strike a second serve, her bigger, stronger first serve having been taken from her. Despite the stature Williams had earned, despite being the strongest, the most aggressive, the world No. 1 . . . the face was of bewildered youth. A passage from Michelle Obama's memoir, which I'd finished reading not long before, came to me, as I thought about that expression on Williams's face. The passage was about how a young Black woman, even a successful young Black woman, in the undeserved moments every young person faces—and regardless of whether those moments were ultimately racially charged or not, but just *might* be—how a young Black woman could, in such moments, feel and register the "quiet, cruel nuances of not belonging."

4

The Parisians who watched the French Open from the best seats on Court Philippe Chatrier, the main show court at Stade Roland-Garros, had distinctive viewing habits. If a match began at 11:00 a.m., the tennis might be glimpsed from time to time over the top of a broadsheet newspaper. At 1:00 p.m., whatever the stage of a match, the courtside seats began to empty: it was time for lunch, and not simply something grabbed at a concession stand. Bistros were within walking distance, out on the narrow streets off the Porte d'Auteuil, and a new restaurant on the grounds, along a cobblestone pathway that led toward the adjacent botanical garden at the southern tip of the Bois de Boulogne. Salmon tartare? Mussels with fennel and leeks? *Framboises* were beginning to show up on menus. Tennis watching would resume around three.

Thus, many courtside seats—new hand-finished chestnut seats—were empty when Serena Williams's second-round match against Japan's Kurumi Nara got underway on a midweek afternoon at two twenty. Nara was just a bit taller than five feet. Her ten years as a pro had been spent mostly on the ITF circuit, the women's tour's minor league. She was ranked No. 238 when she took the court against Williams. Those lingering over their espressos before heading back to Chatrier would have nothing to regret. It took Williams just a little over an hour to dispense with Nara, 6–3, 6–2. Williams's serves and returns were too much, which meant Williams was in control, from the start, of most of the points in most of the games. She ended the match with three straight aces, walking as slow as slow could be along the baseline from one side of the center service line to the other. Her left knee—whether painfully sore or tenderly prone to reinjury—went untested.

5

Williams, in her late twenties, began spending a few months a year in Paris. She had an apartment on the Left Bank, in a quiet street in the Seventh Arrondissement. What drew her to the city?

She never spoke of it as a haven from American racism, in the way literary- and jazz- and artistic-minded African Americans had, and continued to, sensing, as Richard Wright once put it, "more freedom in one square block of Paris than there is in the entire United States." It surely, for Williams, wasn't an affinity for the French *état*. Just days after the US-led invasion of Iraq, in March of 2003, in a postmatch press conference in Key Biscayne, Williams had been asked about the burst of anti-French sentiment in America—France having opposed the war and refused to commit troops to the coalition fighting to topple Saddam Hussein. She'd replied mockingly, in a French accent, "Well, we don't want to play in the war. We want to make clothes." Ten years later, with her apartment in Paris making her liable for "social charges," she'd rail against French income-tax rates to an interviewer: "Seventy-five percent doesn't seem legal." Then, echoing her father's bootstrapping sentiments, she'd added, "Nobody does anything because the government pays you to be broke. So why work?"

The essayist John Jeremiah Sullivan has made the compelling case that among the things Williams was doing in Paris was gaining some distance from her father and his views. Sullivan visited her in Paris in the summer of 2012 for a piece on the Williams sisters that would be published in August of that year in the *New York Times Magazine*. She was starting to work on her tennis game with Patrick Mouratoglou, and, it would seem, beginning to be involved with him, but Mouratoglou does not figure in Sullivan's story. It's essentially a visit with Williams—and one of the best. It's early in the evening, and she's home alone in her apartment. She comes downstairs to greet him when he rings the bell. There was a mix-up about what time he was expected; they set off on a walk together to get some takeout to bring to her place. They return, she pours him a Jack Daniel's, they talk. He admires the furniture she'd bought mostly on wanders through outdoor markets, and the used books she'd brought back from the stalls along the Seine to line her bookshelves. The window behind them offers Paris in the twilight. Williams gives the view a look and says, "I love how the city's all even. I love how you can see the sky. You can't have too many tall buildings. I mean, there are a few, but for the most part, it's old-world. I like it." She liked being alone in the apartment, she told Sullivan. She came to Paris "just to be around nobody."

Sullivan took it from there. He observed no trace of Richard Williams in the apartment. He realized he had sensed a distance from Richard, too, in an earlier meeting he'd had in Cincinnati with Venus, the way she continued to call him "Daddy" but rolled her eyes when Sullivan brought up things Richard had said or claimed to have done. Venus also admitted to ignoring her father's lengthy emails. Richard and Oracene had been divorced ten years by then. Richard was nominally still the sisters' coach, but he was less and less around. And here was Serena, in Paris, in the summer of 2012, far from Richard, and with Mouratoglou, reviving a career that had faltered in the previous two years—winning Wimbledon; winning an Olympic gold medal in London weeks later in singles, and one in doubles with Venus. And here was Serena, in Paris, in her thirty-first year, strolling through the city, shopping in the neighborhood, speaking French with the merchants and speaking it well, admiring the view from a place all her own. Sullivan wrote that he had the sense Serena was "hiding" there—from her father, and maybe from an America "that couldn't decide if she was a goddess or a threat." Or maybe, I thought, reading Sullivan: maybe, in Paris, she was free finally to be herself, or to begin to be; as free, in her own way, as Wright or James Baldwin had felt, in Paris in their time, in Paris to escape.

6

Williams resolved all doubts about the state of her left knee early on in her third-round French Open match. Fifteen minutes into the match, she looked as though she might need that wheelchair. She was moving gingerly, when she was moving at all. It made matters worse that she had never before played her opponent, wasn't familiar with her patterns and proclivities, and was guessing, mostly wrong, on where to best establish her court position and in what direction a next shot coming at her might be headed. Williams was leaning, or standing frozen along the baseline, as the ball, a yard away, passed her; she was lunging or hitting off her back foot feebly. Too often, when she did reach a ball, it was late, her preparation untidy, the resulting shot errant. It was hard to watch.

I was sitting in Philippe Chatrier's press section next to Christopher Clarey, the dean of tennis reporters. He'd been covering tennis, for the *International Herald Tribune* and the *New York Times*, for twenty-five years—since around the time Williams turned pro. He was an old-school journalist, at pains to be fair and complete, though he was comfortably new-media when it came to his work methods: he was watching, and from time to time chatting, with an open laptop in front of him, typing out notes and, frequently enough, tweets. He also had a boyish way of grinning and widening his eyes, at you or his laptop screen, when what he saw transpiring on court was painful. It was his way of wincing, and he was doing it a lot. Williams hadn't looked this flummoxed—*infirm* and flummoxed—since the beginning of her comeback, when she'd lost in Miami in March of 2018 to Naomi Osaka. (She had never before played Osaka, either.)

Her opponent, this unseasonably warm-for-Paris Saturday, was Sofia "Sonya" Kenin, a twenty-year-old American comer. She'd been brought to Florida from Russia as a five-year-old by her parents, who were devoted to making her a tennis player. Kenin had, like Williams, spent time at Rick Macci's academy, but had, unlike Williams, been a regular on the junior circuit through her teens and, there, a perennial US No. 1. She had a backhand with which she could change direction with deft disguise, and a drop shot (as Williams would learn) she could feather across the net from anywhere on the court, including from back behind the baseline. She was confident and relentlessly animated on court. She stomped her feet when she missed a shot and marched to her chair after dropping a game like a child being sent to her room for a time-out. She spent a fair amount of the match being booed by the lively French crowd—the match had started as afternoon was giving way to evening, and the stadium was full—because she seemed to be contesting nearly every close line call. But the jeering only seemed to spur her on.

Kenin ran away with the first set, breaking Williams's serve twice, and confounding her especially with her gossamer drop shots. It looked as though she might run away with the second set, too—she broke Williams at love in the first game—but Williams broke Kenin in the sixth game to even things at 3–3. Williams was staying in the match, as only she could, with her returns and her serves. Still, Kenin was dictating most of the points, and Williams was chugging toward balls, especially when Kenin drew her forward. When Williams, serving with the score tied 5–5, ran down but wildly overstruck still another short ball, she screamed and awkwardly kicked the air. Clarey shot me that look of his. Soon enough, Williams saw her serve broken again. Kenin, in the following game, serving for the match, struggled with nerves, but when Williams sprayed one more backhand—she made thirty-four unforced errors in the two sets, double Kenin's total—Williams was done (6–2, 7–5) and out of the French Open.

Kenin would lose in the following round to Australia's Ash Barty, who would go on to win the women's title, defeating a nineteen-year-old Czech hopeful, Markéta Vondroušová, in straight sets. Barty had reached the final by winning a terrific, three-set semifinal match over a seventeen-year-old American phenom, Amanda Anisimova. Anisimova, like Kenin, was the daughter of Russian immigrants. She, like Kenin until her French Open match with Williams, and like Barty, Vondroušová, and a number of other young top players—Canada's Bianca Andreescu, Aryna Sabalenka of Belarus, Croatia's Donna Vekić—had yet to play against Williams. Which, for Williams, meant that if and when she did play any of them, she wouldn't know their games. And which, for these young newcomers, meant they had no history with her, hadn't been overwhelmed by her—had never had to face her in her prime. Williams, her game no longer what it once was, couldn't intimidate them, as she had so many players when she was at her best—as all great tennis players at the top of their game did to their opponents. The psychological pressure in these matches would be *Williams's* to carry, as it had been against Kenin, and against Naomi Osaka, back at the US Open. The knee problem wasn't the only thing Williams needed to overcome.

7

Whoopi Goldberg was worked up in that peculiarly daytime-TV sort of way, manufacturing, as she did most weekdays, a little controversy for the audience of *The View*, feigning anger for laughs. She was discussing Williams's exit from the French Open. Not her match with Sonya Kenin, but the press conference that followed. And not what transpired during the press conference, actually, but . . . what to call it: the heightened sense of confusion that preceded Williams's meeting briefly and sullenly with reporters after her loss.

After that loss, Williams had gone directly from the court to the media center nearby. She wanted to get things over with, as players who've lost distressingly, in an upset, tend to. Players of Williams's stature, who attract the most reporters, usually command a tournament's main pressroom, where the most seats are, and where the questions and answers are videotaped and transcribed, as they're not, as a rule, in the smaller interview rooms. But Dominic Thiem, a young tennis star and the world's second-best clay-court player, was still in the main pressroom, speaking in German about his third-round win that afternoon with reporters from Austria, where he's from. At official tennis press conferences, the first twenty minutes or so are in English, the tour's lingua franca, followed by a home-country Q&A. When Williams arrived, hovering with her people outside the main-room entrance, Roland-Garros media officials cut Thiem's German presser short, and Thiem left fuming. Shortly thereafter, he went after Williams, who he presumed had bigfooted him, telling a TV reporter from German Eurosport, "Every player has to wait—it shows a bad personality, in my opinion."

In Whoopi Goldberg's opinion, Thiem was a "bonehead." She offered Thiem some perspective: "Listen, man, don't anybody know *who you are!*" (The studio audience loved that.) One of her cohosts, the Hispanic Republican strategist Ana Navarro, expanded on this theme: "They moved him to let the Queen come in. Just have a little self-awareness here. Serena Williams is in a class by her own. Maybe one day you'll be the King of Tennis. But right now, we don't know who you are." Sunny Hostin, another of the hosts, a progressive commentator, concurred, "Serena *is* the Queen."

When CNN's Tara Setmayer, the last of the cohosts to weigh in, tried to stir up a bit of give-and-take—"This is not the first time she's been a bit of a diva"—it got lost in a fresh commotion. A fly had buzzed on the set, and Whoopi did her best to swat it.

I'd missed the whole Serena-Thiem contretemps. By the time I'd ambled over to the media center from Chatrier, Williams was already winding up her cursory meet with reporters. But *The View*, like much of the rest of the media, had, in its take on the matter, missed a couple of things. Williams had requested Interview Room 2, a smaller room—she just wanted to be done with her press duties. And when Roland-Garros media officials ushered Thiem out of the main press room, Williams said softly, but loud enough to be overheard by those hovering around her, "*Whoa*, that's rude."

Which represented a stubborn if quiet truth about Williams, a counterintuitive facet of her makeup. She *is* a celebrity, and a powerful woman who can make a fierce impression, and one who mostly gets her way and can get angry if she doesn't—the aspects of her identity that captivate *The View* and its audience. But she was, once and formatively, a young Black girl in an aspirational family. She, like her sister Venus—like countless Black children in America raised cautiously to rise by their parents—was inculcated from the earliest age that "bad manners" could put you at risk vis-à-vis white people. Unmannerliness could injure your reputation—and not only *your* reputation, but that of your family, even that of your people. This has been written about extensively, perhaps with no more felt sagacity than what the cultural critic Margot Jefferson brought to her award-winning memoir, *Negroland*. Jefferson, the daughter of a doctor, was born in Chicago, in the late 1940s, into the educated, upper-class "colored elite" of segregated America. But what was instilled in her was, by the time Serena was born, an understanding of how the world worked that was accepted not only by Black elites but by all kinds of ambitious, endeavoring African American households—an acceptance, if not an embrace, of a mode of being that would make whites *comfort-*

able with them, or begin to. "You were never to act undignified in their presence," Jefferson writes. The "motto," as she summarizes it, was "Achievement. Invulnerability. Comportment."

Williams, on a tennis court, would be permitted, by the conventions of sports, to act in ways deemed unacceptable outside an arena (though even there, in a match, it would not be *anything goes*). But in situations such as what transpired at the French Open media center, Williams would forever be sensitive to what might be perceived as discourteous, crass, disrespectful. The situation brought to mind something Claudia Rankine had written in an essay about Williams: "But of course, once recognized, black excellence is then supposed to perform with good manners and forgiveness in the face of any racist slights and attacks." Perhaps *any* slight or attack. Since their arrival in tennis, the Williams girls had been observed and remarked upon, by a tennis world as white as any realm, as courteous. They were taught by their parents, in Jefferson's words, to "excel through deeds and manners." Among those things Williams carried, being Serena? Being someone who needed to be vigilantly well-mannered, and was.

Part Six

Wimbledon

1

The lawn was a seventeenth-century English invention, cultivated first on the vast estates of the wealthiest landholders. It was to be understood as a sign that its owner could afford to tend to land not needed for crops. Mown grass declared that not only could nature be transmuted, as it had through the breeding and growing of crops, but agriculture, too. Here was a field from which to harvest nothing save tranquility: a soft, eye-pleasing carpet of green, opening beyond to vistas of hills and sunsets. Here was an expression of the unnecessary, of beauty, of *culture*. Here was a landscape of leisure.

That's certainly how the greensward was subsequently absorbed into English life. It would be strolled upon, picnicked upon, and bowled upon. In the mid-nineteenth century, there came the craze for croquet. Not long after, in 1873, a British major, Walter Clopton Wingfield, designed and patented a game he gave the name "sphairistiké" (from the Greek for "skill at playing at ball"), which drew on a number of other games, including court or "real" tennis (the history is endlessly disputed), and which was, with kits Wingfield mailed out in crates, designed to be played on those very sections of lawns that comfortable Victorians had devoted to croquet, either on their properties or at their recently founded clubs. Wingfield's game came to be called lawn tennis. One of those clubs that turned some of its croquet lawns into tennis courts was the All England Club,

159

established in 1868 on four acres of meadow, south of the Thames and central London's bustle, in the village of Wimbledon. By 1877, the male members of the club, swept up by Wingfield's game, had revised the rules a bit and announced All England's first tennis tournament. Here was *leisure* transmuted. At the subsequently instituted Championships, most club members would sit or stand watching as only a select few, the best, actually played the game on the grass.

The Championships remain the professional game's most revered tournament and prestigious Grand Slam, the All England grounds hallowed, the fortnight of match play appointment-viewing for tennis fans worldwide. Serena Williams was just sixteen in 1998 when she first played in the women's main draw at Wimbledon. The grass game—with its skidding balls, its low and often erratic bounces—was alien to her. She won her first two matches but withdrew from her third-round match during the first set, citing a calf injury. She did win the mixed doubles that year with her partner, the Belarusian Max Mirnyi. And she did make an impression. Her multicolored beads in her braids flew up as she followed through on her strokes; this was noted in press reports, as Bjorn Borg's long, whorling locks had been noted a generation before Serena had emerged. She was Black, at a club where Black men and women were not invited to play until the early 1950s—a powerful Black woman in the white Puma tennis dress she wore, all-white-only being the dress code the genteel All England Club had long ago prescribed, white deemed better at masking unsightly sweat stains.

Williams got comfortable with the grass surface soon enough. Entering the 2019 Championships, she'd won the ladies' singles title seven times. Only Martina Navratilova had won more times (nine) in the Open era. Grass is the fastest of surfaces, and big servers such as Williams tend to thrive on it. Which is why—despite the knee injury, which had hobbled her for months and so marred her play at the French Open just weeks earlier—commentators and oddsmakers placed Williams, seeded No. 11, high among the favorites to win Wimbledon. Her coach, Patrick Mouratoglou, said days before Williams's first-round match that she had received therapy in Paris after consulting with the French orthopedic surgeon Gilles Daubinet, a former medical director for the French Tennis Federation. The knee was no longer swelling, Mouratoglou told the *New York Times.* Williams herself seemed upbeat. "I've had a good week and a half," she said when she met the press before first-round play began. She said, for a laugh but not only a laugh, "I know how to play tennis."

Williams's first-round opponent was a little-known Italian player, Giulia Gatto-Monticone. She was not even what could be described as a journeyman, or journeywoman. She had never before played at Wimbledon in her nearly fifteen years as a pro. She had earned a spot in the draw by winning her qualifying matches. Her world ranking was No. 161, her highest ranking ever, when she walked on court to face Williams. She was thirty-one and had hung around on the lower ITF pro circuit all those years, playing more than eight hundred professional matches, winning ten small satellite tournaments and earning a total of about $300,000—less than a player earned for reaching one Wimbledon quarterfinal. Gatto-Monticone was not going to reach a Wimbledon quarterfinal. But she was a better tennis player than so many, many women who picked up a racquet, just not better, in the summer of 2019, than 160 of them. Among the things advanced tennis players face is the pitiless disposition of their talents: there were good players, and better ones. That Gatto-Monticone had withstood this, along with numerous injuries over the years, was a testament for sure to fortitude.

It was agreeably mild, as weather tends to be in London the first days of July, as the match got underway just past 5:00 p.m.—the last match of the day on Centre Court. Williams got to play all her matches on show courts, being a former champion with a big following everywhere she played and commanding a large TV draw, especially back in the United States, which had the TV market that mattered most. Gatto-Monticone didn't appear nervous. She was simply overmatched. Williams showed a couple of signs of lack of match play in the first set. She wasn't hitting her spots with her second serve, and her footwork was sluggish. Nevertheless, she won set one, 6–2, in under half an hour. When Williams held in the third game of set two without Gatto-Monticone so much as putting a ball in play, the writing was on the wall. Williams took the match, 6–2, 7–5.

A couple of Williams's first serves in the second set topped 125 mph, a speed she hadn't before approached all year. When I brought this up with her afterward, she said, "I can actually use my legs now. It's been a while." She went on to say, "I think also mentally, if you're serving without legs, you're paranoid of hurting your shoulder, so you take a little pace off. But, yeah, now that I can actually use my legs, it just all feels better." She often remarked that the one thing she *knew* she knew was her body. Athletes have to know their bodies. They count on them—find their *selves* in them, as most of the rest of us can't imagine. Williams had spent her days pushing her body, learning what it had, understanding what it didn't, since she was a child. She knew more than she wanted to know about that left knee of hers. Now she was relieved. It showed in the absence of tension in her face as she spoke. The knee wasn't keeping her from being, on court, whom she knew she could still be.

2

In 1996, just months after a fourteen-year-old Serena Williams had played her first professional match in Quebec, a Harvard psychology professor named Frank Sulloway published a book titled

Born to Rebel. Sulloway's thesis, at once provocative and familiar enough to plenty of parents, was that birth order shaped the personalities of children and, further, led to fundamental patterns of development in the psychological makeups and temperaments of siblings. Sulloway's inquiry drew on Darwin and the nascent field of evolutionary psychology, among myriad other sources, and his foundational insight was that brothers and sisters have varying personalities because, in their essential and persistent desire for the attention of their parents, they adopt different strategies, depending on whether they were born first, second, third. . . . What made the book a bestseller, and a controversial one, was Sulloway's finding that, in modern life and throughout history (he drew upon a lot of biography), the eldest child identifies with parental authority and tends to be conscientious, while the younger child is prone to rebel. The book was widely praised by reviewers, and then, in the years that followed, subjected to all manner of debunking by social scientists. Birth order had, nonetheless, found a place in the public imagination. Sulloway's conclusions about family dynamics became a way of seeing the differences between siblings. It's hard not to discover proof of his notion, anecdotal though it may be, when considering Venus and Serena Williams.

Venus *is* the conscientious one. It was memorably on public view the first time the sisters played each other at Wimbledon, in the 2000 ladies' semifinals—the fourth time the two had met on court (Venus had won two of the previous three), but the first time in a widely televised match. Their run to the Wimbledon semis was showing the world that they had arrived, were no fluke, and were on the verge of commanding women's tennis and remolding it. The match was highly anticipated. It was their global coming out. It would be a prototype of most Williams sisters square-offs that would follow through the years: hard fought, with flashes of arresting power tennis, but strained and uneven overall, and at key moments marked by anxious errors. Venus won the first set 6–2, and the second, for the match, 7–6 (3) when Serena double-faulted, as she had done too many times before that afternoon. Venus did no celebrating of her victory. When the two came together at the net beneath the umpire's chair, with eighteen-year-old Serena near tears, Venus draped her arm around her sister and could be heard to say, "Let's get out of here." Here was their relationship, encapsulated, broadcast. Later, Venus would talk to reporters about how emotionally hard it was for her after taking a match from her sister: "I felt sad because I'm the big sister and I'm supposed to take care of her."

Venus had been taking care of Serena since they were children in Compton. When Serena would crawl into bed with her at night, they would talk tennis, as they had done most of the day with their father. "You'd think we'd get enough talk of tennis during the day from Daddy," Serena recounted in *On the Line*, her autobiography, "but Venus used to take the time as we drifted off to pick me up and set me right. She could see when I'd had a tough day, when I need a lift." When they played practice points against each other in the park in Compton, Serena would "hook" her—call balls out that Venus had clearly hit in—and Venus would say nothing. When they walked to school together and approached a busy street, Serena would reflexively reach for Venus's hand. From the beginning of their professional careers, Serena has let it be known, to players and reporters, that Venus took care of her. They spoke on the phone daily. For years they lived together in Florida; now they each have their own Florida homes, but near enough for casual drop-bys. A year after that semifinal match at Wimbledon, Venus beat Serena solidly, 6–2, 6–4, in the US Open final, and the two said the sorts of things they'd continue to say and say again. "I love you. I feel so bad. I feel like I haven't won," Venus told Serena. Serena, a short time later, said of Venus, "She always goes extra, sometimes too much, worrying about Serena." (Serena also warned that she would soon enough defeat Venus and make a habit of it, which turned out to be true.)

Venus, as Serena would be the first to acknowledge, also cleared paths and showed the way for her younger sister. Venus first drew the uneasy attention as an African American junior phenom coming from where nobody played tennis. Venus first turned pro and faced the wariness, and at times hostility, from crowds and even some players. At the US Open in 1997, her first (she was seventeen), a Romanian player, Irina Spîrlea, appeared to deliberately collide into Venus during a changeover, whistling and looking away as her knee drove into Venus's leg. Venus never made much of it, but Richard Williams called the incident racist.

Venus, too, and not Serena, was first to speak publicly of race. After defeating Serena in that 2000 Wimbledon semifinal, Venus went on to beat the defending champion, American Lindsay Davenport, in the final in straight sets—becoming only the second Black woman to win the ladies' championship, and the first in the Open era. Althea Gibson had won in 1958, and Venus acknowledged her and her victory afterward. "It had to be hard," she said of Gibson's journey to the highest reaches of women's tennis, "because people were unable to see past color." But Venus—who had just turned twenty and had never before faced so many postmatch reporters from around the world—didn't stop there. "Still, these days, it's hardly any different because you realize it's been only forty years. How can you change years and centuries of being biased in forty years?"

Serena has spoken often and with force in recent years about the need for equal pay and workplace treatment for women, but here, too, Venus led the way. Of all Venus's victories at Wimbledon— she would eventually win the singles championship five times and, partnering with Serena, the doubles championship six times—it could be said that her most important victory came off court. In 2006, on the eve of the Championships, she published an essay in the *Times* of London, calling on the All England Club to establish equal prize money for men and women through all rounds of play. Club officials maintained that, because men played best-of-five-set matches and women best-of-three, the men deserved more money. Venus argued that women would be happy to play five-set matches; that the public views the men's and women's games equally; and that broadcasters, from whom a lot of the money was extracted, did, too. "I feel so strongly that Wimbledon's stance devalues the principle of meritocracy and diminishes the years of hard work that women on the tour have put into becoming professional tennis players," she wrote.

Among those who bought her argument was the British prime minister Tony Blair. He and members of Parliament called publicly for equal pay, and later that year the Women's Tennis Association and UNESCO teamed up on a campaign promoting gender equality in sports, which Venus led. Early in 2007, Wimbledon announced that it was instituting equal prize money for men and women across competitions. Venus, in her way—quietly forceful and charmingly persistent—assumed the mantle long held by Billie Jean King. It was clear, and not just to women, that her conscientiousness extended beyond her family role to her sport.

Finally, it has been Venus, fifteen months older than Serena, who's been the first to face the diminishment of her game and a sense of greatness ebbing. For years now, Venus has been playing tennis while struggling with the effects of Sjogren's syndrome. This long-term autoimmune disease can cause numbness in the limbs, muscle and joint pain, and chronic fatigue. There is no cure. Venus takes medications, has adopted a vegan diet, and is careful not to play too many tournaments because it takes her longer to recover from matches now. She never knows when a symptom of the syndrome will visit her. The mental strain of that alone must be trying, but she doesn't talk about it.

She entered the first round at the 2019 Wimbledon Championships as an unseeded thirty-nine-year-old drifting outside the top fifty. Perhaps for the last time, on a tennis court, anyway, she played the role of harbinger for her younger sister, and, in a sense, for the women's game. Inflection points in the history of a sport, as in the history of anything, are seen clearly only in retrospect. Still, you *feel* something is happening at certain moments, *in the* moment—a sense of import in the lead-up to the event and then of consequence in its outcome, beyond the score line. You think, *There was a* before, *and now there will unfold an* after *that represents a shift.*

If you were watching the Wimbledon Ladies' Singles Championship in 2000 and saw Venus Williams defeat Lindsay Davenport, you might well have sensed that the Williams sisters had arrived, after years of anticipation and scrutiny, and you would have been right. They would, between them, win *eleven more* Wimbledon singles titles, and the kind of tennis that they played—imposing serves, raw athleticism, attacking offense from anywhere on the court, fiery determination to intimidate and dominate—would reconfigure the women's game. If you were watching on the opening Monday of the 2019 Wimbledon Championships, as evening fell and a stiff breeze drove thickening clouds over Wimbledon's Court One, you saw Venus Williams losing her first-round match in straight sets to the fifteen-year-old American Cori "Coco" Gauff, 6–4, 6–4. It felt like an inflection point.

After the match ended, Venus said it was her plan to be back at Wimbledon next year, but she said it in the same choked and whispery voice she said everything that evening to the reporters she appeared to be pained to be having to meet with. This reticence was not new. It had more or less been the case since June of 2017, when news broke that a car crash in Florida that Venus was involved in, near her home, had resulted in the death, two weeks later, of an elderly man, Jerome Barson, who'd been in the other car. His family blamed Williams and soon after sued her. She was not issued a citation of any kind at the crash site, and an investigation later found she bore no responsibility for the crash. But news outlets had rushed to publish accounts of Venus's previous minor traffic citations and had welcomed the Barson family's attempt to make its case against a celebrated and wealthy athlete. Williams eventually reached a settlement with the Barson estate and would not discuss the matter. Meanwhile, she had stopped discussing much of anything at length with reporters.

In the years before all this, Venus had begun to emerge as the closest thing tennis had to a sports philosopher, thinking out loud at press conferences about the nature of sport and why it mattered as it did. After an Australian Open match, just months before that car crash, she'd had this to say, for example:

> What I will say about sport . . . I think why people love sport so much is because you see everything in a line. In that moment, there is no do-over, there's no retake, there is no voice-over. It's triumph and disaster witnessed in real time. This is why people live and die for sport, because you can't fake it. You can't. You either do it or you don't.

Would that Venus had been moved after her match with Gauff to muse on the nature of sport's in-built, ongoing turnings—the succession of moments, large and small, that mark time's passing, and, with it, at once rousing and tinged with melancholy, the waxing and waning of capability. But that was not to be.

• • •

Gauff would also meet the press, but she'd said all she'd had to say on the court in the moments just after Williams brought the match to an end by dumping yet another ground stroke into the net—her twenty-sixth unforced error of the evening. When Williams came forward to shake Gauff's hand, Gauff seemed unwilling to let it go. "Venus told me congratulations and keep going, she said good luck, and I told her thanks for everything she did," Gauff recounted to the BBC in her postmatch interview. "I wouldn't be here if it wasn't for her—I told her she was so inspiring and I've always wanted to tell her that, but I've never had the guts to before." Then Gauff sat in her chair and cried into a towel. Then she knelt and, bracing herself on her racquet, prayed. Then she left the court wiping tears from her eyes with her forearm, as an overcome child might.

Gauff had held her serve to close out the match, largely on the strength of two fearless second serves, both topping one hundred miles per hour. *Second* serves. From a *fifteen*-year-old. (She had come some way, or so it seemed, since I'd watched her three months earlier on an outer court in Miami.) Those serves, their speed and daring, were pure Williams. But some aspects of Gauff's game hinted not only at where women's tennis had been—the Williams era—but where it looked to be headed. She dashed in to catch a short ball at the very top of her racquet early in the first set and gently coax it aloft: a perfect lob winner just beyond Williams's reach. Gauff can hit her forehand flat or loopy with topspin; can mix in a drop shot; can swing all or nothing or patiently construct a point; can, increasingly, slice her backhand as well as come over the ball with two hands. Which is to say that Gauff, like Australia's Ash Barty, who entered Wimbledon ranked No. 1, and the Canadian phenom Bianca Andreescu, who had won Indian Wells, was not only a Williams-style baseliner. Women's tennis could be entering an era of amalgamation: that of the power all-courter.

That's speculation. As the 2019 tennis season began, women's tennis was entering the era of Naomi Osaka, but she, like Venus, crashed out of Wimbledon in the first round, this following a string of early exits. If nothing else, Osaka's struggles showed just how remarkable it was that the Williams sisters could prevail as they did for twenty years. And if Gauff keeps developing, as expected, and stays injury-free (always an issue in tennis), she's likely to be, among so many other things, a thriving reminder of just how great and consequential Venus and Serena had been.

Meanwhile, as the first days of Wimbledon came and went, one could catch a glimpse of Venus and Serena together, as they'd so often been over the years. I think Venus and Serena were headed to the gym one morning when I spied them in one of those hallways that snake among the areas designated for players: locker rooms, cafeterias, lounges, interview rooms. Serena was animated, saying something with a laugh, grabbing Venus's arm, and Venus was rolling her eyes. Frank Sulloway, the research psychologist with conclusions about siblings, wouldn't have had to hear what was being said to understand the personalities of—and dynamic between—the sisters.

3

Serena Williams followed her first-round Wimbledon victory over Giulia Gatto-Monticone with three more wins, securing a spot in the quarterfinals—her best run since the Australian Open six months earlier. She was moving well on court, in toward the net and back, side to side toward the corners. She was serving steadily and, at times, dazzlingly. She was winning efficiently: in only one of the three matches did she drop a set. "The rust is definitely wearing off," she said after winning in the fourth round, thrashing the Spanish veteran Carla Suárez Navarro, in just over an hour, 6–2, 6–2. "Most of all I feel confident that I can actually move and I don't have to, like, go for winners so soon because I'm in pain."

But going for winners, or at least going big, was Williams's game, and it was what was working for her—particularly, in those first four rounds, on her service returns. Returning a serve at the elite reaches of tennis may be the most difficult shot there is. A first serve coming at the returner is the hardest-hit ball she'll face in a match. A first serve and, if necessary, a second are shots the player hitting them has complete control of—the only such moment in a tennis match. She, the server, has any number of options. She can hit it flat or with slice spin or brush hard up the back of the ball for a kick serve that bounds shoulder high and strangely sideways. She can aim the ball out wide; or up the T; or into her opponent's body, crowding her and preventing her from extending her arms. These days, she's likely to have a first serve of at least 105 mph. Which means the returner has just over half a second to determine what type of serve it is, spin-wise, and where it is headed before moving (if necessary), adjusting her grip (if necessary), and beginning a swing she hopes will not only keep the ball in play but at least neutralize the point—not land too short or softly, which would put the server in control of the point—or perhaps gain *her* control of the point, if the return is clean and hard or gets the server on the run. In the men's game, Novak Djokovic came to dominate in the 2010s, and a key reason was the strength of his return game. On the women's side, no one can intimidate and bully a server like Serena Williams, even late in her career, when she is on her game.

From the point-by-point notes I made courtside, during the first week of Wimbledon, as I'd been making of all Williams's matches during the season:

- Round 2, versus Kaja Juvan, an eighteen-year-old Slovenian qualifier whom Williams had never before faced, Round Two, Set 2, Game 7: *SW earns 2nd break with a hard BH return right to KJ's feet. KJ does her best to scoop it with a BH but it sails long. 5–2 SW.*
- Round 3, versus the German Julia Görges, Wimbledon semifinalist a year earlier, eighteenth seed, who'd never won a set from Williams in four previous matches, Set 1, Game 6: *SW earns two bk. pt. opps. w punishing BH return. JG barely gets racquet on. 15–40. SW breaks—crushes 2nd serve. JG can't handle w FH. 4–2 SW.*
- Round 4, versus Suárez Navarro, Set 2, Game 1: *SW earns quick bk pt opp w FH winner on 1st deuce game. 2nd serve 81 mph SW CRUSHES w BH. BREAKS.*

These moments fail to take into account the presence of Williams, how she positions herself right on the baseline to take a first serve—taking the ball early, on the rise, to rob her opponent of time—and inside the baseline to pounce on a slower second serve. There is no mention made that she hits her backhand returns, like her forehands, with a shorter backswing when receiving first serves, and that on all serves she is bent low, with a forward-facing fully open stance, feet wide apart for better balance, which allows her to wait just a moment longer and smack the ball off her hip if necessary, and to nearly undetectably drive her backhand inside out, surprising opponents who expect backhands to be hit crosscourt. Nor does this small sampling reveal how Williams's returning prowess often forces a server to go for more on her serve, strike her first serve or even a second just a little harder or with a mind to placing it right on the line, "redlining," as it's called. This, in turn, can lead to faults and double faults, and, even when not, to pressure.

Causing stress, incessant stress: this has been an aspect of Williams's game, over the years, as important as any. It can't be tabulated like rally length or service placement, but it's clear enough to those who have watched Williams that she can undo an opponent by mentally and emotionally straining her. Complete a follow-through on a serve, take the hop back to the baseline as you've been schooled to, and watch helplessly as Williams's return is already angling, in a flash, too far from reach, nicking the line, a clean winner, and the crowd is roaring its marvel and approval, and Williams is tucked in a crouch, roaring, too—"*Come ON!*"— and now there is nothing to do but serve to her once again.

4

The day after Williams defeated Suárez Navarro to book her spot in the Wimbledon quarterfinals, *Harper's Bazaar* published online an essay by Williams from its upcoming August issue. CNN and other outlets thought it news that the essay quoted a brief note Williams had sent to Naomi Osaka the previous fall, apologizing for what had transpired during their US Open final. In the print edition of the issue, Williams's essay was announced by a cover photograph of her in a gold Stella McCartney gown. Inside were more photographs of Williams in gold, one showing her exposed buttock beneath a Ralph Lauren cape. All the photographs were promoted on the issue's cover as being "unretouched." To the uninitiated, *this* might appear to be an apology—an apology for years of the magazine's publishing retouched photographs that have manipulated its readers, fostering unreal expectations of attractiveness with images of women thinned and smoothed and otherwise impossibly beautified. That would be a naive reading. As Roland Barthes wrote years ago in his brilliant defense of theatrical pro wrestling, those drawn to it could care less whether it's "rigged or not"; they abandon themselves to the "spectacle." And so it mostly was with fashion magazines. The young readers, or anyway lots of them, that *Harper's Bazaar* wanted to continue attracting were already using Facetune or some other app or photo filter to retouch or "enhance" the photos of themselves they posted on Snapchat or Instagram.

Williams's essay, like *Harper's Bazaar*'s decision to "explore the concept of 'real beauty'" with its unretouched photographs of Serena, was a case study in how celebrity "authenticity" is packaged and publicized now, akin to the sharenting social-media portraits and videos, and, for the biggest celebrities, carefully superintended cable-TV documentaries that had more in common with advertorials than cinéma vérité documentaries. The message was, I control the messaging. A number of younger reporters on the women's tennis tour have a term for this, with regard to Williams. They call it her Beyoncification. When Williams had something she wanted to say, she mostly said it not to the journalists she met with after each of her matches, but via media in which her point of view would neither be questioned nor mediated. She had stopped talking about the US Open final controversy with reporters, but, in *Harper's Bazaar*, she had her own way of having a last word.

The writing took the form of an apology, responsible and confessional. Williams clearly felt uneasy in the aftermath of the US Open final that Osaka won—a narrative she, Williams, was never in control of, then, later, something un-undoable. She felt uneasy about her public image, at the least. Why publish such an essay otherwise? But the essay was not, in any way, an apology for her actions or behavior on court during the match. There was no personal remorse. She once again expressed her belief that the chair umpire had singled her out as a woman for the coaching violation, the racquet-smashing violation, and the third code violation for insulting him and his integrity. No editor at *Harper's Bazaar* apparently thought it her responsibility to her readers that they understand that Williams's coach had continued to acknowledge he was, in fact, coaching; or that racquet smashing was an automatic code violation; or that repeatedly insulting a chair umpire and questioning his integrity have often led to a code violation. What kept Williams awake at night, she wrote, in the days following the match, and what led her eventually to speak with a therapist, she said, was not anything she might have done. It was the forfeiting of a game to Osaka in the second set—a forfeit that was not the decision of the chair umpire but was mandated by the rules, after she, Williams, picked up her third code violation of the match.

Williams nevertheless continued to blame the chair umpire for the forfeiting of the game and remained frustrated and hurt by what he had done to her—done to her for feeling "passionately compelled to stand up for myself." She was frustrated and hurt on Osaka's behalf, too, because "the debacle ruined something that should have been amazing and historic." To Osaka, she wrote, "I am truly sorry"—sorry for what the chair umpire had done; and sorry, as well, for the behavior of the media, which "I had no idea would pit us against each other." Blaming the media was a hallmark of the celebrity nonapology apology, as it had come to be called, mostly by the public-relations people who fashion them or help to.

Osaka responded to Williams's note, writing, according to Williams, "People can misunderstand anger for strength." It is not clear that this rather cryptic formulation represents Osaka's accepting Williams's interpretation of what went down during their US Open final or conveys empathy for Williams's feelings. Osaka is quoted as adding, "No one has stood up for themselves the way you have and you need to continue trailblazing," and reading this, Williams was, she said, moved to tears.

5

The unwritten brand promise of professional tennis is that, for its largest events, it alone among sports of its reach brings together men and women at the same venue, at the same time, to play the same game. Was it doing enough, as a business, to reinforce this value proposition? Were tournament officials putting enough women's matches on the big show courts? Were the broadcasters who carried tennis matches showing enough women's tennis? Were the C-suite tournament and TV executives seeing courtside the clusters of men sitting together watching women play; or the groups of women watching a men's match; or the thousands of men and women commingled, as you will seldom glimpse in such numbers at any other global sporting event, happily watching men or women, so long as the tennis was outstanding and competitive?

Fourteen thousand or so men and women were filling nearly every seat on Centre Court at Wimbledon early one soft summer evening, and they stood and roared, whistled and popped champagne bottles—yes, at Wimbledon, you can bring bottles, or your beer or Pimm's in a proper glass, to your seat—when the players walked on court to begin a mixed-doubles match. One of the pairs was Andy Murray and Serena Williams, which explains why almost no one had left her or his seat when the previous match, between Roger Federer and Lucas Pouille, concluded. Which explains, too, why the match was on Centre Court and not one of the small, bleacher-lined outer courts where mixed doubles is normally found at Grand Slam tournaments, the only tournaments on the tour where mixed doubles gets played. (Mixed doubles is also played at the Olympics.) Mixed doubles, with its close-range clashes among and between men and women, may heighten and reinforce what makes tennis unique, but for the most part it's treated as an afterthought. Even with Williams and Murray partnering, ESPN signed off after Federer's victory over Pouille, choosing to offer the mixed-doubles match only on its streaming service, ESPN+.

Too bad. It was that day's most entertaining tennis, brightening the gloaming with quick-twitch scrambling and keen, strategic shot-making. The Murray-Williams team won easily enough in the end, 6–4, 6–1, largely on the strength of their serving, beating the doubles specialists Andreas Mies, of Germany, and Alexa Guarachi, an American-born Chilean, neither of whom were used to the big-stage attention or the firepower. (Williams had at least one serve of 122 mph, a speed that neither of her opponents could match.) It was great to see Murray back on court, blistering that coiled two-handed backhand of his, and moving, at least in the half court that was his responsibility to defend, as if he had not undergone hip-resurfacing surgery in January. He had ended the year 2016 as the No. 1 men's singles player in the world, but his cumulatively damaged right hip would force him from the game within months, and it remained unclear, postsurgery, whether he'd ever again reach the top of the singles game. His satisfaction, though, at playing and winning with Williams was unmistakable. His body language, so often hunch shouldered and downcast during his years playing singles, was that of a man with gratitude to convey.

Williams looked sanguine, too, and sharp. (She used to partner with her sister Venus for doubles at majors, and they'd won more than a dozen titles. But now the two, in their late thirties, were careful to preserve their energies for singles.) When Williams was at the net, with Murray serving or returning, her volleys were crisp and well placed, her bang-bang reflex volleys surprisingly nimble: she still had fine hands. However, her ability to approach the net from the baseline and, on the move, get low for volleys was never a strength and remained a challenge. In the middle of one point, she slipped while coming in to pick up a short ball and tumbled toward the net and onto the grass. She made a move to get up, then appeared to duck and roll, laughing as shots whizzed above her.

"I just remember I slipped—then I was going to get back up," she said afterward, seated next to Murray in the interview room. "I saw a ball coming towards me, so I just kind of went back down. Then I couldn't get back up after that."

"Did you see the video?" Murray interjected, deadpan.

"Yeah. It was hilarious." Then, to the reporters: "I decided to just stay down and let Andy do all the running."

Murray and Williams liked and respected each other. Williams had long had a rapport with male players—practicing with them, joking among them—that didn't appear to be the case for most women players. Also, she, along with others on the women's tour, appreciated Murray's outspoken support for the women's game and women's issues. He was coached growing up by his mother, Judy, and his abiding sense that women deserve equal treatment in all aspects of the game was unmatched by any other current male player of his stature. Williams also related to the anger that could combust during his singles matches, though Murray's rage tended to be self-directed. Murray, in turn, admired Williams's competitive drive: unflagging, like his own. They were playing together not on a lark but to win it. (They wouldn't win it, losing their third-round match, in three sets, to the top-seeded mixed-doubles pair,

Bruno Soares of Brazil and the American Nicole Melichar, both longtime doubles specialists.)

Would that tennis configured itself to make mixed doubles more inviting to its stars. Imagine Serena Williams playing mixed doubles among men and women at all the Grand Slams. Or imagine an event that combined the men's Davis Cup national-team event and the women's Fed Cup national-team event in a mixed World Cup of Tennis, with not only mixed doubles but mixed teams of men and women. Instead, the Association of Tennis Professionals, which oversees men's tennis, was set to launch the ATP Cup, a ten-day men's national-team competition, to be held in Australia, that essentially duplicated what the newly redesigned Davis Cup final was going to provide six weeks before, in Madrid. One of the cities hosting the ATP Cup matches was Perth, where the event would displace—and doom—the Hopman Cup, an exhibition tournament that for thirty-one years had brought together eight national mixed teams to play men's singles, women's singles, and mixed doubles. It was there, at the Hopman in January, where Roger Federer and Serena Williams had met across the net from each other in mixed doubles. It was memorable. It, or anything much like it, was unlikely to happen again.

6

"Serena is very good at giving you what she gets," Courtney Nguyen was saying. Nguyen wasn't talking about Williams's game, but about the way she relates to players in the locker room. "When Serena gets that deference and positivity, she's going to open up," Nguyen went on. "From the younger players, she's getting that now."

Locker rooms at tennis tournaments are not like locker rooms in stadiums for team sports. In tennis, you dress and get yourself into game mode within a few feet, perhaps, of the player you're about to battle; then you wind down, undress, and shower in proximity to the player you just defeated or lost to. It's intimate. Even at Wimbledon, where the top sixteen women have their own, more luxurious changing area, the players commingle, upstairs, downstairs. The press has no access to the locker area. It's off-limits. There is no postmatch crush around Serena's locker, the way you see reporters, their smartphones out and arms extended, recording the after-game thoughts of LeBron James or Steph Curry. I was trying to get a sense of Williams's relations with other women players by talking with someone who knows the players on the tour well enough to know. Nguyen was one of them.

Nguyen was working on the tour as a journalist of sorts in the employ of the WTA. She blogged and tweeted for the WTA and, at press conferences, asked questions of players along with the other reporters. After months on the tour, I saw clearly that the women players were comfortable with her, and that she knew them as well as anyone else writing about them. Sports leagues in the digital age were all-in on providing their own media to reach fans and influence perceptions, at a time when traditional media outlets such as newspapers and magazines were continuing to trim their staffs. Not that many publications or news outlets had had tennis reporters to begin with.

Nguyen had been a lawyer in her late twenties in San Francisco ten years ago when she'd decided she'd grown more interested in the tennis she was streaming on her laptop than the briefs she was supposed to be finishing for one or another tech client. She thought she might go back to school to get an MFA in writing. "That's what an Asian American does when you have a career crisis," she said. "Get another degree." But she'd already begun her own tennis blog, as a fan, and her father suggested the money she'd spend returning to school might be better spent just traveling with the tour and blogging, if writing about tennis was what she wanted to do. "So I flew to Australia in 2011, and by the time Wimbledon was over I had this offer from *Sports Illustrated.*" She was blogging about tennis for *Sports Illustrated* when the WTA offered her a better deal in 2015. *Sports Illustrated* had since been sold by Time, Inc., and was, in the summer of 2019, on the verge of being resold and gutted of longtime staff.

Nguyen and I were sitting on a second-story wooden deck of the Wimbledon media center, the grass courts arrayed below us sun-honeyed and still lightly dewed, the grounds quiet in the morning hour before the gates opened for spectators and play began. She spoke to me, as she would again later, at the US Open, of how Williams's relations with her fellow players had evolved over the years. Nguyen hadn't been around in the late 1990s when the Williams sisters arrived on the tour, but her sense of how it had been aligned with what others had told me, and what the Williams sisters themselves have said. They stuck together in the locker room and kept their distance—a distance the other players also did their part to maintain. Some players, particularly from the former Eastern Bloc, had never encountered a Black woman and, in some cases, were prejudiced and phobic. As well, some top players looked at Venus and especially Serena with foreboding.

"When Serena was younger, she was like this threat in the locker room," Nguyen told me. "For the Capriatis, the Justines, she was someone who might thwart their dreams, stop them from doing something great. So it was, both ways, 'us against them.'"

The first real friendship Williams forged on the tour was with Caroline Wozniacki, nearly a decade younger than Williams is. She's a Danish player of Polish descent who has lived for years near Manhattan's Union Square. (Such is pro tennis.) Wozniacki had reached No. 1 early in her career, which meant she had Williams's respect. The friendship between them deepened in the spring of 2014, when Wozniacki's then fiancé, the golfer Rory McIlroy, abruptly broke off their engagement in a brief phone call. Williams consoled her in text messages and on the phone, Wozniacki has said, and the two spent time together at Williams's place in Florida. When, just weeks before I sat talking with Nguyen at Wimbledon, Wozniacki married the former NBA player David Lee in a Tuscan vineyard, Williams was a bridesmaid and her daughter, Olympia, the flower girl.

"Woz was the first," Nguyen said, "and still the best friend, after Venus. But, you know, in recent years, Venus has not been around as often deep in tournaments, and Serena, more generally—she's a different Serena than she was as a teenager. That's just maturation, like it is for all of us. And tennis—it's a lonely place. . . . It's also transparency today, with social media, for all the players. You say something to a player in the locker room, and if that player has a problem with it, she tweets it—know what I mean?"

The younger players, especially, have found Williams more approachable and warm, ready with advice and even a locker-room hug after a tough loss. "She gets that deference from the younger generation, and positivity, she opens up—it's natural," Nguyen told me. "They see her more as a celebrity. These kids—Osaka, Andreescu, others—they have never known the sport *without* Serena. I mean, Naomi—she grew up on a steady diet of *only* Serena. You ask them, the younger ones, who they most want to play: Serena. She *is* Serena. She's *Serena*. And she's not going to thwart their dreams. She will at some point be gone. So, no threat. Reverence."

7

The 128-player women's singles draw at Wimbledon, as at the other Grand Slam tournaments, is organized both carefully and randomly. First, thirty-two seeded players are chosen; these are, usually, the thirty-two top-ranked players in the weeks before a major begins, though Wimbledon maintains and sometimes expresses its right to juggle the order of those thirty-two, elevating (or lowering) a player a few positions based on her success over the years when playing on grass. Next, the other ninety-six players in the draw—ranked players on the WTA tour, qualifiers, wild-card entries—are, by computer software, randomly assigned their placement in the draw. The draw has a top and a bottom half (the winners of each meet in the final), and each of these halves is further divided in half to create quarters (with the winners of each of these reaching the semifinals). Once the nonseeded players are distributed, the software distributes the seeds, with each of the top four seeds placed in one of the four quarters. The remaining seeds are similarly distributed. The quarter is where a player must win her fifth match to advance, beyond her quarter, to the semifinals. The quarter is where, at a Grand Slam, she goes to die or live on to the semis and, just maybe, the final.

When the 2019 Wimbledon draw was announced, Williams's quarter was immediately dubbed the Group of Death. Chris Clarey of the *New York Times* tweeted, "One of the craziest, nastiest Grand Slam quarters in the Open Era." Along with Williams, among the thirty-two players in her quarter, were four other players who had once been ranked No. 1; six others who had won a Grand Slam tournament; and three others who were former Wimbledon champions. If there were no upsets along the way—if the higher-ranked seeds survived into the second week at the All England Club—Williams was to have a fourth-round match against fifth-seeded Angelique Kerber of Germany, who'd defeated her in the Wimbledon final the previous year. And if Williams survived that meeting and advanced to the quarterfinals, waiting for her was projected to be Australia's Ash Barty, who'd won the French Open early in June, and then, weeks later, took the title at the Birmingham Classic, a perennial Wimbledon tune-up held in England's West Midlands—a victory that elevated Barty to world No. 1. What were the chances of Williams beating both these women and making it out of her quarter?

The English philosopher Simon Critchley, writing of sport (he's an avid Liverpool football fan), suggests that part of its appeal, its tug on players and fans alike, is its invitation to subsume oneself in the "twisting elaborations of fate." Williams's fans bemoaned her fate in the draw, and maybe Williams did, too, but she wasn't about to say anything about it. But then fate twisted: Kerber was upset in the second round. Barty was upset in the Round of 16 by the unseeded American Alison Riske. Riske, at twenty-nine, was having her best season as a professional; she'd arrived at Wimbledon having just won her first tournament in more than four years, on grass in the Netherlands. Riske was now what stood between Williams and a semifinal match on Centre Court.

The Williams-Riske quarterfinal match was lengthy and close, with Williams going for broke on nearly every shot (and making lots of errors), and Riske trying (with mixed success) to force Williams off the middle of the baseline, where she could dictate points, and get her uncomfortably on the move. Williams rolled an ankle and needed attention, but also struck nineteen aces. Riske had stretches of clean tennis, particularly in the second set, yet even then the outcome of the match somehow never seemed in doubt. It took two hours and felt longer for Williams to prevail 6–4, 4–6, 6–3. One key to the outcome was that Riske double-faulted six times, five of those in the deciding set. The last of those occurred on a risky 97 mph second serve up the T that landed long, put Williams up 5–3, and provided her the opportunity to serve out the match, which she did, blasting, on match point, her own 121 mph serve up the T, an ace.

When I spoke a bit with Riske after the match, she brought up those double faults of hers, and how Williams had caused them. "It's no secret that Serena has an amazing serve," Riske began, "but Serena has an equally as amazing return. I've never played anyone that has a return like Serena." (This was the first time they'd ever played each other.) "That puts a lot of pressure on my serve." She paused. "I was then more cognizant of when I was missing my first serve. 'Wow, here I go, serving another second serve, she's probably going to throw this down my throat!'" Riske laughed. "It does put a lot of pressure on you just because she starts points unlike anyone else on tour. I was definitely feeling the pressure."

So would Williams's next opponent, two days later. Barbora Strýcová was a five-feet-five-inch, thirty-three-year-old Czech who had for years been a top doubles player. In most of the Wimbledon singles draws she'd entered, she had not made it past the second round. But her quarter, like Williams's, had opened up, as they say in tennis, with many of the top-seeded players falling early. Strýcová herself had knocked off fourth-seeded Kiki Bertens of the Netherlands in the third round.

Strýcová more or less played singles the way she played doubles: changing up pace, looking for sharp angles, scrambling on defense, and, in particular, following her serve with an approach to the net. Her serving-and-volleying undid her in her semifinal against Williams. Strýcová served-and-volleyed forty times in the match and won the point four times. Williams's power was simply too much. She lasered a crosscourt shot past Strýcová to earn her first break and kept it up for the rest of the match, which would be hers in less than an hour: 6–1, 6–2. Serena Williams was into her first Grand Slam final of the year.

Williams kept mentioning, in her press conference after the match, how calm she was, how important it was for her to remain calm in the final, how, as she put it, "not getting overpumped, but at the same time not getting underwound" would be key to her winning a coveted twenty-fourth major title, and her first as a mother. "I was actually thinking this morning, when I won my first Wimbledon—I think it was against Venus," she said at one point. (It was against Venus: 2002, in straight sets.) "I was really calm."

It was as if Williams was channeling and attempting to deflect what many of the reporters in the room had on their minds—had had on their minds since her return to tennis after giving birth. *She wants one more Slam trophy too much. She comes into finals anxious and tight. She defeats herself.*

8

The Friday before the last weekend at Wimbledon is traditionally when the two men's semifinal matches are played. I woke up in my hotel in Chelsea to a near-cloudless midsummer morning and decided to spend a day away from the All England Club. Sportswriters on the tour speak of "match fatigue," brought on by all the sitting and watching and waiting; I was suffering a slight case. After breakfast, I wandered instead up to Kensington Gardens, strolled through a new wildflower meadow thick with red poppies and palepink ragged robin, and kept walking east without any fixed intent along a path that led me, eventually, to the entrance of the Serpentine Gallery, housed in a former tea pavilion and dedicated to exhibitions of contemporary art. The current exhibition was a retrospective of the work of the African American artist Faith Ringgold.

I had a hazy sense of who Ringgold was. I'd written about art when I first got to New York in the mid-1970s. Ringgold and her work were then on the periphery of the New York contemporary-art world, which was centered in Lower Manhattan; dominated mostly by conceptual art and the latest work of younger artists grappling with conceptualism's implications; and very, very white (like tennis). What I could recall of Ringgold's work were figurative paintings of Black men and women with overt political messages about race. She was also, I remembered more clearly, involved with a number of feminist art groups, protesting the lack of works by women in museum shows and collections, and exhibiting their work in women's cooperative galleries. Feminism in those years was basically white, too, with a deep-felt debate among Black women writers and activists about feminism: Did it redirect energies from the battle for racial equality? Was it a movement to empower more white people? Ringgold was a Black feminist figurative artist, an outlier in so many ways.

That Ringgold, approaching ninety, was now having the first retrospective of her work, and at a prominent, cutting-edge London art center, spoke to a broader cultural moment taking hold internationally, an understanding that too many artists of color—along with too many writers and filmmakers and performers of color—had been overlooked. Ringgold's time had come. Much of the Serpentine show was given over to quilts Ringgold had begun making in the 1980s. Quilting, socially and aesthetically, has long been an important practice among African American women, especially in the South. Through quilting, Ringgold has said, she found a way to escape the European male tradition of paint on canvas, and to sew and weave (and paint on what she'd sewn and woven) autobiographical stories—stories of her Harlem childhood, of her struggles as a woman, of the concerns and predicaments of being a Black woman in America. The story quilts, as Ringgold called them, were her most compelling works. Some she'd reimagined and remade as children's books. She'd found, in midlife, her medium and message.

Something bigger was to be sensed, though, in roaming the galleries and looking at years of Ringgold's work. Art's teleology, since the nineteenth century and the advent of modernism, had been the search for aesthetic and intellectual originality, through formal exploration and experimentation—a search to find art's essence, through transgressing and transforming what art had been and was meant to be. The Ringgold show spoke of a different sense of art's purpose and place and unfolding. Here were works devoted to the portraits and stories of those who hadn't much made it into the art that got shown in leading cultural institutions. The aim was to fill the gallery walls with images of the long marginalized and overlooked. For some, the work would be an encounter with difference, with lives lived elsewhere; for others, it would be a seldom-available-before museum encounter with those who "look like me."

For me, there was no way to wander through Ringgold's show and not think about Serena Williams. There was one story quilt especially, which Ringgold had made in 1986 when she was fifty-six and titled *Change: Faith Ringgold's Over 100 Pounds Weight Loss Performance Story Quilt*. It's about a middle-aged Black woman struggling with norms of beauty (which art had helped to create and reinforce) and a desire to feel good about herself—and, because Ringgold was keen and conscious, about a woman struggling with *why* she finds herself struggling with those things. Wander the Louvre or any other place art gets hung and you won't encounter anything like what this quilt portrays.

Nor have the likenesses to be found in Ringgold's work been traditionally the stuff of fashion-magazine covers, where today's idealized portraits of women tend to be found. Which is one more way of seeing, and thinking about, Serena Williams. The cultural critic bell hooks had argued years ago that the Black liberation movement was as much a struggle over images as anything else. All those cover shoots Williams loves to do and that help to promote her personal brand are something more than her attending to the attention she seeks. They do resonate with women who have seen nothing but tall, thin white women when they glance at the magazine rack.

But resonate *how*? Does Serena literally look like them? Represent for them a kinship of social identity? Or does she represent a yearning—for success, wealth, power? "How identity relates to identification is, of course, a complicated matter," as Kwame Anthony Appiah, a professor of philosophy at New York University who has written much about this, carefully and searchingly, has put it. Images such as that of Williams on a magazine cover conflate representation and aspiration. For everyone, identity is a deeper, more manifold thing than skin pigment and body type. You, viewing Serena on a magazine cover, are not Serena—*whoever* you are. Still, why not have Williams's image to look at to start a conversation about representation and identity? Why not be encouraged and reassured by seeing Serena, if only to more confidently begin the tangled and unceasing venture of figuring out what you look like to whom, and who, in the end, you are?

9

Pete Sampras, slowing and struggling and contemplating retirement, at age thirty-one, in the summer of 2002, brought back his old coach Paul Annacone before the start of the US Open. Stunning much of the tennis world, Sampras, seeded seventeenth, won it, defeating Andre Agassi in the final, and retiring shortly thereafter. Annacone, who'd later coach Roger Federer, among others, has a theory about how a tennis great ages: "I always felt that and still feel that you can't take away greatness. In other words, you're not, all of a sudden, not great anymore. But what happens, I've seen, is that you can't sustain it for long periods of time."

Not all aspects of a great player's game diminish at the same pace, nor do the ineffables of greatness—the self-belief and hunger to win and the ability, under pressure, to find yet a next gear—wane steadily and irrevocably like fast-twitch muscle fibers. Greatness, Annacone suggests, comes, with time, to flicker. It can flare in late career but will never again glow every week, and don't count on finding some switch for it in the moment that nothing short of greatness is what's required to win.

Serena Williams faced Romania's Simona Halep in the Wimbledon ladies' final, on an overcast Saturday afternoon before a crowd roaring for her as she came on court and, if they'd read the oddsmakers (the English do), fairly assured she would win. In the ten matches Williams and Halep had played previously against each other, Williams had won nine of them, most recently at the Australian Open. Williams was an all-time-great grass-court player. Before reaching this final, Halep had never gotten further at the Championships than a quarterfinal. Having begun the year as world No. 1, she'd seen her ranking drop to No. 8 after losing in the quarterfinals at the French Open, which she'd won the year before. To reach the Wimbledon final, she'd defeated only one seeded player. It might have been Naomi Osaka standing across the net from Williams (Osaka lost in the first round), or Karolína Plíšková (she lost in the Round of 16), but it was Halep. Here, on paper, anyway, was the opportunity Williams had been waiting for since her return to tennis after giving birth to her daughter—the chance to win her a record-tying twenty-fourth Grand Slam title and her first as a mother.

Major finals are not played on paper. Approaching her thirty-

eighth birthday, Williams never summoned a flicker of greatness in a lopsided, 6–2, 6–2, loss to Halep. The pace of Williams's
first serve was not what it had been in previous matches (not one
reached 120 mph), and she had only two aces. Her returns, particularly on the backhand side, were not punishing, and neither,
for the most part, were her ground strokes. Williams often starts
slowly, but *slowly* doesn't do justice to how she started out this
match. Williams was down 0–4 in the first *eleven minutes*. That
this wasn't going to be Serena's day was all but certain by then.

Maybe it was just nerves. Wanting one more major championship as badly as she does has weighed on her. Maybe she just
didn't have enough match play in a season that had seen her hobbled by a knee. Or maybe working her way rather easily to the final
through a draw in which so many of the best players got knocked
out by the quarterfinals lent a false impression of how ready she
would be to face Halep. Halep *was* a top player, a champion. She
had been dominating opponents through the Wimbledon fortnight, moving on the slippery grass as if it were clay, and stepping
firmly into her ground strokes to generate more pace.

On this Saturday, Halep brought greatness with her to the
final, and it never wavered—she herself called it the best match
she had ever played. Her serve had unusual pop, particularly up
the T. (Williams, who had been scorching returns in her previous matches, earned just one break-point opportunity and didn't
convert.) Halep consistently redirected Williams's ground strokes,
something you don't often see—and Williams, more than once,
stood surprised and flat-footed as resulting winners landed yards
from her or hissed past her. Halep's defense sent ball after ball
back, forcing Williams to rally, and when the rallies extended,
Halep mostly won them. Halep broke Williams's serve four times.
She silenced Williams—there were few screams, only one or two
self-encouraging shouts of *"Come on!"* It was over in fifty-six min-

utes. It was the worst drubbing in a Grand Slam final of Williams's long career.

Halep, afterward, was as easeful and joyful as I have ever seen her. She laughed. She smiled broadly and often. She could not stop using the word "happy," which is not a self-descriptive word she has reached for much over the years. When asked by a reporter, "At what point in your career playing Wimbledon did you feel winning Wimbledon could be a possibility for you?" she deadpanned, "Today," and laughed some more.

Williams, understandably, was downcast. She'd reached three Grand Slam finals since returning to the tour after giving birth to Olympia. She hadn't won a set in any of them. She talked with reporters not long after the match ended. She couldn't explain or wasn't in the frame of mind to try to explain the shortcomings of her performance—why her greatness, as Annacone would have it, did not show itself. She did manage, nevertheless, to summarize things: "I don't know. *She* just played great."

Part Seven

New York

1

In 1957, the year she won women's singles championships at both Wimbledon and the US Nationals, the forerunner of the US Open, Althea Gibson told a reporter, "I don't consider myself to be a representative of my people. I'm thinking of me and nobody else." (Serena Williams would say something similar, though fundamentally not the same, to an interviewer in 2015: "I play for me, but I also play and represent something much greater than me. I embrace that. I love that." But "ultimately," she ended by saying, "when I am out there on the court, I am playing for me.") Gibson's victories back then at the All England Club and at the West Side Tennis Club in Forest Hills, Queens, places where she had broken the color barrier in the years before triumphing in those 1957 finals, nonetheless meant a great deal to many African Americans. They urged and helped secure for Gibson a ticker-tape parade up Broadway in Manhattan after her Wimbledon victory, a match they never saw: television wouldn't begin broadcasting tennis tournaments until the 1960s. She was celebrated in the Black magazines *Ebony* and *Jet* and appeared on the covers of *Sports Illustrated* and *Time*. Still, Gibson was determined not to be remembered as the Jackie Robinson of tennis. For many years, sadly enough, she got her wish.

Tennis lacks the mnemonic organizing principles and rituals

that, in other sports, have a way of keeping historical memory alive—place-based teams with old-timers' days; stadiums or arenas with their trophy cases and championship banners, visited and revisited across months and seasons each year by fans and their descendants. After retiring, Gibson worked as the director of recreation in East Orange, New Jersey, where she lived alone. She had played her tennis before the Open era, when there was no women's professional tennis, and earned little from the game. By the time she died, in 2003, at the age of seventy-six, she had long drifted away from tennis, and tennis from her, though Richard Williams had made sure his daughters knew of her and her example. When Wheaties put Serena's image on the front of its orange box for the first time early in the summer of 2019, Serena posted a photo on Instagram of a 2001 commemorative box with a time-softened old photo of Althea Gibson, hoisting a trophy. "Althea Gibson was the FIRST Black Woman tennis player to be on the box," Williams wrote. "Today, I am honored to be the second."

On the Monday morning that play began at the 2019 US Open, on the grounds of the Billie Jean King National Tennis Center in Flushing, Queens, a cool morning that hinted of fall's imminence, a colossal eighteen-ton mounted granite bust of Althea Gibson was unveiled outside Arthur Ashe Stadium. Billie Jean King, who had lobbied the United State Tennis Association, which ran the US Open, to recognize Gibson in a formal way, was on hand, as was the sculptor of the work, Eric Goulder, and, in a wheelchair, Gibson's former doubles partner, an Englishwoman named Angela Buxton—herself, as she has related, an often shunned outsider to women's tennis in the 1950s, being Jewish. They, along with hundreds of others in attendance, heard speakers talk of Gibson's remarkable career, in which she won more than fifty singles and doubles titles. Her parents had come north to Harlem from South Carolina in 1930, when Althea was three, and the first sport that got her attention was boxing. It was at Harlem's famed Cosmopolitan Tennis Club, a cornerstone then of the American Tennis Association and its Black professional players, where Gibson got her first tennis training, before eventually heading back south, to North Carolina, to hone her game with Dr. Hubert Eaton. Dr. Eaton, along with another Black physician and tennis coach, Robert Walter Johnson, would carefully guide Gibson to the US Nationals and her breaking of the color barrier.

It was Dr. Johnson, a Virginian, who also coached and mentored the great Arthur Ashe. Ashe came along in the mid-1960s, ten or so years after Gibson—rising to the top of the men's game in an era that witnessed the advance of the civil rights movement, the dawn of tennis's Open era, and the first national TV broadcasts of major tournaments. As a result, and because men's tennis, then as now, was given greater prominence than the women's game—and, too, because Ashe eventually became the activist Gibson never was—Ashe would come to be generally understood as the game's African American trailblazer and have the world's largest Grand Slam show court named for him. Katrina Adams, a former president and CEO of the USTA, alluded to this in her remarks at the dedication of the Gibson sculpture: "Recognizing for me as an African American woman and recognizing what Althea stood for and understanding that she truly broke the color barrier for tennis—a lot of people think it's Arthur, but it was Althea, eleven years before him."

It was, perhaps, easy to be skeptical about what the statue of Gibson might or could mean to the tens of thousands of ticketholders who would walk past it in the coming weeks of the US Open, and in the years to follow. Statues seemed of another time. Much of the energy focused on statues in America just now was on having ones dedicated years ago to honor men who were racists and slaveholders removed from college campuses and city parks.

The biopic had superseded the statue as a visual repository of historical memory. (Whoopi Goldberg was said to be in discussions to produce an Althea Gibson biopic.) Yet in my dozens of comings and goings from the US Open media center, abutting Ashe Stadium, I seldom passed the Gibson bust without seeing people posing for a picture in front of it: older African American women, mostly, but also Black families and mixed groups of tennis friends. There were plenty of selfies, too.

2

Serena Williams thumped Maria Sharapova, 6–1, 6–1, in their US Open first-round match. It should have come as no surprise. Williams versus Sharapova had long been less a tennis rivalry than a marquee event—that, and a personal feud. In 2004, when she was just seventeen, Sharapova upset Williams in the Wimbledon final and then beat her again later that year. Sharapova didn't register another victory against Williams until the 2018 French Open—and it was by default, Williams having withdrawn with a pectoral injury. Before this latest match in Flushing, the two had played twenty-two times, and Williams had won nineteen of those matches. Since 2004, Sharapova had won four *sets* against Williams. Both being power-baseline players, they've lacked even the contrast in playing styles that can make for something like a rivalry, however one-sided. Their matches have tended toward the brutal and brief.

What's made things interesting is their evident mutual animus. In her as-told-to autobiography, *Unstoppable*, which was published in 2017, Sharapova traced her discord with Williams to that Wimbledon final in 2004. She describes hearing Williams "bawling" in the locker room after the match and claims that Williams knew that Sharapova had heard her sobbing, angering her—and that she, Williams, later told "a friend" of Sharapova's, who is quoted anonymously in the book, "I will never lose to that little bitch again." Whatever the truth of that story, there was bad blood for sure by 2013, when a reporter for *Rolling Stone* heard Williams, speaking on the phone with her sister Venus, describe a "top five player who is now in love" as "boring" and persuasively speculated that Williams was talking about Sharapova. At a Wimbledon press conference soon after that piece was published, Sharapova remarked, in a reference to Williams's relationship with her coach Patrick Mouratoglou, "If she wants to talk about something personal, maybe she should talk about her relationship and her boyfriend that was married and is getting a divorce and has kids." It also understandably irked Williams that, for years, Sharapova, being willowy, blond, and white, brought in more endorsement money than she did, even as Williams was throttling her on the court. But, these days, Williams was outearning her off the court, too.

Sharapova, who was now thirty-two, had won five Grand Slam tournaments and was a former world No. 1. She had won the US Open once, in 2006. In her prime, even as Williams was defeating her again and again, she was a fierce competitor who seemed to will victories against other players and possessed a corner-seeking backhand that, when she had time to step into it, was hard and flat and dictating. Injuries, particularly one to her shoulder that robbed her of an effective first serve, were diminishing her game even before she was suspended in 2016 from the tour for many months, after testing positive for meldonium, which had been recently banned as a performance-enhancing drug. (For this 2019 Williams-Sharapova match, Williams's husband sat courtside, mischievously, in a T-shirt bearing the slogan D.A.R.E. KEEPING KIDS OFF DRUGS.) Sharapova returned to the tour in 2017 and, in the first round of the US Open, upset Simona Halep, who was then ranked No. 2 in the world. But Sharapova's shoulder has continued to cause her pain and trouble her serve, and she'd arrived in Flushing for this US Open ranked No. 87 in the world. How far off could retirement be? (She would announce her retirement in February 2020.)

Williams, meanwhile, approaching her thirty-eighth birthday, had not only reached the final at Wimbledon, in July, but, a month later, reached the final at the Rogers Cup, in Toronto, where, in a quarterfinal match, she'd decisively defeated Naomi Osaka in a rematch of their notorious US Open final of 2018. Williams developed back spasms in the final in Toronto, against the Canadian phenom Bianca Andreescu, and had to retire, tearfully. Andreescu walked over to the chair where Williams sat quietly weeping; knelt; put her arms around Williams; and consoled her with words that not so long ago would not be understood as consoling: "You're a fucking beast."

With no hints of back problems against Sharapova, every sign was that Williams's fitness was the best it had been since giving birth to Olympia, nearly two years ago. She never once seemed out of breath, even in the handful of longer rallies that dotted a match of quick, cannon-shot points. Williams's lateral movement along the baseline appeared unstrained, her first steps quick enough to ensure that she'd get to shots out wide in time and with proper spacing, neither crowding the ball nor—as had often been the case this past year—being forced to lunge and stretch for it.

Williams had, too, a calm focus that she sometimes lacks in the first match of a tournament. Her serve was there from the start. Sharapova was putting most of her first serves in, too, but to little effect; they were not making Williams move, and she was punishing them. She broke Sharapova in the fourth game and again two games later. Neither time did Williams show any celebratory zeal—there were no shouts of "Come on," no fiery fist pumps. She held at love to take the first set, in twenty-four minutes.

It went much the same in the second set. Sharapova had two break chances in the fourth game, but Williams saved both. On the first one, Williams hit a kick serve that Sharapova mistimed, driving the ball into the net. On the second, Sharapova followed to the net one of her best backhands of the match—deep and sharply angled—only to see Williams pass her with a spectacular down-the-line backhand of her own. The crowd, filling Arthur Ashe Stadium for this celebrity square-off, roared and rose, and Williams, at last, raised her fist and shook it.

Sharapova lost that game and never won another. She won few points on her serve in what remained of the set, and just one as Williams broke her in the final game, for the match.

Neither player showed any signs of enmity in their press conferences that followed. Maybe they're past that. Or maybe the match had said everything that there was to say. Williams succinctly summed up the rivalry that has never really been a rivalry: "I always said her ball somehow lands in my strike zone. I don't know. It's just perfect for me."

3

Doreen St. Félix's father, a Haitian-born surgeon, was obsessed with tennis and, in particular, with the story of Serena Williams. "I think for my father, who had a lot of ideas about African Americans, Serena was not just this powerful Black athlete, which she was, but was *intelligent*," St. Félix said, and gently laughed. "Being young, all my dad wanted for me was to play tennis."

St. Félix did not play tennis, or anyway not well enough to get anywhere playing tennis. She was, however, intelligent, very intelligent. She graduated from Brown in 2014 with a lot on her mind about Black women. A year later, she published a searching essay about Rihanna in the online music journal *Pitchfork* that got a lot of attention, and not only from pop cognoscenti. She kept writing and was now, at twenty-seven, a staff writer for the *New Yorker*, and among the most important young cultural critics of color at work in America. We were sitting in a Tribeca café on a hot afternoon, sipping iced tea, and St. Félix was talking—or better, perhaps, thinking aloud, over the café din—about Serena Williams, what she meant and to whom.

St. Félix's essay on Rihanna explores the role—a liberating, empowering role, as St. Félix saw it—that money can play in the lives of Black women. And not just wealth, hidden and abstracted in investments, but money flaunted, in opulent fashion looks and thick rolls of cash stuffed into designer bags. "Sprawled amongst her earnings, the moneyed Black girl is an enlarged version of herself necessarily taking up the space of her debtors," she wrote in her Rihanna essay. "She's an image of material liberation."

St. Félix believes that this power of money for Black women is not limited to the likes of Rihanna, whose net worth, according to *Forbes*, had reached $600 million. "I think financial independence is a means for Black women to assert their sense of themselves, their independence," St. Félix told me. "Financial independence allows them to live fully in the world, and not just as tertiary beings: Black, but not a man; a woman, but not a white woman. If you grew up like me, a Black girl, you heard story after story of Black women who, without their own money, just got fucked over." She paused. "Aretha Franklin . . . I was lucky to see one of her last shows. Her thing about being unwilling to perform unless she got paid up front, in cash. That purse she carried her money in. I *saw* it!" St. Félix paused again. "You grew up with a lot of cautionary tales of women not getting their due."

St. Félix grew up, too, with the story of Serena Williams. "She worked so hard to get what she has. She, Serena, and Rihanna and Beyoncé, they are building generational wealth. Generational wealth just doesn't exist in Black America. For Blacks in America, forever, there has been nothing to pass down. These women, they are businesswomen beyond being musicians, or a tennis player. They are creating family wealth. They are investing, or can, in other Black women, which can end up generating wealth in communities."

I asked St. Félix what she thought would be the legacies of these women, beyond their money and its potential influence.

"I'm not sure. I think Serena is like Beyoncé in this way: she's ubiquitous, everywhere, but no one really knows what she thinks. She's ubiquitous. Her daughter is ubiquitous. The daughter's doll is ubiquitous. I mean, for older Black women, there is a great deal of understanding of Serena's struggle, the suffering involved in becoming who she became. There's an attachment to the narrative. But celebrity—and it's as a celebrity that Serena reaches her wider, younger audience—celebrity ubiquity has a way of watering that narrative down."

As St. Félix saw it, Williams will at some point have to begin speaking out on broader social and political issues. "Being a work-place feminist—equal pay, more women on corporate boards—that's important, but not enough in Black America. To maintain her cultural status, she's going to have to take a stand on things, issues in Black America. I mean, take Oprah: she's had to. There are so many Black celebrities who have been forced in recent years to begin taking a stand on criminal-justice reform, get active. But that hasn't been the case with Serena. Compare her to LeBron. No one knows what she thinks. And then what happens is that there will be no one who seems to *care* what she thinks."

4

I watched Williams's second-round match in Flushing on TV. Her opponent was the seventeen-year-old American Caty McNally, whom I'd seen lose to Coco Gauff in Miami in March. I was seeing Williams the way most people who have seen Williams have seen her—on television. No other tennis player of this era has kept Americans glued to their sets like Serena.

TV has ways of distorting tennis. The main cameras, positioned above the court, somehow conspire to make the speed of the ball appear slower than it actually is and don't register the range and rates of spin pro players apply to their strokes. From a courtside seat, you feel the terrifying pace of a 125 mph serve and can, at times, hear the spin-hiss of a whirring slice. What television *can* deliver, though, is an intimacy with a player, midmatch—a glimpse of emotions, not just shots and points—that only spectators in the finest, most expensive seats can hope to have. The grimace after she double-faults. The quick, confident nod she shoots her coaching box after breaking her opponent's serve. The glower she fixes on an opponent who's just darted a volley off her knee. Or the slump-shouldered, head-hung body language that signals to coach and opponent alike that she's been drained of energy and self-belief.

Williams has been one of the most emotionally expressive players the game has ever known. And pretty much from the start, her career has unfolded in front of big television audiences—big for tennis in this century, anyway. Tennis never drew the viewership of baseball, football, and basketball, or even, by and large, golf. Back in the 1970s, the US Open was watched in 4 to 5 million households, when America went through a craze of tennis playing, and when the stars of the game included Jimmy Connors, Chris Evert, John McEnroe, Billie Jean King: America's first TV-age tennis celebrities. The ratings drifted down in the years that followed and were showing no signs of growth until the Williams sisters broke through on the tour. By the summer of 2001 they were such a phenomenon that, when they both reached that year's US Open final, tournament officials and CBS, then the US Open's exclusive American broadcaster, decided Williams versus Williams was suitable for prime time and moved their match from Saturday afternoon to Saturday evening. It proved smart thinking: the match, which Venus won in straight sets before a sold-out crowd in Arthur Ashe Stadium, was watched by an estimated *22.7 million* viewers. That's more than the Lakers and the 76ers averaged for the NBA finals that year, and in the neighborhood of all but Game 7 of that year's baseball World Series between the Arizona Diamondbacks and the New York Yankees—one of the most widely watched World Series in years.

Was it the size of the audience that night that convinced Serena she had a future as an actress? She began taking acting classes the following year. She was twenty years old. She dreamed of a movie role, of working with, as she told an interviewer in August of 2002, Morgan Freeman, or maybe Sean Connery. "With my time schedule, I'd have to have a small role," she suggested, "but I'd like it to be all about me. So maybe I can get hurt in the beginning of the movie and I can just stay in a coma until the end." She did land a part, as a schoolteacher, in one episode of the Damon Wayans sitcom *My Wife and Kids*, and another in an episode of the grittier short-lived Showtime drama *Street Time*. Since then, for the most part, she has played herself on TV (in reality shows and documentaries) and played a lot of tennis on TV.

Her matches no longer draw anywhere near 20 million television viewers—few broadcast sporting events draw what they once did in our age of four hundred channels, streaming services, and social media. ESPN, and not one of the Big Three networks, was now broadcasting the US Open. Still, a Serena match tended to get watched in the United States by more people than any other player's matches. There's her celebrity, her quest for a twenty-fourth Grand Slam title (and first as a mom), and those moments when her big personality animates her. Her controversial 2018 final against Naomi Osaka was watched by 3.1 million viewers, which is a million more than watched that year's men's final (Novak Djokovic's straight-set victory over Juan Martín del Potro). It was the second-largest audience that ESPN, which began televising the US Open in 2009, ever drew for a tennis match. The largest remained a 2015 quarterfinal—between Venus and Serena Williams.

Serena's match against Caty McNally was not going to attract a record audience. The second match of a Wednesday night, it continued past what a reasonable adult with a job to get up for considers bedtime. It did make for compelling Serena viewing. She winced and muttered through the first set, as McNally's old-school backhand slice and net rushing unsettled her. Disbelief settled on Williams's face as McNally broke her serve, waved her arms to get the crowd behind her, *got* the crowd beyond her, and took the first set 7–5. Williams turned it around in the second set, winning it 6–3, and as she did, you could see in the close-ups, as she rocked awaiting McNally's serves, the focus and confidence emerging, that deadly stare she addresses across the net. In the third set, Williams turned the match into a rout, losing not a single point on her serve, winning the crowd back, and exaggerating, or seeming to, that signature slow walk of hers to the service line, as if she could not be calmer or in greater control. The broad, broad Serena smile came when it was over, 5–7, 6–3, 6–1, the royal wave to the upper reaches, and she was on her way to round three.

5

Fifteen-year-old Coco Gauff was a first-week sensation at the US Open, as she'd been at Wimbledon. She won her first two matches before being thoroughly undone by Naomi Osaka, in the night-match glare of loud and LED-flooded Ashe Stadium, 6–3, 6–0. (The two players fought back tears and embraced movingly on court after the match: a memorable moment for them, the spectators, the viewers at home watching, and tennis.) Another player on the women's side was creating a stir in the early rounds: Taylor Townsend, a young African American who, like Gauff, had been a teenage champion and a precocious tour presence, reaching the third round in doubles at the US Open in 2011 as a fifteen-year-old. Townsend, too, had been inspired by Serena Williams, not by her playing style (which was the case with Gauff), but because Williams, for Townsend, showed the game of tennis could be played by women who weren't thin. (Townsend: "When you see people that look like you in a sport and you have representation, it gives you hope that that can be you.") Townsend was five feet seven and listed her weight as 170 pounds.

She had no sooner turned sixteen than her body, her weight and fitness level, became an issue. She was the top-ranked junior player in the world, but the United States Tennis Association declined to cover her travel expenses to the 2012 US Open juniors—Townsend, who'd been born in Chicago, was by then training in Florida—because those coaching her at the USTA believed she hadn't slimmed down and gotten into match-ready shape. Patrick McEnroe, the general manager of the USTA's player-development program, explained his decision to the *Wall Street Journal* this way: "Our concern is her long-term health, number one, and her long-term development as a player. We have one goal in mind: for her to be playing in [Arthur Ashe Stadium] in the main draw and competing for major titles when it's time. That's how we make every decision, based on that."

The decision was immediately criticized by a number of players, including Serena Williams, who'd go on to win that year's US Open women's title. Williams said, "Everyone deserves to play. She's so sweet and she works so hard. For a female, particularly, in the United States, in particular, and African American, to have to deal with this is unnecessary. Women athletes come in all different sizes and shapes and colors and everything."

Townsend's family wound up funding her trip to that year's US Open juniors, where Townsend reached the quarterfinals before losing to a future WTA top-twenty player, Estonia's Anett Kontaveit. The USTA eventually reimbursed Townsend's family for those travel costs. But Townsend's struggles continued, less a result of her weight and fitness, it would seem, than her choice of game style. Plenty of women on the tour today were neither thin nor ripped, if few the size of Townsend. But no one played Townsend's kind of tennis, not anymore. She played the kind of tennis that Martina Navratilova more or less took with her when she retired from the singles tour, twenty-five years ago. Townsend served and volleyed relentlessly. She followed a lot of her returns to the net, too. Her opponents—with their light alloy racquets and high-tech fiber strings; with their power and topspin—hit passing shots the likes of which Navratilova never had to deal with. Serving and volleying, chipping and charging, were no longer a ways to get to the top of the tour.

Townsend, now twenty-three, arrived at the US Open ranked No. 116 in the world. She had spent most of the years since emerging as a junior prodigy playing, when she was playing at all, on the ITF circuit, the second tier of the women's pro tour. She had to play a week of qualifying matches to earn a spot in the

US Open main draw. She won her main-draw first-round match against twenty-five-year-old Kateryna Kozlova of Ukraine, who, like Townsend, had spent most of her career on the ITF circuit. Townsend's win brought her to Arthur Ashe Stadium for the first time for a main-draw singles match on a Thursday afternoon of week one. Her opponent was Simona Halep, seeded No. 4 and the new Wimbledon champion. The crowd, thin as the match began, expected Halep to make short work of Townsend—extend points, get her on the run, wear her out. Halep had played Townsend three times and won three times. But a player ranked just outside the top one hundred is not an unexceptional player; she is, for the most part, an elite player who can't quite put together all the elements of her game—and tennis is a multifaceted, complicated game—in very many high-level matches. It does happen once in a while, though. It's what happens in what gets called an upset.

Those on hand for the Townsend-Halep match were standing and roaring by its end. Fans love an upset, but perhaps they were caught up, too, in the easeful, full-focused joy of Townsend's play. The Hungarian-born psychologist Mihály Csíkszentmihályi identified and coined the frame of mind and form Townsend was exhibiting: the flow state. Townsend was feeling the ball and in the zone (those are the terms players use for flow) as she glided to the net more than one hundred times, more than sixty times alone in the third and deciding set, which went to a tiebreak. She was sticking her volleys firmly, angling them sharply, and more often than not anticipating the direction of Halep's passing shots and cutting them off. Halep was thrown and, being Halep, getting down on herself for being thrown. Townsend sealed the 2–6, 6–3, 7–6 (4) victory with a deep forehand volley, forked crosscourt to Halep's backhand. Halep reached it but netted it. Townsend lifted her arms to the sky.

She was still feeling it as she met with the press afterward. "It's been a long road, a lot of haters, a lot of people who weren't sure," she said with her particular effervescence. "I've heard it for a really long time that I was never going to do this or do that." In the coming days she would win one more match, then lose in the Round of 16 to Bianca Andreescu. Townsend wasn't thinking of any matches to come, though, in the hours after she defeated Simona Halep. In the flush of that victory, she was thinking, she said, "that I belong here."

6

Williams played her third-round match on an azure-skied Friday afternoon that began the Labor Day weekend. Her opponent was Karolína Muchová, who had just turned twenty-three and was from the Czech Republic. Muchová was among the younger cohort of fine Czech players, one that included twenty-year-old Markéta Vondroušová, who had in June reached the French Open final. (She withdrew from the US Open before it began, citing a wrist injury.) Muchová lacked the powerful serve of her fellow countrywoman Karolína Plíšková—though she had defeated Plíšková, a perennial top-five presence, in the Round of 16 at Wimbledon in July, in as good a match as there'd been this year in women's tennis. Nor did Muchová have the commanding ground strokes of Petra Kvitová, another top Czech. (Here in Flushing, Kvitová was upset in the second round by the German Andrea Petkovic.) What Muchová had was the kind of all-court game—changes of pace and spin and shape to the struck ball—that had emerged this year as the way the women's next gen came to play.

I'd spoken with Muchová briefly the previous afternoon, after she'd defeated Taiwan's Hsieh Su-wei. The match was out on Court 4, at the edge of the tennis grounds, from whose sun-spangled bleachers you could watch, between points, the passing traffic on the Grand Central Parkway. Su-wei, a veteran in her thirties, was a longtime and deft practitioner of what might be described as a rococo heightening of all-court style. She hit from both wings with all kinds of spin. She never saw a ball she wanted to hit squarely. She defined *tricky*.

Why were there so many Czech women players? I'd asked Muchová. Four Czech women were among the thirty-two women seeds when main-draw singles play at the US Open began. There were also four Americans—no other nation had more than four—but the population of the Czech Republic was around 3 percent that of the United States; it was only half that of Florida, where most Americans on the women's tour live or train. The top-ranked women's double player in the world, Barbora Strýcová, was a Czech, too. Three Czech women were in the doubles top ten.

Muchová smiled. She said she had no idea why so many Czech women played tennis so well.

Maybe, I suggested, it reflected that the parents of these players came of age in the 1970s and 1980s, the heyday of Martina Navratilova, the greatest Czech export to the game. Maybe, in the years after the Velvet Revolution of 1989, and the freeing up of Czech broadcasting, it reflected the inspirational presence on TV of Helena Suková, who won doubles championships at each of the four Grand Slam tournaments, and Jana Novotná, who reached No. 2 in the world in singles and won Wimbledon in 1998—though the women in the game today were but small girls back then. Maybe, as some other Czech players had offered over the years, it resulted from the support system for junior players, or the coaching.

Muchová smiled again. I sensed it was meant as an eye roll. She was tired. She needed to rest, she said. She would be playing for the first time the following afternoon in Arthur Ashe Stadium. She would be playing Serena Williams.

She started out strong enough against Williams, but the third time she served in the first set, she had to struggle to hold, saving two break points. The next time she served, Williams broke her easily and went on to take the set, 6–3. The following set Muchová was broken the first game she served and looked weary. Williams would break her two more times (and be broken once herself in a sloppy game); win the set 6–2; and finish the match in an hour and fifteen minutes. She looked anything but weary.

7

Two days after efficiently eliminating Karolína Muchová, Williams did much the same to Croatia's Petra Martić, defeating her in straight sets. That fourth-round win put Williams into the quarterfinals. She was playing like someone—confident, in form, determined—on a path to another Grand Slam final, and a chance to win a coveted twenty-fourth. Williams had rolled her ankle early in the second set against Martić, sending a buzz of concern through the Sunday-night crowd filling Ashe Stadium. But afterward, in the main interview room, Williams was quick to say she could sense the ankle would be fine. She was in a good mood seated before the assembled reporters. It was Olympia's second birthday. Two years before, Serena had been elated to give birth, but had, soon after, developed medical complications that led to a frightening emergency. She'd thought about that earlier in the day, she said. Mostly, though, Olympia was on her mind.

Serena had spoken earlier in the tournament about how their being apart was evolving, but still difficult: "In the beginning she would really be upset when I left, and now she's a little bit better." She'd added, smiling, that now "I think I'm a little more upset." The smile faded. "You know, it's hard. Sometimes my heart literally aches when I'm not around her. But, you know, it's good for me, I guess, to keep working. And just to all moms out there that it's not easy. It's really kind of painful sometimes. Sometimes you just have to do what you have to do."

I found myself thinking of the glimpses I'd had of Olympia during my months on the tour: scampering down a hallway; being held by Williams's agent and friend, Jill Smoller; being held, mostly, by Williams, after a match, in the players' gym, say, keeping her hamstrings loose by slowly pedaling on a stationary bike, Olympia cradled in her left arm, her head resting gently on her mother's shoulder. Working mom.

After her win over Martić, Williams was asked when Olympia might attend a match to watch her mom, as she had as an infant, on the lap of her father in the player's box. "She's a little loud and obnoxious now," Williams replied, chuckling, "so I'm not sure she should come to the matches." Olympia watched on television sometimes, Williams said, and pointed at the screen and said, "Mama." She also pointed at the screen when she saw her Aunt Venus, Serena deadpanned. She said, "Mama," then, too.

There would be no celebrating Olympia's birthday with a party and a cake. As a Jehovah's Witness, Serena explained, as she had the year before at the US Open, when Olympia turned one, Serena didn't celebrate birthdays, or Christmas or Easter or other holidays. Jehovah's Witnesses believe such celebrations displease God because their roots are pagan.

The depth to which Williams identified as a Witness was hard to gauge. Going to meetings three times a week at a Kingdom Hall was woven into her childhood in Compton and, she'd recalled in her autobiography, continued into her early teens in Florida, even as her days were more and more crowded with tennis training. "Yes, it takes up time, but you don't really notice the time when you're at Kingdom Hall," she reflected in her book. "It becomes a part of you, and washes over you, and you're swept up and set down on the other side of the experience in such a way that the time just flies."

She'd gone door to door, "out in service" as it is called, handing out tracts and evangelizing, as Witnesses do. Her mother, Oracene, has said that Serena had "witnessed" in this way even to other players in her early days on the tour. Oracene's taking her daughters to meetings regularly—not just Venus and Serena but Lyndrea and Isha—and reading the Bible with them at home, seemed clearly to have deepened a bond among them. It was something beyond tennis, and without Richard, who never participated much in the family's religious life. Serena would speak in her early years as a pro of how she read the Bible each night, and throughout her career, after her big wins, she has often thanked Jehovah God on court.

Williams has spoken, too, about how after her 2009 US Open on-court outburst against the line judge who called her for a foot fault—"I swear to God, I'll fucking take the ball and shove it down your fucking throat!"—she'd been summoned by church elders, who reprimanded her and showed her passages from Scripture that forbade taking God's name in vain and being foulmouthed. (Letter of Paul to the Ephesians: "Let a rotten saying not proceed out of your mouth.")

Williams married a non-Witness, which violates a church command. Her seminudity in various magazine photographs also violates a Witness command, as did her being pregnant out of wedlock. In recent years various online posts—including posts on Reddit, which her husband cofounded—have called for Williams, "unrepentant" for these "sinful acts," to be formally "disfellowed" from the church. This has not happened, perhaps because, according to other posts by those identifying themselves as Witnesses, no record exists that Williams was ever officially baptized as a Witness—never, as a teenager or an adult, fully immersed in water, clothed, as the rite is carried out by church elders. Her failure to abide by certain church rules, and even her failure to have undergone certain church rites, if true, make her no different from countless other modern-day American Christians who consider themselves good Christians. Williams sees herself as "essentially in line with conservative Christian values," which can be interpreted any number of ways, as she herself can.

The Jehovah's Witnesses take Jesus's admonishing his disciples to be "no part of this world" as a warning to refrain from political involvement and to remain "neutral." Witnesses do not vote, canvass for candidates, or lobby governments; nor are they to spend time better spent with their Bibles on keeping up on current events. Williams's identifying as a Witness has never prevented her from speaking out about racism, expressing her joy at Barack Obama's election (though she didn't vote for him), or defending Colin Kaepernick, the former NFL quarterback who began taking a knee during the pregame playing of the national anthem to protest police shootings of African Americans (though Williams has not expressed support for bills advancing criminal-justice reform).

Nor are there any church strictures on women fighting for equal pay, as William has. Months before discussing why she wouldn't be celebrating Olympia's second birthday, she'd been asked, in the press conference following her defeat of Victoria Azarenka at Indian Wells, about news that day that the US women's national soccer team had filed a lawsuit seeking pay commensurate with that of the men's team, accusing the US Soccer Federation of "institutionalized gender discrimination." Williams began her answer by praising those who came before her and fought for pay equity in tennis, such as Billie Jean King. She went on to say, "I think at some point, in every sport, you have to have those pioneers, and maybe it's the time for soccer."

A journalist in the room raised the name of another pioneer, Ruth Bader Ginsburg, the Supreme Court justice who had, before ascending to the bench, argued hundreds of sex-discrimination cases, including a number before the Supreme Court that concerned women who were not being paid what men were paid for doing the same job. Williams said she was not familiar with Ginsburg's "work." She obviously had no idea who Ginsburg was. It might well have been true that any number of American tennis players, men and women, did not know of the contributions Ginsburg had made in the fight against gender discrimination, or even who she was. Nevertheless, Williams was in her late thirties, intelligent, informed about all sorts of things (movies, fashion, food, real estate, money), and Ginsburg was not Stephen Breyer—Ginsburg had become something of a pop icon, like Williams herself. Maybe Williams's life as a Witness had kept a knowledge of Ginsburg from her.

8

Williams's US Open quarterfinal opponent, China's Wang Qiang, was having a career year. She'd gotten further than she ever had before at the Australian Open; made it to the fourth round at Indian Wells before losing to the eventual champion, Bianca Andreescu; and now, in Flushing, had reached her meeting with Williams, her first, by upsetting the world No. 2, Ash Barty. Wang (that's her family name) had spent years as a pro without getting within shouting distance of the top fifty, and here she was, at twenty-seven, in the top twenty. She'd gotten there with the stamina and tactical prowess she'd always had; working with her new coach, the Frenchman Thomas Drouet, she'd heightened those strengths and deepened their integration. She was China's best tennis player, and looking, at the moment, like the second-greatest tennis player China had yet produced.

The greatest, Li Na, was something of a late bloomer, too, and someone Wang had long spoken of as a source of inspiration. Li was twenty-nine when she won the French Open in 2011, becoming the first Chinese player (the first Asian national, male or female) to win a Grand Slam tournament. She went on to win an Australian Open before retiring at the end of 2014. By then, she was one of the most famous people in China. An estimated 116 million viewers in China had watched the broadcast of her French Open victory. Li's first racquet sport had been badminton, and tennis had only recently been seen for the first time by the vast majority of Chinese (thanks, in no small part, to its reintroduction to the Olympics held in Seoul in 1988) when she took up the game at age eight. Today, some 14 million Chinese were said to be playing tennis. The week the 2019 US Open began, there were, along with Wang Qiang, nine other women from China in the WTA top two hundred. Li Na had led China to a place in women's professional tennis.

And women's professional tennis was, in turn, led by Li Na to China. In 2011, two WTA tournaments were held annually in China. Now there were nine, one more than were held in the United States, and one of them, the China Open in Beijing, was among the most prestigious and lucrative (in prize money) on the tour. The annual Asia Swing dominated the sport in the weeks after the US Open finished up, more so on the women's side than the men's. (Only four annual men's tournaments were held in China, and only one Chinese player was in the ATP top two hundred as the 2019 season drew to an end: Zhang Zhizhen, with a career high of No. 179.) Tennis was said to be a $4 billion industry in China, making it second only to the United States (estimate: $6 billion), and growing at a faster rate, with women the key drivers of that growth. (Chinese men preferred basketball.) That's a big reason why the WTA decided to move the tour's culmination, the WTA Finals, to Shenzhen, for ten years beginning in 2019.

The biggest reason? Shenzhen had outbid a number of other cities in Europe and elsewhere. The successful bid was submitted by Gemdale Corporation, one of China's largest real-estate developers, with a promise of a new stadium and at least $4.4 million for the tournament's singles champion. This represented the largest amount ever promised a player in women's tennis—or *men's*. Total prize money in Shenzhen would be in the neighborhood of $14 million, almost double the prize money to be distributed to men at the 2019 ATP Finals in London. China was betting on tennis: someday soon, perhaps, Wang Qiang or some other Chinese player in the women's game would be among the top-ranked eight who get to compete in the WTA Finals. (Two pairs of Chinese doubles players would be among the eight doubles teams to qualify in Shenzhen.) And the WTA was betting on China: it was where the money was, the big money.

Richard Williams had understood the lure of money, too—that's what had led him to put tennis racquets in the hands of his young daughters. There was money for women athletes in tennis as there was not, then or now, in any other sport women played. The money in 1980, when he says he saw Virginia Ruzici on television with her check for winning in Salt Lake City, was paltry compared with what a top player in the women's game could earn in 2019. But then, it had only been ten years before Ruzici's victory, in the summer of 1970, at an event in California called the Pacific Southwest Championships, when one of the key figures in the creation of professional tennis and the ushering in of the Open era, the former great turned promoter Jack Kramer, offered the newly minted pro men entering the tournament a total of $12,500, and the women just $1,500. Moreover, he proposed paying the women no money at all until they reached the quarterfinals; they should, presumably, play for glory and the good of the game.

That proved the last straw for Billie Jean King, who led a group of players ("The Original Nine") in a boycott of the event—and eventually to the formation of the Virginia Slims Circuit. The WTA tour, launched in 1973, grew out of that circuit, and King always saw clearly that what she and those other earliest women pros were fighting for, with their demand for pay equity, was part of something larger, beyond tennis. It grew out of what now gets called the sixties, as she put forward in *We Have Come a Long Way*, her 1988 history of the women's game, its title echoing the advertising slogan for Virginia Slims, the cigarettes marketed specifically to women, and the sponsor (accepted with ambivalence by King and the others) of the first women's pro tour. King, in her book, used the term "consciousness"—an alertness to injustice and other societal wrongs, and a moral impulse to right them. She saw her push for prize-money parity as a fight for women's rights more broadly, a fight aligned as well with the struggle for racial equality and a wider expansion of human rights. The battle she led was about money, but not only about money.

In the days before tennis fans filled Arthur Ashe for the Williams-Wang quarterfinal, a Chinese paramilitary force had used the Shenzhen Bay Sports Center, where the WTA Finals were to be held until the planned new tennis stadium was built, as a staging ground. Every morning, military transports and armored personnel carriers drove up, hundreds of security officers jumped out, and, once inside, spent hours drilling. Hong Kong was visible across the bay—which was the point. Democracy protests in the semiautonomous city had been going on for months; China's ruling Communist Party was sending a warning across the bay that the use of force from the Chinese mainland to quell the protests remained an option. It might have been understood by WTA officials as a warning of a different sort: Was it a good idea for women's tennis to be building a future that depended, to a significant degree, on financing from a nation whose authoritarian government, with its surveillance technology and unwavering one-party-forever dictates, appeared to be ruling more and more coercively? In the idiom used by the young women playing the tennis, what about the brand?

No worries. That, essentially, was what the WTA's president, Micky Lawler, told the *New York Times*. Her role with the WTA was to drive business development, and she'd overseen the Shenzhen deal. She said, "We've had nothing but a great relationship with China. They have been very good partners. The reason we love working in sports it's not supposed to touch anything but positive human connections." Sports was about sticking to sports, in other words. The WTA had come a long way.

Serena Williams would not be playing the Asia Swing. Richard Williams had seen not only the money but the toll that playing too many tournaments took on a player. He urged his daughters not to cram too many appearances into a season. The Williams sisters had, for years, been limiting the number of events they entered and had become more and more select about where and when they played as they entered their late thirties. Not playing in Asia meant that Serena could not possibly accumulate the ranking points to finish in the top eight and thus qualify for the WTA Finals. But she'd skipped the finals in 2016, the season before she became pregnant, and also the year before that, when she'd finished ranked No. 1. Williams cared now about Grand Slam victories, almost exclusively—and about having a life, which meant time for her family and other business concerns. Come what may, her 2019 season was going to end at the US Open, in Arthur Ashe Stadium.

It would not end with her quarterfinal match. She trounced Wang Qiang, 6–1, 6–0. The match was over, mercifully, in forty-four minutes. In one stretch Williams won eleven straight points—and won them fast. A particular sound is made when a player strikes an incoming ball cleanly—that is, when the timing of all her bodily mechanics on a ground stroke are in sync; when she makes contact with the ball out in front of her; and when that contact is made in the upper-middle third of her racquet-head string bed, where the benefit of racquet speed generated by the swing is maximized. It's a certain *pock*. You hear it all the time when a pro is practicing. Williams created this soundscape in her expeditious vanquishing of Wang.

Maybe its being over in a flash lessened the pain for Wang. Then, too, she'd earned $500,000 by reaching the quarterfinals. Afterward, Wang seemed almost sanguine. She joked with the many Chinese sportswriters who'd remained in New York to see and report on her quarterfinal match. She smiled and explained, in English, that the reason she'd lost so badly and quickly was not complicated: "The power, like, I cannot handle it. Just too much for me."

And what would she take away from her first match against Serena Williams?

"Build my muscle."

9

Marsha Smith was certain, or anyway pretty sure, that Serena Williams would win the US Open final and tie the record, twenty-four, for the most Grand Slam singles championships won by a woman—by *anybody*. Had I seen Williams's semifinal victory two nights ago? Oh, *my*! How she'd thrashed that blond girl—where was she from? Yes, that's right, Svitolina, Elina Svitolina. Ukrainian? Yes, Serena would win the final, Marsha believed, but I should understand that if she didn't win, it would not change Marsha's thinking about Serena at all, not one bit.

"She *better* win," Marsha's friend Fiona said now, and followed her pronouncement with a growl of a laugh. Fiona's last name was Smith, too, but they were not related, just old friends, close friends: two African American women of a certain age who shared, among other things, an adoration of Serena Williams. I had fallen into a conversation with them, sitting, as they and dozens of others were, along the hard gray-stone lip of the fountain at the main entrance to Arthur Ashe Stadium. The US Open's giant electronic scoreboard loomed above the plaza, and us. Only scores from junior matches were being reported up there—the tournament was winding down. And no match from inside Ashe was being simulcast on the big screen at the center of the scoreboard, as was the custom, not yet. The start of the women's final was a couple of hours away.

The Saturday afternoon was pleasant, after a chilly morning, a breeze carrying a hint of summer's end. Before I'd begun chatting with Marsha and Fiona, who were busy with sandwiches and soft drinks when I first noticed them next to me, I'd been taking in the sun and looking over my notes from the Williams-Svitolina match. Williams had won it quickly and decisively on Thursday evening, 6–3, 6–1. Svitolina, on paper, was no easy out, a wear-you-down defender, the No. 5 seed. And she'd faced a tougher road to the semifinals than Williams. That's why Marsha and Fiona, along with the oddsmakers and any number of commentators, thought Williams would, in the final, defeat the nineteen-year-old Canadian sensation, Bianca Andreescu. Andreescu had beaten Williams a month earlier in Canada, in the final of the Rogers Cup. But Serena had had to retire from that match with back spasms.

Now, in New York, Andreescu might struggle, not with any injury but with the fatigue from long, hard-fought battles in the quarterfinals and semifinals. Williams was locked in, deep in the zone. That's why Marsha and Fiona were here to see her.

I learned, soon enough, that Marsha and Fiona had come to Flushing to see Williams play numerous times before. They brought to this day's match a history, Serena's history. There were her great and many triumphs here: six titles, including three in a row, 2012–14, two of them over Victoria Azarenka. Those matches against Azarenka ranked among the best US Open women's finals of the last thirty years. Williams had suffered memorable losses, too, in Arthur Ashe, none more stunning or anguishing than her 2015 loss in the semifinals to Italy's Roberta Vinci. Vinci was aging and unseeded, but in possession of a backhand slice that messed up Williams's timing and messed with her mind when so much was on it: a US Open title that year, after her already having won the Australian Open, the French Open, and Wimbledon, would have earned her an in-year Grand Slam, something that, on the women's side, only Steffi Graf had accomplished in the Open era. However, most of Williams's most memorable battles—and Marsha and Fiona had still-smoldering recall of these—were with umpires and line judges. *2004:* Four wrong third-set calls, including a ghastly overrule by the chair umpire, Mariana Alves, of what was a correct line call, go against Williams and play a significant role in her quarterfinal loss to Jennifer Capriati. As a result, Hawk-Eye, the line-calling technology, is instituted in Ashe Stadium, and its use on the pro tours soon becomes widespread. *2009:* Williams is called for a foot fault, verbally threatens the line judge, is penalized a point for unsportsmanlike conduct, and thus loses the semifinal to Kim Clijsters. *2011:* In the final, against the Australian Samantha Stosur, the chair umpire awards a point to Stosur when Williams lets out a self-encouraging "Come on!" as Stosur is about to try to return what looked to be an unreturnable Williams forehand. Deliberate hindrance, rules the chair umpire, Eva Asderaki. Stosur would win the match in straight sets, and Williams would be fined $2,000 for telling Asderaki, "You are out of control. You're just a hater, and you are unattractive inside." *2018:* The Naomi Osaka final. Marsha and Fiona were not much interested in rehashing *that.*

Truth be told, they weren't, on the whole, all that interested in tennis, I was coming to realize. Serena Williams was their interest.

"You don't know about a Black woman's life," Marsha said to me at one point without a trace of malice, or hesitation. "She"—Serena—"means something to a Black woman."

"What she grew up with," Fiona said, nodding. "We know about that."

"She came from humble beginnings," Marsha said, "and she went on to be a winner. She has a story to tell."

"Yes," Fiona said. "A story that African Americans need to hear. You can *make* something of yourself." She paused. "Serena Williams has the urge to win. She is a winner. I *associate* with winners."

Marsha expanded on this. "She is successful, and she provides for and protects her family. Protects her family and her family name. Nothing is more important."

I was about to head into the media center and grab a sandwich of my own before the final began. Before I did, I pointed toward Ashe Stadium and asked the women where their seats were.

A smile began spreading across Marsha's broad face. "Right *here!*" They'd purchased grounds passes for the final, for $25 apiece. They were going to watch the match on the giant scoreboard. "We never go inside," Marsha explained. "Too expensive! That's why we got here early. We're right in front of the screen up there. We are always fine, the two of us, right here."

10

The US Open had a message for the ticketholders pouring down the steep aisles of Arthur Ashe Stadium for the women's final. The scoreboards were displaying, in what amounted to jumbotron fine print, the code of conduct for professional tennis: when violations were enforced and penalties assessed by the chair umpire. The United States Tennis Association had held a two-day conference at its main campus in Orlando earlier in the year to discuss how to avoid a repeat of the Williams-Osaka fiasco. Carlos Ramos would be kept away from umpiring any matches including Williams. And maybe, if the rules were posted, the spectators would be more aware, and less confused and angry, if any player (Williams in particular, it went unsaid) was penalized. Umpires or others involved in officiating were to be available to broadcasters and ready to post on social-media sites. Like the implementation of Hawk-Eye for contested line calls, here, in a sense, were other Serena Williams–inspired innovations.

Who knows what the midafternoon throngs made of all that as they settled into their seats. Their noisy ovation for Williams's entrance onto the court made clear they were here for her, here to see her win, to win her twenty-fourth Grand Slam and tie the record, to win one as a mother and close that narrative. They were here to potentially get caught up in a suspenseful out-of-time present—a palpable promise suffusing any sports arena in the minutes before play begins—but also to feel a part of something larger, a historic moment. That's why even the cheapest seats still available, a handful of them in the high-far expanses of the stadium, were going for more than $300 on

StubHub. That's why the grounds outside the stadium were as crowded as they were. That's why Marsha and Fiona had wisely arrived early.

Sun-slant shadows were already beginning to ink the court as the players warmed up. Warm-ups reveal nothing—not to an onlooker in a good courtside seat, and not, it was generally understood inside tennis, to the players about each other. Williams was in violet, Andreescu in black with white-and-purple trim. Williams had strung together back-to-back-to-back commanding wins to reach the final, the best week of tennis she'd played since returning to the game after giving birth to her daughter. She was nursing no injuries, injuries of the sort that had plagued her at various times during the season and kept her off the court for weeks on end. Andreescu had had an injury-marred year, too. After winning at Indian Wells, she'd retired midway through her fourth-round match in Miami with a torn rotator cuff in her right hitting shoulder. She attempted a return at the French Open in May, but was again forced to retire, during her second-round match, because of shoulder pain. She wouldn't get back to match play until August, at the Rogers Cup in Toronto, which she won when Williams retired in the final. Andreescu was here now having won and won for two weeks running and gotten herself to the US Open final. The uncanny fact was, Bianca Andreescu had not lost a match that she was able to complete injury-free since *February*! Most of those watching the players wind up their warm-ups by practicing their serves could not be expected to know that. Serena Williams would, however, make a point of knowing that kind of thing.

Williams was greeted with another surge of crowd cheer when she strolled to the baseline to begin the match, and still another, louder and throatier, when she arced her first serve out wide, the side-spun ball brushing the line and continuing on its way untouched—a clean ace. It would prove the last unclouded moment Williams's fans would have that afternoon. A chasm suddenly opened. Minutes after her opening-point ace, the Williams who'd spent a week playing her season-best tennis suddenly gave way to the Williams who struggled to keep it together in a Grand Slam final. Up 40–15, just a point from holding her serve, she made two dismal errors in a row—backhand shanked, forehand netted—to bring things scruffily to deuce. Then Williams double-faulted twice in a row, and like *that*, her serve was broken.

A pro player double-faults when she is (a) concerned her opponent is hammering her second serve and so goes for too much with it, "redlines" and misses; or (b) is anxious. Williams? Correct answer: (b). Maybe she wanted it, the twenty-fourth, too much. Maybe she was being nerve-racked by the memory of the Osaka final the year before—or by the inchoate undermemories of all the volatile weirdnesses that had visited her here on Ashe in big moments through the years. Or maybe she had no idea what had gotten into herself, which would have her thinking too much: a tennis-match death spiral. If you are forced to hit second serves at all on crucial points, your first serve is not working either.

Double-faulting, especially the anxiety-induced kind, has a way of darkening everything for a player, all aspects of her game. She grows preoccupied with her serving, downcast, mind-muddled. She wonders, *What is it with me?* She finds her legs not wanting to move when she needs them to move. She finds the shots she can rely on are suddenly not reliable. If she is Serena, she keeps the crowd in the match with patches of ferocious power tennis, even as too many of her shots miss the mark. The crowd spent much of the seventh game of the first set, with Andreescu up a break, 4–2, cheering deliriously for Williams as she fought to hold her serve, fending off one break point (with an ace up the T), then another (when Andreescu netted a backhand), then another (with a pure-Serena backhand winner), then *another* (one more ace!), and still *one more* (with a short, beautifully rolled and angled forehand winner), before holding, finally. But Williams couldn't hold the next time she served: Andreescu took that game and the set, 6–3, when Williams, facing a break point that was set point, too, once again double-faulted. As the players sat and toweled, the stadium crowd collectively groaned and murmured. *Not another final, not again. . . .*

Set two picked up where set one left off. Williams was broken, without winning a point, the first time she served (double-faulting on break point!); broken the second time she served; broken the third time she served. She was getting her first serve in maybe 25 percent of the time, and with nothing like the pace she'd consistently summoned in previous matches. She did break Andreescu's serve once; she was not going to get bageled. But it was looking like a rout. A particular sort of rout. Andreescu was not playing great tennis. She was playing aggressive, big-strike tennis—Serena's power, and maybe the momentous pressure of the final, had Andreescu playing with little of the variety (slice, lob, net rushing) she normally brought to a match. She was having scattered minutes of remarkable high-octane tennis, getting low and exploding into inside-out forehands and backhands that more than once caught Williams leaning the wrong way. But mostly Andreescu was playing good enough tennis against an opponent playing miserable tennis. Williams knew it. She was hanging her head. She was pleading with herself. *She* was miserable.

With Andreescu serving, up 5–1, serving with the game at

40–30, serving for the match and the championship, Serena crushed a return winner: match point saved. She then earned a break point (but couldn't convert it), and then a second, which she did convert when she watched Andreescu's third-shot put-away sail past her, long. Williams then held her serve; then broke Andreescu once more; then held again: Williams had evened the set at 5–5! By then, the crowd in the upper reaches had been on its feet for ten minutes, and the noise inside Ashe was as loud as I'd ever heard it—a sustained roar that seemed to have a near-physical presence, shoving you, shaking the place. Whistles and wails came of *"Serena!"* midpoint from the crepuscular high tiers (afternoon was giving way to twilight), and schadenfreude cheers for every Andreescu mishit. At one point, Andreescu could be seen putting her fingers in her ears. "I could barely hear myself think," she would later say. She did manage to gather herself and hold to go up 6–5. Could Williams answer that, do the same, hold, and bring the set to a tiebreak?

She could not. A backhand of hers sailed wide, the score was 15–40, and now she had two championship points to save. She saved the first, but not the second: Williams could only lunge and watch as an Andreescu forehand winner skipped past her for the game, the set, and the championship. There would be no twenty-fourth Grand Slam victory for Williams in 2019.

11

Williams had lost and was at a loss. That was clear soon enough, as she seated herself at the table on the dais in the main interview room and began taking questions from the many reporters on hand. She had kept them waiting, thirty minutes, forty minutes beyond the scheduled time of the press conference, time the reporters passed sitting silently, mostly, some of them poring over the match scoring they'd done in their own notebooks, others studying stat-sheet handouts that had been distributed. They understood Williams had put 44 percent of her first serves in play, to Andreescu's 66 percent; had made fifty-eight total errors, to Andreescu's thirty-five; had double-faulted *eight* times. Williams understood all this, too, if less exactly. She understood it emotionally, continued to feel it. It was in her eyes, downcast and dulled, in her deep sighs and sulky pout, in her voice, soft and clotted. She'd lost, and that stark fact could not be undone. No player hated losing like Williams. She had never lost enough to know how to. This loss, like her other big losses, was not fully apprehended by her, not yet, anyway, and maybe not ever. From time to time, she gently stroked her hair away from her shoulders, shoulders left bare by her dove-gray tank top: a woman comforting herself as a girl might, inward-turned and blue.

She congratulated Andreescu. She talked of how she liked Andreescu, her "super-intensity," akin to her own. She thought she heard a radio from somewhere and expressed her annoyance. She was sure she heard the clacking of keys as a reporter toward the back of the room typed on his laptop, and this annoyed her, too. She was fighting back tears as she said, not so much as an answer to any question but thinking aloud, "Honestly didn't play my best today." It had been more her loss than Andreescu's win, in other words, which was true. She had to find a way, she said, to bring her best tennis to Grand Slam finals—which was true, too.

It had not been her day, it had not been her year, and not since she was a teenager growing accustomed to the tour had she gone two seasons in a row without winning a major title. It would turn out to be Ash Barty's year: winning the Miami Open and the French Open, and capping the season by winning the WTA finals in Shenzhen, a tournament in which three of the eight players vying for the singles title would retire from matches with injuries, and attendance would be sparse, which might or might not have had to do with unrest in nearby Hong Kong. It had been Williams's decade, though—twelve Grand Slam trophies—as had the decade that preceded it. No other woman in the Open era, in the history of women's tennis, had dominated like that. (Few in *any* sport had.) Moreover, despite hampering injuries, she had reached two Grand Slam finals during the 2019 season, one more than any other player on the women's tour.

Billie Jean King had said back in June, shortly before Wimbledon got underway, that she hoped Williams would play until she was forty, as King herself had. But she worried that Williams had too much else going on besides tennis to put in the training and play the smaller tournaments (and win them and thus regain the habit of winning) that would prepare her to not only reach Grand Slam finals but triumph. "It's not fair to her," King said, "but I wish she would just make a commitment for the next year and a half to two years and just say, 'I'm going to absolutely devote what's necessary for my tennis so when I look in the mirror when I'm older that I can go back in my mind and know I gave everything I had and be happy.'"

Williams was not going to set aside her business interests. Nor was she about to spend less time with her family. As the WTA finals were wrapping up in Shenzhen, she launched a new jewelry line. A couple of weeks later, in early November, she would be doing what many of the players on the just-completed

2019 WTA tour were doing, relaxing at a luxurious, far-flung tropical resort. In recent years, the go-to Instagram shot for women in the wake of the season's end had become a poolside or beachside portrait, and always in a bikini or swimsuit. Williams was in the Maldives, from where she posted a photograph of herself in a fashionable maillot. She also posted a slo-mo video of her and Olympia plunging down a waterslide. Tennis was a world away.

Still, the 2020 season would begin in less than two months. In mid-January, she'd win her first title since giving birth to Olympia, taking the ASB Classic in Auckland, a small Australian Open tune-up event, and posing for photographers while holding the trophy and her now two-year-old daughter in her arms. Two weeks later, she'd crash out of the Australian Open, losing a grueling third-round match to Wang Qiang—a stronger, more confident Wang Qiang—whom Williams had demolished at the US Open just a few months earlier. "Definitely going to be training tomorrow," Williams said after the loss. But the Coronavirus soon enough changed everything, and there were no next tournaments to train for—no Indian Wells or Miami Open; no clay-court season in Europe; no Wimbledon. In April, the US Open tennis complex, where Williams had failed in her bid to win one more major final, was functioning as a makeshift hospital.

"Honestly, Serena did not show up today," she'd said after that loss in Flushing to Bianca Andreescu. Maybe she meant a younger Serena, a Serena who never had a string of losing, in a row, four Grand Slam finals she'd reached. Maybe it was an instance of pain-easing disassociation. What I heard was a woman sharing an instance of deeply intuitive self-cognition.

Serena was the greatness she carried, the ideal, the potential. Serena could not always be summoned, but Serena would not, could not, be extinguished. So understood, she remained Serena, would always be Serena, and was still becoming, becoming what Serena wanted Serena to be.

Epilogue

"I think we've just done a really poor job in this country, Serena, learning the history of how we came to be where we are," Bryan Stevenson was saying. "We have a long history of racial inequality that most people have not been required to confront." Stevenson, sixty years old and a lawyer by training, was founder and director of the Equal Justice Initiative and had, through his tireless work, saved scores of prisoners from the death penalty; helped secure Supreme Court decisions that prohibit sentencing those under eighteen to life without parole; and spurred the construction of the National Memorial for Peace and Justice in Montgomery, Alabama, which commemorates the estimated four thousand Black victims of lynching in America. It was a Saturday in June, and Stevenson, from Montgomery via video, was joining Serena Williams on her *Serena Saturdays* Instagram Live show. Most Saturdays, the show was devoted to fashion, beauty, and exercise. From her home (she was in Florida this Saturday), Williams would sit before a single camera in front of a rack of her S-line clothing and, wearing a dress or outfit she'd designed, would tend to chat for forty-five minutes about the latest items of hers you could buy or, sometimes, about makeup, jewelry, or her daughter (who might make a cameo). This Saturday was different. Weeks before, in late May, George Floyd had died after being arrested outside a shop in Minneapolis for allegedly passing a counterfeit $20 bill. A white police officer had continued to press his knee on Floyd's neck as Floyd, handcuffed and pinned to the ground, pleaded that he could not breathe. Almost immediately, protests engulfed cities across the nation and, in places, were still underway day and night. Racial injustice was what America was talking about—and what Williams decided she wanted to talk about on her show. In 2015 she had written a brief appreciation of Stevenson for *Time's* annual list of the 100 Most Influential People. She admired "the way his gentle voice pulls you in to listen that much closer to the power behind his every word." They liked each other, it was clear, and were comfortable talking about things Williams seldom discussed with sports reporters. It was a remarkable conversation. It was a Serena I had not seen on the tennis tour—a tour shut down, as it had been since March, by the COVID-19 pandemic. It was, for that matter, a Serena I had not seen in women's magazines or TV interviews or anywhere else.

At Williams's urging, Stevenson was explaining how the abolition of chattel slavery in the South "didn't end white supremacy." It's not possible to know what devoted followers of Williams's on Instagram were expecting when they sought out her show on their feeds, but what they got this particular Saturday was a walk through the failures of the twelve-year Reconstruction Era that followed the end of the Civil War. Stevenson explained how racism persisted, even among the abolitionists; how freed slaves received neither the land nor aid nor rights they were due; and how by the end of the nineteenth century state and local laws, upheld by the courts, sanctioned and imposed racial segregation: the Jim Crow laws that would be enforced until the mid-1960s. What America needed, Stevenson suggested, was a second Reconstruction, another twelve-year process to bring about the legal and economic justice promised to Black men and women in 1865.

"That's so deep," Williams said. "Will we ever get justice?"

Then she brought up her father, who was born and raised in the Jim Crow South. "My dad always told us, 'You have to know your history.' He ended up in California because people were trying to kill him." She and Stevenson talked about, among other things, South Africa, the Bible, and their personal experiences of racism. Stevenson mentioned how from time to time, when he was defending a client, a judge would enter a courtroom, glance at the defendant's table, and reflexively assume Stevenson, being Black, was the defendant. Williams brought up how it was when she first followed Venus onto the tennis tour—two Black teenagers, two rarities in the women's game. Often at a tournament, she related, Venus would play an earlier match than Serena would, and she would sit in the locker room, listening to how Venus was doing. If the crowd was cheering, she knew Venus was losing. If there was silence, she knew Venus was winning. And Venus would do the same thing—listening in the locker room for crowd reaction—when Serena was playing. "I was playing not only against opponents," Williams told Stevenson. "I was playing against crowds, against people."

"You were playing against history."

Later in the show, Stevenson mentioned that he didn't watch tennis until he began watching Venus and Serena. A smile spread across his face, and Serena smiled, too. "People of all different races who have been disfavored or excluded or marginalized identifying with your struggles," he told Serena. He made it clear he meant on the court and off. "When we fight, we endure. When we keep pushing even though it seems like everything is pushing against us, we actually contribute to this movement toward justice." Serena's continuing to play matches and battle, he assured her, "inspires us, it energizes us."

Williams in June of 2020 was continuing to train in the hope she would get to play more matches and battle that summer.

Days before she'd spoken with Stevenson on Instagram Live, the USTA had announced, with the approval of New York's governor, Andrew Cuomo, that despite the cancellation of Wimbledon and the postponement of the French Open until the early fall, it was proceeding with plans to hold the US Open in New York as scheduled, beginning the last day of August. The Western & Southern Open, a tournament held outside Cincinnati each mid-August prior to the US Open, would this year be held the week before the Open at the Open's home in Flushing. The idea was to create one three-week-long, COVID-free bubble: no fans, no journalists such as me, and all the players locked down when they were not at the USTA Billie Jean King National Tennis Center practicing or playing their matches. The USTA had also carefully sought and won assurance from Williams that she would participate. Roger Federer was out for the year following knee surgery. Rafael Nadal, worried about traveling during the pandemic, had announced he had no plans to leave Spain for New York. With the Open limited to a TV audience, it needed stars more than ever, and Williams was that star. She herself saw the opportunity the COVID-summer US Open presented: like Federer and Nadal, many of the top international women's players, whether because of injury or coronavirus fears, would eventually announce they were staying home—six of the top eight, 20 percent of the top one hundred. Would a thinned field provide an opportunity for her to win a twenty-fourth major? The Open would be introducing a new Laykold-brand surface to its hard courts. Williams had a court coated with the same surface built in her Palm Beach Gardens backyard.

*

Williams did not win her twenty-fourth major at the US Open. She did play well enough to reach the semifinals, where, on a rainy Thursday evening under a closed roof in a near-empty Arthur Ashe Stadium, she lost to Victoria Azarenka—racing to a one-set lead, 6–1, before her baseline game began to falter and Azarenka found her range. Two days later, Azarenka would lose in the final to Naomi Osaka in what was one of the most exciting and hard-fought US Open finals in years. It took Osaka three sets and an adjustment of a too-predictable crosscourt pattern to her point creation to prevail and win her third major, and her second US Open, 1–6, 6–3, 6–3. Osaka's boyfriend, the rapper Cordae, was among the several hundred people inside Ashe to watch the match, and when Azarenka drove a backhand into the net on a championship point, he leaped from his chair and raised his arms—and the vest he had on parted to reveal a T-shirt calling for defunding of the police. It was a reminder of American life outside the tennis bubble, and of Osaka's role in bringing it inside.

She'd gone to Minneapolis with Cordae after the killing, in late May, of George Floyd by a police officer. During the Western & Southern Open, she'd boycotted her semifinal match to protest the shooting of Jacob Blake by police in Kenosha, Wisconsin, which led tournament officials to suspend all play for a day. She had arrived on court for each of her matches at the US Open with a mask bearing the name of a Black man, woman, or child who was killed by a police officer (or, in the case of Trayvon Martin, by a member of a neighborhood-watch program). Osaka was twenty-two, bashful at times but also assertive, cultivating an outsider distinctiveness while becoming the highest-paid female athlete in the world, according to *Forbes*, earning $37.4 million in prize money and endorsements in the twelve months leading up to *Forbes* releasing its 2020 list of top-earning athletes—$1.4 million more than Serena. Her mother is Japanese, and her father is Haitian; Osaka was born in Japan and grew up mostly on Long Island and in Florida. She was now living in Los Angeles and had spent much of her summer protesting, and, on social media, urging others to try to understand what life is like for Black Americans. She was a gift to tennis in a fraught time, reminding us that sports cannot and should not simply be an escape, that struggle is everywhere and ongoing—even as she reminded us, struggling early as she did on court in the women's final, that excellence in sports is rare and can be noble.

One thing Williams took away with her from the US Open was an injured left Achilles tendon, the result of an awkward stretch she made attempting to reach a passing shot early in the third set of her semifinal match against Azarenka. She limped to her chair and received medical treatment, and though she finished the match, she would not travel to Rome for the rescheduled (because of COVID) Italian Open. She would give it a try at the French Open, winning her first match in Paris before withdrawing—deciding not to risk doing further damage to the Achilles tendon, which was still causing her pain. She had turned thirty-nine just days before making the announcement. Thirty-nine is not an age for winning on the *terre battue* of Roland-Garros. Thirty-nine is an improbable age for winning a major on any surface. The oldest woman to win a major was thirty-five when she did it. That was Serena herself—and she did it, we learned later, when she was six weeks pregnant, defeating her sister Venus at the 2017 Australian Open. January of 2017, in any sport, was, as 2020 waned, a long, long time ago.

Williams would win her first five matches in February 2021 at the Australian Open: her Achilles injury healed, her fitness better than at any time since giving birth to her daughter, her confidence high, her ability somehow, at times, to chase balls into the corners and return them with pace and tactical daring as electrifying once again as the one-legged, Day-Glo-and-black catsuit she wore on court. But as in 2018 at the US Open, Naomi Osaka—in a tense, error-strewn semifinal that felt like a final—would stand between her and a twenty-fourth major title. At the press conference afterward, Serena, eyes swollen, devastated, had few answers about the match (she lost 3–6, 4–6) or what the future held for her, and she left the podium sobbing.

She had already made history, twenty-fourth slam or not—that needed to be understood, by her devoted fans and maybe by her. She is, clearly, the greatest of all time: the most dominant for the longest stretch of years; the most influential on the way the game has come to be played; the most consequential culturally, too, as an icon for Black women especially. Those fans of hers across the world will rightly continue to root for her to win one more, in 2021 and perhaps beyond, if Williams still has the desire and fitness to play on into her forties. But to watch with too much anxiousness that she win risks distracting oneself from the very components of her greatness, which are still, remarkably, on display, if no longer consistently. Her gift to tennis was that she had continued playing well after her legacy had been secured, playing with sufficing flickers of brilliance, in an arrestive twilight that extended beyond anyone's imagining but hers.

Watching her carry on, striking aces (*twenty* in her quarterfinal match at the US Open against Bulgaria's Tsvetana Pironkova); edging inside the baseline to pounce on a second serve, cracking a down-the-line backhand winner off a ball taken early, on a short hop; and watching, too, as she seemed so often now to be just a half step late coming forward to a drop shot, or, late in a match, as she gasped for breath after a rally of six, seven shots—I found myself thinking of lines written by one of my favorite poets, Jack Gilbert, in a poem titled "Failing and Flying":

EPILOGUE

I believe Icarus was not failing as he fell / but just coming to the end of his triumph. It had been a struggle for Serena Williams, a captivating struggle, from the start, and was a struggle for sure, a struggle of a different sort, though no less captivating, during these last years of hers, as she fell, and fell again. But it—all of it—had been her triumph, too.

ACKNOWLEDGMENTS

My thanks to:

My editor at Scribner, Colin Harrison, for his attentiveness and insightfulness. Also to Nan Graham, publisher of Scribner, who has had an encouraging hand in every book I've written. And to Steve Boldt, for his gently fastidious copyediting, and Sarah Goldberg, for smoothly ushering the book along. And to the others at Scribner who raised questions about and provided comments on the manuscript, which I believe strengthened the book.

My editor at NewYorker.com, David Haglund, and also Michael Luo, the editor of NewYorker.com, and David Remnick, editor of the *New Yorker*. I spent a year on the tour on *New Yorker* credentials, and wrote frequently for NewYorker.com, where my dispatches received the kind of care that is a rarity, and a blessing.

Diane Cardwell, Jennifer Egan, Megan Liberman, Michael Pollan, and Louisa Thomas. They read various drafts of the book at different stages. Their questions and suggestions were invaluable to me.

My literary agent, David McCormick. He believed in this book from the first phone call.

The many reporters from around the world who cover tennis,

ACKNOWLEDGMENTS

and from whom—in the media canteens at tournaments, in the press seats in arenas, and elsewhere—I learned a great deal. Christopher Clarey, Joel Drucker, Ben Rothenberg, and Louisa Thomas (again) were especially generous with their time and knowledge.

David Shaftel and Caitlin Thompson, cofounders of the journal *Racquet*. Writing for them—and having a coffee with them at the Odeon late in the afternoon—never fails to remind me how much I love the game of tennis.

My wife, Barbara Mundy, as ever, for everything.

NOTES

Introduction

1 *Leslie Jones, crashing the "Weekend Update" sketch:* NBC.com, September 29, 2018.

Part One: Melbourne

8 *glimpsed the tacos she was about to have:* Serena Williams Instagram photograph of tacos she made for Sunday dinner, posted October 18, 2018. It got more than eighty thousand "likes."

9 *"We seek attention without quite understanding what the attention is that we seek":* Adam Phillips, *Attention Seeking* (UK: Penguin Press, 2019), 7.

9 *thinking she was ugly, or thinking she was attractive:* Serena Williams with Daniel Paisner, *On the Line* (New York: Grand Central Publishing, 2009), 124; and Serena Williams, "Letter to My Mom," Reddit, September 19, 2017.

10 *The* New York Times *sent a reporter to an obscure tournament in Canada:* Robin Finn, "A Family Tradition at Age 14," *New York Times*, October 31, 1995, Section B, 13.

14 *estimated by* Forbes *magazine to be $225 million:* "The Highest-Paid Athletes 2019," *Forbes*, June 10, 2019, list, #63.

14 *ESPN was producing a list of the world's most famous athletes:* ESPN World Fame 100 2019, ESPN.com, March 12, 2019.

16 *"a too-tall, too-forceful, ready-to-emasculate Godzilla":* Michelle Obama, *Becoming* (New York: Crown, 2018), 264.

17 *Muhammad Ali had slapped his first wife for what she chose to wear:* David Remnick, *King of the World: Muhammad Ali and the Rise of an American Hero* (New York: Vintage Books paperback, 2016), 248.

22 *If you have read many memoirs:* Ken Dryden, *The Game*. 30th Anniversary Edition (Chicago: Triumph Books, 2013).

23 *passage from Joan Didion's novel:* Joan Didion, *Play It as It Lays* (New York: Farrar, Straus and Giroux paperback, 2005), 41.

24 *she had secured an entire floor at St. Mary's Medical Center:* Thomas Forester, CBS12 News, West Palm Beach, FL, September 1, 2018.

24 *Then much of what could go wrong did go wrong:* Rob Haskell, "Serena Williams on Motherhood, Marriage, and Making Her Comeback," *Vogue*, February 2018.

24 *The decor had a theme:* Beauty and the Beast: Brooke Marine, "Serena Williams Married Alexis Ohanian at a Wedding in New Orleans," *W*, November 17, 2017.

26 *just prior to the match she'd learned of the release from prison:* Sean Gregory, "Serena Williams Opens Up about Her Complicated Comeback . . . ," *Time*, August 16, 2018.

26 *suffering from postpartum depression:* Ibid.

26 *On Instagram she stated that she "felt I was not a good mom":* Opheli Garcia Lawler, "Serena Williams Opens Up . . . ," *Cut*, August 6, 2018.

28 *The largest? Serena versus Venus, evening quarterfinal, 2015:* Mary Pilon, "Can Serena and Venus Williams Save Tanking TV Tennis Ratings?," *Fortune*, September 9, 2015.

32 *referred to as Taquanda:* Stephen Rodrick, "Serena Williams: The Great One," *Rolling Stone*, June 18, 2013.

34 *on Fox News, as exhibiting "militant anger":* Obama, *Becoming*, 264.

34 *Dissertations have been written on the anger of Black female characters:* See, for example, Inderjit Kaur Grewal, "Anger and M/otherlove in the Fiction of Toni Morrison" (PhD diss., Royal Holloway, University of London, March 2014).

34 *"Anger is better. There is a sense of being in anger":* Toni Morrison, *The Bluest Eye* (New York: Plume, 1994), 50.

34 *"Anger is a very intense but tiny emotion, you know":* Toni Morrison, interviewed in *Paris Review* 128 (Fall 1993).

35 *writes at some length about Williams's:* Claudia Rankine, *Citizen: An American Lyric* (Minneapolis: Graywolf Press, 2014), 22–36. Quotation here can be found on page 32.

35 *whose rage was focused, whose greatness on court "belongs to all of us":* Brittney Cooper, *Eloquent Rage* (New York: St. Martin's Press, 2018), 6.

35 *"the sort of behavior that no one should be engaging in on the court":* Martina Navratilova, "What Serena Got Wrong," *New York Times*, September 11, 2018.

38 *she stepped on a piece of broken glass:* Kevin Mitchell, "Serena Williams Reveals Details of Her Serious Foot Injury," *Guardian*, September 2, 2010.

38 *hospitalized in Los Angeles for a pulmonary embolism:* Christopher Clarey, "Williams Was Treated for Blood Clot in Lungs," *New York Times*, March 2, 2011.

38 *photographed walking with their arms around each other:* Jonathan Wall, "Is Serena Williams Dating Her Coach?," Yahoo! Sports, September 13, 2012.

39 *Mouratoglou's wife, Clarisse . . . filed for divorce:* John Stevens, "Spurned Wife of Serena's Lover . . . ," *Daily Mail*, June 24, 2013.

42 *he'd already completed a round of golf and quenched his thirst:* Karsten Braasch,

"How to Beat Both Williams Sisters in One Afternoon," *Observer Sport Monthly*, September 2, 2001.

43 *Asked about playing Murray by David Letterman:* Chris Chase, "Serena Tells David Letterman . . . ," *USA Today*, August 23, 2013. For tape of the segment see grabien.com.

44 *Williams published an essay on Reddit:* Williams, "Letter to My Mom."

44 *photograph surfaced of two Australian-football players:* Maya Oppenheim, "Australian Football Players Wear Blackface . . . ," *Independent*, September 20, 2018.

45 *A Twitter storm had erupted:* See also Jon Levine, "*GQ* Magazine Slammed for Serena Williams . . . ," *Wrap*, November 13, 2018.

50 *newfound faith got her through postpartum depression and believed that it cured:* Court's antigay views and their roots in her reading of Christian Scripture have been widely reported. See Giovanni Torre, "Margaret Court, Voice of a Pulpit . . . ," *New York Times*, June 5, 2017; and Paul Karp, "Religious Freedom Review: Margaret Court Claims . . . ," *Guardian*, March 29, 2018.

51 *"I personally don't think she should have her name anymore":* Ben Rothenberg, "Billie Jean King Says Margaret Court Arena's Name Should Change," *New York Times*, January 12, 2018.

56 *In 1999, she'd enrolled at the Art Institute of Fort Lauderdale:* Williams with Paisner, *On the Line*, 131.

Part Two: Indian Wells

70 *"It's going to be because I'm sick of practicing":* Rodrick, "Serena Williams."

72 *Compton was no longer a Black-majority city:* Dakota Smith and Angel Jennings, "In L.A. Historic African American Core, a Growing Latino Wave . . . ," *Los Angeles Times*, February 28, 2017.

73 *"I'm not gonna move to Compton":* Richard Williams with Bart Davis, *Black and White: The Way I See It* (New York: Atria, 2014), 190.

73 *strewn with racquet covers and tennis magazines:* Sonja Steptoe, "Child's Play," *Sports Illustrated*, June 10, 1991. Vault, the *Sports Illustrated* archive, is an invaluable source of reporting about tennis in general, and the Williams sisters in particular.

74 *"I had a lot of hate in me in those days":* Williams with Davis, *Black and White*, 41.

74 *married Betty Johnson, with whom he is believed to have had four or five children:* See "How Many Siblings Does Serena Williams Have?," reference.com; and famechain.com.

74 *he had one son with Johnson:* Williams with Davis, *Black and White*, 157.

74 *she was being handed a check:* Ibid., 161.

74 *tennis was a "sissy" sport:* Pat Jordan, "Daddy's Big Test," *New York Times Magazine*, March 16, 1997.

75 *"someone who knew as much about stealing":* Williams with Davis, *Black and White*, 152.

75 *"They'd be used to combat":* Ibid., 190.

76 *a book about the New York City playground-basketball legend Lloyd Daniels:* Steptoe, "Child's Play."

77 *signs to inspire and urge on his daughters:* See photographs of the signs in Williams with Davis, *Black and White.*

77 *Serena had to crawl into bed with one of her sisters:* For Serena's home life in Compton, see Williams with Paisner, *On the Line,* 29–45.

78 *had the girls heading with her to the Kingdom Hall:* For the role of religion in the Williams family's life in Compton: Ibid., 86–90.

78 *mansion in the guarded and gated Summit estates:* Mackenzie Dunn, "Serena Williams . . . New Beverly Hills Estate," *Domino,* October 28, 2017.

81 *Azarenka took actions then to establish the baby's legal residency as Minsk:* See BelarusFeed, December 19, 2018.

86 *a recounting of the events surrounding the Serena-Clijsters final:* Joel Drucker, "What Happened at Indian Wells?," ESPN.com, March 11, 2009.

86 *trainer "kept telling her to hold off ":* Williams with Paisner, *On the Line,* 65.

87 *a just-published story in the* National Enquirer: "Wimbledon Fixed?," *National Enquirer,* March 14, 2001.

87 *"why don't the Williamses set the record straight?":* Bill Dwyre, "Tilling Over the Garden Soil," *Los Angeles Times,* March 17, 2001.

88 *"His string of wild tales over the years had left his denials hollow":* Selena Roberts, "Serena Williams Wins as the Boos Rain Down," *New York Times,* March 18, 2001.

88 *"Would another family have been treated as mine was?":* Williams with Davis, *Black and White,* 254.

89 *"The booing was just wearing me out":* Williams with Paisner, *On the Line,* 75.

89 *"busting my butt for the blue-haired Palm Springs jet-setter":* Ibid., 76.

Part Three: Miami

97 *a plainclothes police officer named James Frascatore:* Liz Clarke, "NYPD Officer Who Tackled James Blake . . . ," *Washington Post,* September 25, 2018.

99 *Playing basketball in the WNBA:* Selena Hill, "Top WNBA Salaries vs. NBA Salaries," *Black Enterprise,* April 16, 2018.

99 *eight of the top-ten-earning female athletes in the world:* Kurt Badenhausen, "The Highest-Paid Female Athletes 2018," forbes.com, August 21, 2018.

101 *a story in South Florida's* Sun Sentinel *about Naomi Osaka's years in the area:* Dave Hyde, "An Uncommon Dream Came True . . . for Naomi Osaka," *South Florida Sun Sentinel,* March 16, 2019.

102 *Gauff's parents decided to move to Florida:* For more on the Gauff family and their commitment to Coco's development, see Jerry Bembry, "Coco Gauff and Family Following Familiar Path to Greatness," *Undefeated,* July 5, 2019.

107 *Oracene, with the help of tutors, began homeschooling the girls:* Williams with Paisner, *On the Line,* 106.

108 *when she grew to hate the courts:* Ibid., 105.

108 *thought parents of teen phenoms who were okay with that "ought to be shot":* Robin Finn, "Last of the 14-Year-Olds . . . ," *New York Times,* October 27, 1994.

108 *stint at a Miami drug-rehab center:* Robin Finn, "Capriati Voluntarily in Rehabilitation," *New York Times,* May 20, 1994.

109 *Venus Williams . . . played her first WTA tour match:* Sally Jenkins, "Venus Rising," *Sports Illustrated,* November 14, 1994.

112 *first glimpse the world got of Qai Qai:* "Serena Williams Daughter Got into a Fight with Her Grand Baby . . . ," YouTube, August 5, 2018.

112 *interview with Qai Qai appeared in* Oprah Magazine*:* Arianna Davis, "Qai Qai . . . Gives Us Her First Exclusive Interview," *Oprah Magazine,* February 28, 2019.

113 *talking with Beard about Instagram:* Lovie Gyarkye, "The Way We Look Now, according to Instagram," *New York Times,* October 5, 2018.

115 *"haven't considered the potential reach or longevity of what is happening":* Adrienne Lafrance, "The Perils of 'Sharenting,'" *Atlantic,* October 6, 2016.

115 *soon star together in a new ad for Pampers:* Pampers, YouTube, April 3, 2019.

115 *Qai Qai weighed in with an Instagram post shortly thereafter:* Instagram, March 24, 2019.

Part Four: Rome

122 *The meet-cute, which Ohanian and Williams relayed to* Vanity Fair*:* Buzz Bissinger, "Serena Williams's Love Match," *Vanity Fair,* August 2017.

123 *They sold it the following year . . . for between $10 million and $20 million:* Melia Robinson, "Reddit's Cofounders Sold the Company . . . ," Business Insider, November 4, 2017.

123 *It also became increasingly toxic:* Andrew Marantz, "Reddit and the Struggle to Detoxify the Internet," *New Yorker,* March 12, 2018.

123 *in part, because his mother was dying of brain cancer:* Michael Schulman, "Founder of Reddit and the Internet's Own Cheerleader," *New York Times,* November 22, 2013.

124 *he would not seem Williams's type: Serena Williams:* "It's interesting. I never thought I would have married a white guy...." Christopher Clarey, "Serena Williams as Herself," *New York Times,* April 27, 2018.

124 *he flew her to Venice:* Alexis Ohanian Instagram post, July 21, 2018.

125 *"Homosexuals, by and large, constitute the vanguard":* Susan Sontag, "Notes on 'Camp,'" in *Against Interpretation* (New York: Delta paperback, 1981), 290.

127 *the 2016 Pirelli calendar:* Vanessa Friedman, "The 2016 Pirelli Calendar May Signal a Cultural Shift," *New York Times,* November 30, 2015.

128 *announced the founding of Serena Ventures:* Kurt Badenhausen, "Inside Serena Williams' Plan to Ace Venture Investing," forbes.com, June 3, 2019.

Part Five: Paris

134 *I reached her at her home, in Boca Raton:* My interview with Evert took place prior to the 2018 French Open. What she had to say had not dated a year later.

138 *posted by an all-but-unheard-of Belgian tennis player, Ysaline Bonaventure:* @YsaBona, Twitter, May 23, 2019.

138 *a scene in a documentary,* Serena*: Serena,* directed by Ryan White. See also Kelyn Soong, "New Serena Williams documentary . . . ," *Washington Post,* June 21, 2016.

139 *"Under the Sea" remained a go-to karaoke song for Serena:* Shirley Li, "Watch Serena Williams Sing . . . ," ew.com, August 27, 2015.

144 *highlight reels of the match are available on YouTube:* See, for longest of them, one uploaded to YouTube by JOTennisVid, December 12, 2017.

146 *"not my best memory":* Steve Tignor, "French Open Memories . . . ," tennis.com, May 22, 2018.

146 *"someone cheating me & lying":* @serenawilliams, Twitter, February 24, 2011.

146 *A passage from Michelle Obama's memoir:* Obama, *Becoming,* 75. Obama is writing here about her years at Princeton, when she was just a little younger than Williams was when she played the 2003 French Open.

146 *"We want to make clothes":* "Serena's War Jibe Galls French," *Sydney Morning Herald,* March 31, 2003.

148 *rail against French income-tax rates:* Rodrick, "Serena Williams."

148 *Sullivan visited her in Paris in the summer of 2012 for a piece:* John Jeremiah Sullivan, "Venus and Serena Against the World," *New York Times Magazine,* August 23, 2012.

152 *discussing Williams's exit from the French Open:* The View, YouTube, June 3, 2019.

155 *"You were never to act undignified in their presence":* Margot Jefferson, *Negroland* (New York: Vintage Books, 2016), 4.

155 *The situation brought to mind:* Claudia Rankine, "The Meaning of Serena Williams," *New York Times Magazine,* August 25, 2015.

155 *"excel through deeds and manners":* Ibid., 3.

Part Six: Wimbledon

159 *a landscape of leisure:* For more on the history of the lawn, see "Lawn History" on the website of the Planet Natural Research Center.

160 *masking unsightly sweat stains:* Adam Augustyn, "Why Do Tennis Players Wear Whites at Wimbledon?," www.britannica.com.

161 *The knee was no longer swelling:* Christopher Clarey, "Serena Williams's Coach Says She Is Pain Free . . . ," *New York Times,* June 30, 2019.

163 *Sulloway's thesis, at once provocative and familiar enough:* Frank Sulloway, *Born to Rebel: Birth Order, Family Dynamics, and Creative Lives* (New York: Pantheon, 1996).

163 *subjected to all manner of debunking by social scientists:* See, for example, Julie Beck, "Birth Order Is Basically Meaningless," theatlantic.com, October 21, 2015. Beck summarizes the findings of German researchers, who published a study of more than twenty thousand European adults in *Proceedings of the National Academy of Sciences.*

164 *"She could see when I'd had a tough day, when I need a lift":* Williams with Paisner, *On the Line,* 45.

166 *she published an essay in the* Times *of London:* Venus Williams, "Wimbledon Has Sent Me a Message . . . ," *Times* (London), June 26, 2006.

166 *Venus takes medications, has adopted a vegan diet:* Nicol Natale, "Venus Williams Opens Up . . . ," www.prevention.com, July 30, 2019.

168 *Williams eventually reached a settlement:* Associated Press, "Venus Williams Reaches Settlement," ESPN.com, November 20, 2018.

173 *Williams's essay was announced by a cover photograph of her:* Harper's Bazaar, August 2019.

174 *As Roland Barthes wrote years ago in his brilliant defense:* Roland Barthes, "The World of Wrestling," in *Mythologies* (New York: Hill and Wang, 1983), 15–25.

174 *"explore the concept of 'real beauty'":* Harper's Bazaar, August 2019, 24.

174 *The writing took the form of an apology:* Ibid., 114–18.

182 *Wozniacki's then fiancé, the golfer Rory McIlroy, abruptly broke off their engagement:* Dan Carson, "Rory McIlroy Reportedly Broke Up . . . ," bleacherreport.com, May 28, 2014.

183 *quarter was immediately dubbed the Group of Death:* "Wimbledon Draw: Serena Williams Placed in the Group of Death," *Washington Post,* June 28, 2019.

183 *"One of the craziest, nastiest Grand Slam quarters":* Christopher Clarey, Twitter, June 28, 2019.

184 *to subsume oneself in the "twisting elaborations of fate":* Simon Critchley, *What We Think About When We Think About Soccer* (New York: Penguin Books, 2017), 37.

187 *a deep-felt debate among Black women writers and activists about feminism:* See, perhaps most famously, Toni Morrison, "What the Black Woman Thinks About Women's Lib," *New York Times Magazine,* August 22, 1971; collected in her *What Moves at the Margin* (Jackson: University of Mississippi Press, 2008), 18–30.

187 *she found a way to escape the European male tradition of paint on canvas:* See Barbara Bloemink, *Re/righting History: Counternarratives by Contemporary African-American Artists,* a catalog accompanying an exhibition at the Katonah Museum of Art, 1999.

189 *as much a struggle over images as anything else:* bell hooks, quoted in Maurice Berger, *For All the World to See: Visual Culture and the Struggle for Civil Rights* (New Haven, CT: Yale University Press, 2010), 5.

189 *"How identity relates to identification is, of course, a complicated":* Kwame Anthony Appiah, "What Does It Mean 'Look Like Me'?," *New York Times,* September 22, 2019. Also see his book *The Lies That Bind: Rethinking Identity* (New York: Liveright, 2018).

190 *"I always felt that and still feel that you can't take away greatness":* Paul Annacone quoted in Christopher Clarey, "Novak Djokovic Can Regain . . . ," nytimes.com, October 25, 2018.

Part Seven: New York

195 *"I don't consider myself to be a representative of my people":* Sally H. Jacobs, "Althea Gibson, Tennis Star Ahead of Her Time . . . ," *New York Times,* August 26, 2019. Jacobs is writing a biography of Gibson.

195 *"I play for me, but I also play and represent something much greater":* Claudia Rankine, "The Meaning of Serena Williams," *New York Times,* August 30, 2015.

196 *"Althea Gibson was the FIRST Black Woman tennis player to be on the box":* Sheryl Estrada, "Serena Williams Pays Tribute," diversityinc.com, June 25, 2019.

196 *Angela Buxton—herself an often shunned outsider:* For more on Buxton and Gib-

son, see Bruce Schoenfeld, *The Match: Althea Gibson & Angela Buxton* (New York: Amistad, 2004).

197 *It was at Harlem's famed Cosmopolitan Tennis Club:* Gibson's development as a player is detailed in Jacobs, "Althea Gibson."

199 *"I will never lose to that little bitch again":* Maria Sharapova, *Unstoppable* (New York: Sarah Crichton Books/FSG, 2017), 191.

199 *"top five player who is now in love" as "boring":* Rodrick, "Serena Williams."

199 *"her boyfriend that was married and is getting a divorce and has kids":* Simon Cambers, "Wimbledon 2013: Maria Sharapova Reacts Angrily . . . ," *Observer,* June 22, 2013.

205 *watched by an estimated 22.7 million viewers:* Pilon, "Can Serena and Venus Williams Save Tanking TV Tennis Ratings?"

205 *"With my time schedule, I'd have to have a small role":* Derrick Whyte, "Serena Prepares for Acting Career," *Independent,* August 10, 2002.

207 *"Our concern is her long-term health, number one, and her long-term development":* Tom Perrotta, "Why the USTA Benched America's Best Junior," *Wall Street Journal,* September 8, 2012.

208 *"Everyone deserves to play":* Alexander Abad-Santos, "Serena Williams Defends Taylor Townsend . . . ," theatlantic.com, September 11, 2012.

209 *coined the frame of mind and form Townsend was exhibiting:* the flow state: For more on the flow state, see Kendra Cherry, "'Flow' Can Help You Achieve Goals," verywellmind.com, January 14, 2016.

213 *"you don't really notice the time when you're at Kingdom Hall":* Williams with Paisner, *On the Line,* 87–88.

214 *Serena had "witnessed" in this way even to other players:* Kimberly Winston, "Serena Williams' Secret Weapon . . . ," washingtonpost.com, July 11, 2015.

214 *she'd been summoned by church elders:* Sullivan, "Venus and Serena Against the World."

214 *no record exists that Williams was ever officially baptized as a Witness:* "Is Serena Williams a Baptized JW?," Reddit, August 30, 2018.

217 *An estimated 116 million viewers in China had watched the broadcast:* Jonathan Landreth, "Record Chinese Television Audience . . . ," hollywoodreporter.com, June 9, 2011.

217 *some 14 million Chinese were said to be playing tennis:* David Waldstein, "For Li Na, Another First in Tennis," *New York Times,* July 19, 2019.

219 *Tennis was said to be a $4 billion industry in China:* Ibid.

219 *proved the last straw for Billie Jean King:* For the founding and history of the Virginia Slims Circuit, see Billie Jean King with Cynthia Starr, *We Have Come a Long Way* (New York: A Regina Ryan Book/McGraw-Hill, 1988); and Grace Lichtenstein, *A Long Way, Baby* (New York: William Morrow, 1974).

219 *King, in her book, used the term "consciousness":* King with Starr: *We Have Come a Long Way,* 120.

220 *what the WTA's president, Micky Lawler, told the* New York Times: Cindy Shmerler, "The WTA Finals Settle Down in China," *New York Times,* October 25, 2019.

231 *Williams was in the Maldives:* Instagram post, November 5, 2019.

Epilogue

237 *It was a Saturday in June:* "Serena Interviews Bryan Stevenson," YouTube, June 23, 2020.

238 *In 2015 she had written: Time,* April 16, 2015.

241 *Osaka was twenty-two:* "*Forbes* Reveals Naomi Osaka Is World's Highest Paid Female Athlete Ever," press release, May 22, 2020.

243 *I found myself thinking of lines:* Jack Gilbert, *Refusing Heaven* (New York: Alfred A. Knopf, 2005), 18.

ABOUT THE AUTHOR

Gerald Marzorati writes regularly about tennis for NewYorker .com. He was the editor of the *New York Times Magazine* from 2003 to 2010. He previously worked as an editor at the *Soho News*, *Harper's*, and the *New Yorker*. His writing has appeared in the *New York Times* and many other publications. His first book, *A Painter of Darkness*, won the PEN/Martha Albrand Award for a first book of nonfiction. He is also the author of *Late to the Ball*, a memoir about tennis and aging.